RUSSELL M NASH

YELLOW
FEVER

An Englishman falls under the
spell of The Far East

RUSSELL M NASH

YELLOW
FEVER

An Englishman falls under the
spell of The Far East

MEREO
Cirencester

Published by Mereo

Mereo is an imprint of Memoirs Publishing

1A The Market Place Cirencester Gloucestershire GL7 2PR
info@memoirsbooks.co.uk | www.memoirspublishing.com

Yellow Fever
An Englishman falls under the spell of China

ISBN: 978-1-86151-124-9

To Jason, for making me believe,
and to Ping, for everything

CONTENTS

Foreword

Chapter 1	The beginning	P. 1
Chapter 2	First contact	P. 4
Chapter 3	Shanghai here I am	P. 23
Chapter 4	Shanghai nights	P. 38
Chapter 5	Minhang	P. 65
Chapter 6	Banquets and booze	P. 96
Chapter 7	Language and things	P. 113
Chapter 8	Medicine and things	P. 125
Chapter 9	Visas	P. 133
Chapter 10	Big Ron revisited	P. 143
Chapter 11	Turn down, turn on	P. 148
Chapter 12	Geoff	P. 155
Chapter 13	Life and living	P. 163
Chapter 14	Hangzhou	P. 186
Chapter 15	Taxis, trains and things	P. 197
Chapter 16	The 'Ways'	P. 211
Chapter 17	Alice Li – a Chinese brief encounter	P. 234
Chapter 18	Celebrations	P. 246
Chapter 19	Chocolate fireguards and Aussies	P. 256
Chapter 20	Travels	P. 272
Chapter 21	Shanghai limbo	P. 304
	Pronunciation guide	

FOREWORD

It's a time to reflect and a time to think. Has all that's happened to me over the last few years been for a purpose and led me to where I am now, and who I am now? Is there more to come, or have I finally hit the ground and come to rest after my long, uncontrolled fall? I hope there's no more rolling and tumbling, as I'm not sure if I can take any more. I'm not young any more; even though some of me feels young – younger than before - and I need to settle down again. The mirror tells me this, more than anything else, every morning – lines on the face, hair going – rapidly - muscles softening and so forth. Yes. Slow down, conserve and preserve.

In 1997 I came to China, having agreed to take on the task of opening a new feed mill in Shanghai. At that point I had no clear idea of anything in my life. In my late forties, I was at yet another of life's crossroads. My family was grown and so the purpose that had existed in my life for so long, though not gone, was shifting. I became more important. What I wanted for myself became more important. The only problem was that I had no clear idea what I wanted.

My wife was still important, as she should have been after twenty-five years of marriage, but we wanted different things. She wanted to drift into old age, it seemed, and look forward to grandparenthood, pipe and slippers (for me), TV, garden; wash the car on Sundays and holidays in the sun. Nothing wrong with that except that personally, I wasn't prepared to begin to die. Mind you, I had no clear alternative in mind, and had I not come to China, I might have drifted down the same path beside her.

I had been vaguely discontented, uncertain and dissatisfied for about the last ten years of our marriage and, in the darker moments, couldn't countenance spending the remainder of my life with her. I think our children, Michael and Sarah, knew it or suspected it, but said nothing until later. I put it down to the 'male menopause', if there is such a thing, and got on with life as best I could, burying myself in work, both in my job and at home, with my sex drive gone and my feelings for my wife dwindling. Trying not to think. Trying to be conventional.

Had I become selfish? Had I always been selfish? Maybe. It could be that all I'd ever done was for my own satisfaction and that making people happy and being a good husband and father was for my own gratification. Was what I'd done in my life and helping to make my children the people they became reflecting back at me and making me feel good and that's what I did it for? Maybe.

It's civilization and evolution that are to blame. In nature the purpose of any and every life form is to procreate and, purpose in life achieved, to die. We procreate, and then what do we do? Hopefully, we procreate and then continue to create in some form or other. Some procreate and then vegetate, and I wasn't prepared to do that. My fall, jump, slide began well before China, although China was and still is blamed for it.

Thinking about it, how many men are the same as I was, but their lives didn't change because there was no catalytic happening or cathartic experience to push them into the blind leap? If the incidence is the same as the broken marriage rate amongst the others in my company who went to China, there are a lot. Out of six 'China long-term stayers' (two years or more) in my company, three ended up getting divorced. Of the other three, two had their wives with them, so they didn't really count. One of them, I know, was affected by 'yellow fever'. Had he been on a free rein, he would also have succumbed, I'm sure.

Within a month of going to China I felt things changing and sap beginning to rise again. I knew my life would never be the same again, wherever it led, and now I'm here, back in China again via Vietnam with a short, enforced, painful, year's absence in the UK in between. Here now, but where will I be tomorrow? Still here, I hope and pray. Enough. I think I've drifted in the wind as much as I want to, or need to.

Drifting can be pleasurable, but after a while there is a need to be anchored in a safe port. Sheet anchors were tentatively put down a couple of times, but nothing heavy enough to hold me in one place or with one person. I think now, though, I am well and truly grounded. Not shipwrecked, foundering or hooked on a reef, but firmly anchored and moored.

Is there such a thing as 'the love of your life', or is every love 'the one' when it's happening? Even the wisest can't say, so what chance have I got? I feel now as I've never felt before, or as I never remember feeling before. Memory is a strange thing. The body forgets pain and remembers pleasure. If it were not so, women would never have a second child, and I would have stopped playing rugby after my first broken bone. Emotions and feelings, however, can be different, with pain and pleasure equally recalled and a measurement made, a balance, between the two. Periods of black depression, despair and pain compared, weighed and judged against the equivalent pleasure, happiness and pure joy.

The sad thing is that it's incredibly difficult to stay happy for extended periods, unless you're insane, whereas it's easy to sink into and stay in depression. Instances of pure joy in my life seem to have been few and fleeting; my son's first smile and first words (his birth was a horrendous experience.); the birth of my daughter with me as assistant midwife; the first time I kissed Ping and then seeing her in Hangzhou after we had been apart for two months. Ah. I want more of this feeling in the rest of my life. Wish me luck.

As I write, it is February 2006 and I first, literally, put pen to paper in the summer of 1998. That was on a Majorcan beach on a brief holiday with my wife (it was to be our last), having read all my books and become tired of looking at fat Germans. I was even bored with looking at big tits. Possibly the first signs of 'Yellow Fever'. The holiday was not good. I was changing and my wife could sense it. Looking back, it was a terrible time – I was torn between the past and an unknown future.

The initial writing was purely a tongue-in-cheek information sheet for my company – pitfalls, observations, suggestions and advice - but to my surprise, it was well received by the Personnel Director in the UK and I was asked to 'keep them coming.' Thereafter I carried on supplying bits and pieces to him until, one day, the CEO picked one of my more irreverent renderings off the fax machine. For some reason he was 'not amused' – probably the humourectomy he had to undergo to get the job. I was advised to 'be more careful' about what I wrote and where I sent it.

I was, by that time, somewhat cynical with regard to the UK end of the company's views, opinions and complete lack of understanding about China or 'how it was'. Unfortunately, the 'The Queen thinks everywhere in the world smells of new paint' syndrome was firmly entrenched in the company and sunshine was blown up too many senior arses most of the time. When the Olympian gods descended, everything had to be pretty, sweet and nice, with no bad or disturbing news. Messengers do get shot, so I thought, 'Fuck them.' and continued to write for myself and for those people whom I deemed worthy.

Readers will notice that sex is a major feature in my

writings, both in China and Vietnam and, even Scotland (more so in Vietnam). So be it. I do not apologise for any of it. I'm not a sex maniac, deviant or pervert, it's just that sex and women played a large part in what happened to me after I came to the East. That and the friends I made and found out here. Everything I write is true or based on things that happened to me and to others and is not apocryphal in any way. I hope you enjoy it. I know, for the most part, I did.

CHAPTER ONE

THE BEGINNING

It all began in a casual, innocuous way with a phone call. It was 5.30 in the evening in early January 1997 and I was still at work. There must have been some problem that kept me there, but I can't remember what. For some now forgotten reason I called my boss, Paul. I had known him for more than twenty years, so he and I were friends as well as colleagues and the relationship was good. My greeting was, "Hello there, Paul. What are you up to?"

"Very busy, Russ. I'm off to China tomorrow for two weeks, so I've got a lot to sort out before I leave. What do you want?"

(The Animal Feed Industry was going to shit in Britain, so the company were moving into China – new factory in Shanghai and possible joint ventures elsewhere.)

"Fucking hell. Another holiday for you, you lucky bastard."

"Fuck off. I've got to go to six different places and China is fucking BIG. It's not like flitting about the UK or Europe and you now what that's like. I'll be knackered."

I knew what he meant, having done my share of the same in Europe. It looks like a good life but it can be absolute shit. "Mm, yeah, I know" I replied. "Still, it must be interesting over there. I wouldn't mind having a look myself."

There was a pause - Paul had a stammer, so I wasn't sure if the delay in answering was due to this or because he was thinking – then, "So, if I asked you to go to Shanghai for three months, it wouldn't be a problem?"

"Mmm, no."

"OK. Right, we'll talk when I get back. Got to go now. Bye." Click.

Never, never volunteer. What had I done? I drove home in something of a daze. For all my married life I had been unwilling to be away from home for more than a week - at the most. I know that this had held me back career-wise, but it was a conscious and deliberate choice that I had made. Family first. Why now?

At home I tried to be casual about it when I dropped it into the usual 'How was work today?' conversation. Played it cool. I didn't mention the three months, thinking that this might be too much for them to handle. I was right. "Yes, we'll manage. Two or three weeks will be fine."

I was probably the least excited about it all. Even the dog caught the mood, running round the dining room table barking until everybody got pissed off and threw her out into the garden. I managed to get everyone to slow down, telling them I had to wait for Paul to come back before I knew any details, thinking all the while what it might mean to my life.

Paul returned and things began to take shape. I was to be 'the man' to start up and commission the new factory in Shanghai and train all the staff. The time it was to take was revised down, from three to two months (little did I know.) which suited the family. I had been gradually bumping up the length of my being away from 'two or three weeks' to 'maybe a month' to 'possibly a month or two' rather than drop it all on them at once, so they were happy enough.

When August 97 arrived, I was off to the Far East for a first taste.

FIRST CONTACT

The day had arrived and I was on my way. British Airways Business Class to Beijing and my first real taste of long-haul, work-related travel. Pleasant enough as a first experience, but soon to be something I loathed, particularly on Air India and Air China. Being confined for twelve hours or more drives me up the wall – more so if it's in Economy Class rather than First or Business. I do like seeing and being in a new place, but if it takes any longer than two hours to get there, forget it. I was travelling with my boss, Paul, and a lunatic called Len Styles. Len worked in the Purchase Department at the Head Office, but had somehow managed to get himself involved with activities in China. He was a piss-head and had more than a touch of the wide boy about him, but he had been seconded to be part of the joint venture negotiating team. He was a good man for a piss up and a wild night, but not your ideal company ambassador. It was yet another of life's and my company's mysteries.

Anyway, all was exciting, new and different. My trip

was to involve a visit to Anshan in Liaoning Province in Northeast China, before going down to Shanghai for a first look at the new factory. It was more than a familiarisation trip, in that we were to do an asset register check on a prospective joint venture partner, the Liaohe Company, in Anshan. i.e. we had to check that they owned what they said they owned. It's called 'due diligence'. I was excited and full of anticipation and my mind was open to new experiences – any and all new experiences.

Towards the end of the flight I looked, again, out of the window and there it was. We were flying over the Great Wall. We were there.

As a first experience of China, Beijing Airport, the old one, was daunting. It was cramped, disorganised, confusing, unfriendly, dirty and HOT, and gave rise to my first, but not last, 'What the fuck am I doing here?'

Len had a bad start. He pissed off the girl whose job it was to tell people 'Do not cross the yellow line.' by insisting on crossing it, and was then sent to the back of the immigration queue for not filling in his entry card and health declaration form. After he had finally negotiated immigration without pissing anyone else off, we still had a three-hour wait before our onward flight to Shenyang. What to do? Then Len had one of his few good ideas and said, "Come on. I know where the bar is." That was it. The tone of the trip was set. Go with the flow.

After more beer than was good for us in our jet-lagged state, we decided to make our way to the departure gate. Not that easy. It had been changed and the only information to that effect was on a small chalkboard, which was being carried around the airport lounge and it was also only in Chinese. Anyway, we found it eventually and settled down to wait. It was my first opportunity to study Chinese people close up, so I studied.

As usual with me, the women were the first to get my attention. I had my first sight of shiny black forests of straight, underarm hair, along with tantalising flashes of thigh, crotch and escaping foliage as skirts were lifted unselfconsciously and wafted, with legs wide apart, in a futile attempt to keep cool. Then there were the flashes of dark, protruding nipples on small firm breasts as they stooped and bent to rummage in their bags. Ah. Get thee behind me, Satan. It had begun.

Then, of course, there were the men. Trousers rolled up to the knees for the same purpose – keeping cool, that is - nothing Masonic about it. I witnessed, for the first time, the Chinese habit of hawking and spitting in public, either on the floor or in the nearest waste bin. Disgusting, but you got used to it. 'Food' was being consumed. I say food, but, at the time, I couldn't work out what the hell they were putting in their mouths.

Everything was strange, alien and different, and it continued to be so for a long time. It takes about six months to get your head round it all and accept what you encounter. I say accept rather than understand. Understanding takes longer – a lot longer.

The flight was called and for the first time I witnessed and became part of a Chinese phenomenon – the pyramid queue. They are getting better at it, but slowly. Queuing is something that Chinese people have difficulty grasping as a concept. 'I want to be first. I'm most important. I have to be first.' is how they see it. I found myself next to a Hong Kong Chinese man who was rather irate. "These fucking people make me ashamed to be Chinese. When will they ever fucking learn? They're here. The fucking plane won't go without them." were the words he uttered in perfect English, as he shook his head in disgust.

Looking around, I also began to wonder why I wasn't carrying my thirty-kilo baggage allowance under my arm like the rest of them. "How is he going to get that tea chest in the overhead locker?" I wondered.

On the plane it settled down, apart from the total disregard for instructions like 'fasten your seat belts', 'no smoking' etc. The worst offenders were two schoolteachers who were shepherding about twenty small children. They were all over the place, taking photographs, looking out of windows and using the toilet until the stewardesses threatened them. Fine example.

I was intrigued by the in-flight announcements. They were supposed to be in English as well as Chinese, but all I got was, 'Than' yo for yo coarashun.' 'Food' was served.

We made it to Shenyang and were met by a guy called Bob Wilson, Business Development Manager for China, who could speak fluent Mandarin Chinese – a rarity in those days. It could have been the only reason he got the job, because he was about as much use as glass eye. He shunted us off to Anshan, about an hour and a half away, filling us in on the way.

My first view of Chinese countryside was extremely disappointing. Liaoning is a corn-growing region, so all there was to see was an endless ocean of waving green. Very pleasant, but, very quickly, boring. If it had been a month or two later it would have been worse, though. After the harvest everything is a boring, uniform brown, changing to white when it snows. Thankfully Liaoning isn't typical of most of China.

Anshan. God preserve me from Anshan. What a shithole! It is a 'steel city' and everywhere has the smell and colour of sulphur dioxide and even on good days the people roam the streets in face masks. Four hundred thousand of them work either directly or indirectly for Anshan Steel, so the company controls the city – schools, hospitals, shops, hotels… the hospitals are a must, given the higher than average incidence of lung disorders in steel cities.

We were to stay our nine or ten days in Anshan, in the Anshan International Hotel. It was a good hotel, for Anshan, but suffered badly in comparison with Shanghai. The rooms were big barns of places with two king-size beds and bathrooms like indoor swimming pools. It was, however, a place of paradoxes, as I find many Chinese and Vietnamese hotels are - excellent and frustratingly bad at the same time. The view from my window on the eighteenth floor could have been better, but as I wasn't a tourist, the vast expanse of Anshan steelworks two miles away, filling the horizon, wasn't a big problem. The coating of sulphur dioxide on the outside of the windows, however, was, and gave me some pause for thought. Thank God I was only there for a few days.

After checking in, exploring the room and taking a shower I ventured down to the lobby to see if anyone was about. It was two thirty, the bar was open and I made a bet with myself. I won. Len was already in residence and on his second beer and he shouted, "Come on, get some down you! Tomorrow's Sunday, so we can have a few." As I said – the tone was set.

Paul and Bob joined us shortly after and we began in earnest. After about two hours we were mellow and beginning to feel the jet-lag creeping up on us. However, we decided that, given that we had a day to recover, a good session would sort us out. Either that or kill us, so we went for it.

Time passed. It reached 6 pm and things began to happen. 'Ladies' began walk through the lobby to the lifts. Lots of ladies. Lots of attractive ladies. Lots of very attractive ladies... I raised my eyebrows in query and Bob enlightened me, "They're the girls from the karaoke bar on the third floor. In-house hookers."

I was puzzled. "But in the room it said... the hotel rules and things. No entertaining women for immoral purposes and stuff."

"Ha!" Bob laughed. "You're in China, mate."

I had just encountered my first 'Chinese double standard'. There would be more – a lot more.

Curiosity got the better of us, so before we fell over, around 9.30, we decided to check out the karaoke bar. We wandered in and took a look. We were immediately the centre of attention, as foreigners were still a rarity in those days. All the girls were gorgeous and, we found out later, had been hand picked, as the hotel was used by the police, Mafia (same thing) army and government officials in the city as a place of 'relaxation'. A couple of them wandered over and sat with us, probably because they were the only ones who could speak English, and asked us questions – questions that I was to become all too familiar with: 'Where you from?' 'What your name?' 'Why come China?' 'How long you stay Anshan?' etc.

One of them, a Miss Fu, had caught my eye earlier in the night, as she was crossing the lobby. She was tall for a Chinese girl, short hair, long, long legs and a fantastic shape. She also had a sweet, sweet smile and a delightful, childlike, broken English accent. I was captivated, and even in my jet-lagged and drunken state, felt warning twitches from somewhere that had been semi-dormant for a long time. We talked with them for a while until we decided to call it a night and headed for bed, with a promise to return. Hmm. The bug had bitten me and the infection had started its course.

Sleep came easy, even with Miss Fu running through my mind, and I heard nothing until an alarm call, which I hadn't booked, woke me at 8 am. It was different. 'Ni hao, thisa you wake up call. Wisha you have a nice day.' It was so lovely that I wasn't even pissed off at being wakened up early on a Sunday. I was soon to find out that the alarm call was one of the few good things about the hotel's services. I headed downstairs for breakfast and my first mystery tour. Breakfast? What the fuck was fried hyacinth? It turned out to be mange tout peas. Sack the translator.

The buffet was a conglomeration of Chinese and Western food. I use the term 'Western' advisedly. An attempt had been made to produce bacon, eggs, sausage and toast, but only the scrambled eggs came close, cold though they were. As for the rest of it – cream cakes for breakfast? I was amazed to see Chinese guests with plates overflowing with everything, and I mean everything. The Chinese are still coming to terms with buffets and seem to think you have to grab as much as you can in one visit. My initial thought was, 'Fucking pigs'. Sadly, after eight years, my opinion has only modified slightly, from 'Fucking pigs' to 'Pigs'. It reminds me of an episode from my teens, after my first appearance for the local rugby team. The team was a mishmash of veteran boozers, fit young lads and useless 'enthusiasts'. In the changing room, after the game, a giraffe-like, myopic veteran called Dick approached one of the 'enthusiasts' and put a fatherly arm around his shoulders. "Well, John, I'm glad to say that you've improved."

"Thanks, Dick."

"Yes. Last season you were fucking useless, but this year you're just useless." Anyway, back to China.

We spent the morning sitting in the lobby chatting, drinking coffee and watching the activities in the hotel. The first thing that struck me was the number of people working, but seeming to do very little. In Britain, staff everywhere, not just in hotels, is trimmed to the bone, but in China it doesn't matter – yet. As soon as wages begin to grow it WILL matter. However, for now it's OK for a girl to spend a whole day pacing back and forward in the cathedral-like hotel lobby, polishing the same piece of floor, or for other girls to sit on every floor and press the button on the lift when they hear a guest leave their room.

There was also a 'toilet ghost' – an old man in the gent's toilet whose only job was to turn on the tap and offer you a towel. It was somewhat scary, at first, to have someone give you a broad smile as you entered the toilet and then hover behind when you were having a piss, but you got used to it. In China you get used to many things, and reach a point where nothing shocks or surprises you too much any more – sad really.

After a club sandwich lunch we took a stroll outside, but quickly decided that it was too hot. That was the problem with Anshan – you either broil or freeze your nuts off, with very rarely an in between. What to do? A couple of hours 'crash' was the general consensus, to be followed by a meeting to sort out the plan of attack for Monday morning.

We met again at around 4.00, had our meeting and were still in the lobby when the 'ladies' came in for work. Fu gave me a wave as she passed by and she shouted a question, "See you later?"

"Maybe" I replied. Maybe not tonight, but certainly sometime. What a body.

Common sense took over, fortunately, and we all decided that, discretion being the better part of valour, we should have a quiet night in preparation for the morning. It was probably a good idea for me personally, as it stopped me from rushing headlong down the path which had, invitingly, presented itself. I would tread it soon enough and too often. So it was dinner, a couple of drinks, bed and sleep.

Sleep? My phone rang at midnight. Fu. "Why no come?" I explained that we had to work and that I would see her soon enough. Eventually she understood, but it didn't stop her from calling me again at two in the morning and every night until... later.

Morning came and we started to work. Well, we attempted to start work. We were ferried to the Liaohe Company and got our first glimpse of the business in which we were aiming to purchase a controlling share. What a first glimpse. A grand entrance gate, massive statue of a soaring eagle, impressive reception area and then - nothing. Like a movie back-lot, there was nothing behind it. As I found out is typical in China, the offices, facilities and factory were very, very basic. All fur coat and no knickers.

We were shunted into the owner, Mr Huang's, office – it of course was opulent, lavishly furnished and even had a bed. We soon found out why.

He welcomed us as only the Chinese can and I had my first taste of baijiu, which is a usually colourless spirit made from wheat, sorghum or glutinous rice. I'd been warned, but – FUCK. I got used to it, though. We spent the day thereafter in meeting people, looking around the place, eating and drinking and drinking. The day, therefore, was a blur of new faces, most of them called Wang, seen through a haze of alcohol. Pleasant, but tiring. Bob told us to be on our guard. "Be careful. Most of the prettier women don't do a lot of actual 'work' work. Mr Huang believes in having as much 'comfort' at work as possible. Yes. The bed. If he offers you the opportunity to have a nap at lunchtime say no, unless, of course, you want a quick trip home. We can't afford to compromise ourselves."

It became apparent that each of us had been allocated a 'comforter' should we feel the need. Mine, a Miss Wang, made it very, very obvious what was available when she sat opposite to me in a meeting wearing a short, short skirt and a pair of crotchless knickers. She sat there doing a 'Sharon Stone,' giving me tantalising flashes of a beautiful bush and a glistening pussy. She was either anticipating me, by her come-on smile, or Mr Huang had already split her whiskers at lunchtime – probably the latter. The rest of her was OK too.

Bob had a direct route to the CEO, which he used when the pressure was on and when he had something or anything to report, so it was wise, highly recommended and, indeed, essential to take heed. I didn't find most of this out until later, after a few snippets of bad news found their way back to the UK faster than a rat up a drainpipe. Bob was not to be trusted, bastard that he was. In fact he was 'as slippery as a pork butcher's prick', to quote an old workmate.

In between all the socialising, entertainment and 'distractions' we actually managed to get some work done and achieved most of our objectives and even some things that weren't on the list. The company was sound, if a little strange to our eyes. It was a dictatorship, which should have been no surprise, given that Mr Huang was a self-made man. Initially he had dragged himself up from the dirt by hauling cattle bones and carcasses from Inner Mongolia, to supply the local feed industry with meat and bone meal. He had Chinese mafia connections, as was obvious from the black-shirted, silent, unsmiling and immobile characters who haunted reception areas and any banquet he arranged on our behalf.

There were many new experiences and only a foretaste of doing business in China. I was the only China novice in the team, but most of the things we came across were new to all of us, even Bob. I didn't know it, but I was being assessed as well as Liaohe. This came out in a quiet moment towards the end of our stay in Anshan, when we were relaxing over a first beer of the evening. There was a lull in the conversation and Paul said, "Well, Bob, do you think he'll be OK?"

"Yeah, nothing we've come across seems to have thrown him too much since we've been here. He'll be fine." Len nodded in agreement.

"Mmm, thought so. Good. Right choice" said Paul with a grunt and a smile.

My 'volunteering' had only been part of it. Paul recognised that I was OK at a distance and didn't need anyone to hold my hand. I was also good at what I did, which helped. I had once complained to him that he didn't visit me in South Wales very often. "If I have to be there every month, you've got a problem. I know you're OK, so I leave you alone. I don't like the fucking Welsh anyway. You get on well with them." That was his explanation.

This last was very true and I could also cope with being surrounded by people speaking a different language without going nuts. That was good training for China, along with the slightly different way things operate in Wales. Difficult to define, but it was just different. Not as different as China, but enough to make it easier for me.

In between work, when we could fend off the hospitality, other things were going on. The work was stressful, so we needed to relax away from it and the people involved – let our hair down on our own. We had been advised against venturing out too much in Anshan because, unlike most Chinese cities, it wasn't 100% safe. True this. Most cities in China are very safe. I have wandered the streets alone in Shanghai at all times of night and never once felt threatened, or worried about my safety. You cannot say this about any city in Britain. So, the hotel it was, and there was enough there to keep us happy. Fu kept up the late night phone calls until I worked out that the only way to stop them was to take away the need for her to make them.

On Friday night we hit the karaoke bar, having avoided yet another Liaohe banquet by claiming that we had a progress report to compile and send to England. It was partly true, and the best lies should always contain some element of the truth. We had a good time and entertained others as well as ourselves. My renditions of 'The Banana

Boat Song' and 'Sailing' received encores and will be long remembered.

Fu joined us, along with three other girls. Fuck it! We were all on expenses and my boss, Paul, signed off on mine anyway. Fu said she was feeling tired, but she said it with that smile on her face. Twenty-five years of fidelity about to be blown away. A big step. Rather like a parachute jump, I imagine, in that there's no undoing it. So it was with mixed emotions that I went back to my room.

There was a preamble, but it was very short. She was gorgeous – everywhere, and in every way. About all she said in English was, "I like make with foreigner".

She was good at it, and I was mesmerised and fascinated. After we had both used our mouths on each other for long enough, she pushed me onto my back and impaled herself, taking my full length inside her with no problem. She 'went for it' and gave up trying to speak English. "Aiya! Hao! Hen hao! Da! Da! Wo xi huan! Hen hao! Aiya!" I found out, much later, that this meant, "My god! Good! Very good! Big! Big! I like! Very good! My god!"

It didn't last very long – my fault – but long enough for her to have at least one climax before I did. Wow. We slowed down and took our time after that. Conversation was difficult, because her English was limited and my Chinese was, at the time, nonexistent. Our hands and bodies did the talking for us, and what a body she had. Now I've seen more than a few, but I couldn't have done better on a first venture if I'd had a hundred lined up to choose from. She didn't have any fat on her and she was fit and strong. I found out later that she had been a gymnast, but had damaged a knee and been forced to give it up prematurely. It's an ill wind… God, she was fit. Her breasts were small, but her nipples were big and dark. Perfect. Moving further down, her stomach was flat and muscular and her pubic hair was straight, black and profuse. Her legs were long and she could put them anywhere – full splits or behind her head. Wow!

We slept when we were both exhausted and she eventually left around nine in the morning, giving indications that she wanted to see me again at night. She wanted, and I wanted. I went down to breakfast feeling, apart from being wrung out, a few twinges of remorse and fear. It was too late for remorse, as it always is, but fear? For many reasons.

I was more than a bit sheepish when I joined Paul and Len for breakfast, but Paul put me at ease. "How was yours, then?" was the first thing he said to me.

"Mine?" innocently.

"What do you think Len and I did after you left with a hard on? Sat and talked?"

We all laughed and swapped details. After a while I asked Paul where Bob was.

"Hmph. Still up to his nuts, I suspect. He's been coming here, off and on, for about six months. He's got a regular. He phoned me last night desperate for a condom. He'd fucking well run out."

I was somewhat relieved. I had been worried about Bob and didn't trust him to keep his mouth shut, but 'People who live in glass houses...' etc. He appeared after about half an hour, but gave no indication as to what kind of night he'd had, so we didn't ask. Some things are very useful to know, however.

The weekend progressed and Fu took up semi-permanent residence, so we did a lot of it. The infection was heading straight for chronic and bypassing acute completely.

The rest of the time at Anshan continued very much in the same vein until we left. The business was done and we were one step nearer to agreement with Liaohe. I, on the other hand, had taken my first step down a road that I didn't even know I was on. I went back to Anshan fairly often and carried on seeing Fu whenever I was there, but there was never any relationship other than sex. One day, about a year later, I made a trip there and she was gone – moved to Beijing and better things - and I never saw or heard from her again. I hope her life is good now. There were plenty more fish in the Anshan sea anyway, as I was to find out.

Our work done in Anshan, we said our farewells and set off for Shanghai. It was a Chinese internal airline again and the trip was very much the same as the flight from Beijing to Shenyang – fucking chaos and mayhem. I hasten to add that they have improved since then. The only way is up? The only difference was that this flight had cabin TV, so the Chinese were slightly quieter – only slightly. It was all in Chinese, of course, but the figure on the screen was English. It was Chris Patten, ex-Governor General of

Hong Kong, and the programme was a rerun of the handover ceremony. Patten was getting all emotional at the lowering of the flag etc. Hong Kong had been handed back only a few weeks before we arrived in China, and the Chinese people were still very excited about it. I watched for a while and then Bob shook his head and moaned, "Here we fucking go again."

"What?"

"What a load of shite." Then he translated, "Chris Patten hangs his head in shame as the last bastion of the British Empire disappears from the mainland of China."

We all laughed out loud and received several puzzled glances. Since then I've tried to explain to Chinese people that British people didn't give a shit about Hong Kong, but they only shake their heads in disbelief. It was SO important to them. Macau was bad enough as well, so God help us when Taiwan comes back. Note that I say *when* and not *if.* All Chinese people refer to it as 'Taiwan Province', never just 'Taiwan', and they always correct you when you say it wrong. I do it now, on purpose, to wind them up. I also point out to them that Korea, Mongolia and Vietnam all used to be part of a greater China. Some of them see the joke, but many – too many – look very thoughtful.

We made it to Shanghai unscathed and unsullied, to be met by Henry, the Shanghai General Manager. He was a good guy and no doubt still is. We were to get on well for the short time we worked together. Henry had overseen the initial stages of the joint venture and the building of the new factory, but now he was almost done and I was to take over and start the thing going. Henry took us for a meal and a few beers and a gossip before we decided to have an early night, to catch up on some sleep. It had been a long day and we had an even longer one ahead of us.

I did have time to see a little bit of Shanghai by night, though. It was unbelievable to see for the first time, and me a country boy. We were staying in The Holiday Inn Crowne Plaza – the best hotel, at the time, that I'd ever stayed in. It was to be my first home in China when I went there to work proper.

The next morning Henry picked Paul and me up from the hotel, Bob and Len having business elsewhere in Shanghai, and took us out to the site. We had to travel to Minhang, about an hour away, on the outskirts of Shanghai, take a look at the new factory and have a progress meeting with Henry and the site engineer, Geoff Smithson (More about Geoff later). It also gave me an opportunity to take a look at Shanghai by day. It is BIG and spectacular – not beautiful. In particular, the view from the Xupu Bridge, looking east, still sticks in my mind. There will be more about Shanghai later.

Our visit was good and everything seemed fine and on target. Henry, however, expressed his misgivings about our partner Mr Mao. He didn't trust him one little bit and was certain that he had a hidden agenda. It turned out that Henry was right and Mao eventually made a play to take control. By that time, unfortunately, Henry was long gone, his expressed opinions about Mao getting him an early return home. When shit and fan came together, Henry never even got an apology or an acknowledgment that he had been right. Bastards.

The day came to an end, and Paul and I were taken back to Shanghai and our last night in China, before heading home via Hong Kong the next morning.

We had a quick shower and headed for the hotel bar – Charlie's. You will hear more about Charlie's – a lot more – but this was my first visit and all was new. There was a live band playing and the place was about three quarters full. Most were foreign men and what was left was made up of hookers – classy hookers. We fended off a couple of girls, bought a drink and found a seat from which we could scope the place. It was interesting and different. It was also a foretaste of a place that was going to become my 'local' in Shanghai. I couldn't wait.

Bed beckoned after our long, hard day, with the prospect of an early flight to Hong Kong and then home. It would be back home for a few months or so and then back to Shanghai. Home - it seemed a long, long way away and a long time since I'd been there. A lot had happened to me already, and a lot more was going to happen.

CHAPTER THREE

SHANGHAI HERE I AM

Full of expectancy, and trying not to let anyone see how excited I was, I was off to Shanghai on my own at last. 'Bon voyage,' everybody said, and they meant it – I think. Was it going to be the experience of a lifetime or just another pain in the arse and disappointment? I'd become accustomed to things turning out to be less than I thought they would be, so I tried to keep my expectations as well under control as possible.

Difficult. One or two alarm bells had rung already, as the cynical side of my nature expected. I'd been given my ticket to Shanghai and a piece of paper. A piece of paper? Yes, a piece of paper with the address of the hotel on it in Chinese. I asked, "Why?" but knew what was coming.

"There'll be nobody to meet you at Shanghai, so you'll have to get yourself to the hotel. You've been there already, so you'll be fine."

"Fucking great" I thought. Had I been a financial, administration, sales or technical type I would have been picked up at the airport, looked after and coddled.

However, being a production-cum-engineering type, I was deemed to be qualified in woodcraft, able to live off the land, resourceful, able to speak fluent Chinese and, therefore, capable of getting myself from the airport to the hotel by myself. Not the best of starts.

I made it to Shanghai without any problems, via Hong Kong, courtesy of Cathay Pacific - gorgeous girls – and Dragon Airlines, safely negotiated immigration, yellow lines, entry cards and health declarations and then suffered my first instance of being ripped off by a taxi driver. As soon as I made it through the exit I was accosted by a smiley-faced one. I gave him my piece of paper and he scrutinised it for a few seconds before saying, hopefully, "One hundred. OK?"

"OK." I'd been travelling for thirteen hours, so I'd had enough and I wouldn't have cared if he'd asked for twice as much.

Had I turned right and walked the fifty yards to the official taxi ranks, I could have got there for thirty. There would have been some arguing of course, as taxi drivers are obliged contractually to service the airport and have to sit and wait. Sometimes this wait can be up to two hours, during which time they are not making any money. When you get in and they find that you aren't going very far they are not very happy. They argue, but there's nothing they can do, except try to drag the journey out by taking you where you want to go as indirectly as possible. They usually manage to get it up to a more acceptable, for them, forty or fifty. I, however, was still a China virgin and didn't know any of this at the time. Next time, though?

Even in my befuddled state, my trip to the hotel grabbed my attention. It was my first Chinese taxi ride and, as such, worth remembering. I'm not a nervous passenger by any means, but I was gripping my seat by the time we had moved a hundred yards. After a short while I eased and cast my fate on the mercy of Saint Christopher, when I realised that it wasn't just my guy who was crazy – shenjing bing. They were all crazy. They drove as if they were pedestrians.

Imagine, if you will, that you are in a city shopping centre on the last shopping day before Christmas and the place is heaving with last-minute shoppers. You walk out of a shop and join in with the throng on the pavement. You don't look or hesitate. You just do it. That's how people drove in Shanghai and, generally, everywhere in China. The traffic worked on the 'constant flow' principle – just like a flock of birds – with no real problems unless there was contact. Contact resulted in confrontation, crowd entertainment and a traffic jam, with the police lounging in the background till it cooled off. It has improved to a degree, with things like lane discipline and observance of traffic lights now more normal. Before, if anyone was driving correctly, it caused a major problem because they were the odd ones out.

I got used to it quickly – some never do – and used the 'first taxi ride' as an introduction and initiation for China first-timers, by making them sit beside the driver, so I could watch their reactions. Cruel bastard. Apart from the way the traffic moved, there was the traffic itself. 90% of it was taxis and 99% of those were VW Santanas. At first I wondered how the Japanese let this happen until I found out about the general dislike, even hatred, towards Japan, softened only by a pragmatic liking for Japanese money. The Chinese have long memories, as I was to find out.

I made it to the hotel in one piece and with my nerves still intact – just. There was a message for me – 'Can't meet you tonight. Had to go to Hangzhou. Geoff and the rest of the boys should be back at the hotel by 8.00. See you tomorrow. Henry.'

I got my room sorted out, showered, changed and lay on the bed flicking through the TV channels. I couldn't believe it. Fucking 'Neighbours' was on the Aussie channel. Was nowhere safe? Was there no escape? What to do next? It was eleven in the morning, but for me it was only three in the morning. Sleep was the best option, so I took it.

I woke three hours later, feeling like shit, with my head thumping and a taste in my mouth like sweaty armpit. What to do now? Anything to get rid of the taste in my mouth and the headache, so I decided to explore the hotel, starting with the club lounge – deserted. Down to the lobby and coffee. Coffee? What time was it? It was 2.30 in the afternoon, which made it 6.30 in the morning by my fucked up body clock. Breakfast time. I ordered a chicken sandwich along with the coffee and watched the world go by for an hour or so.

I like people watching, and there were a lot of people to watch. I concentrated on the women, of course, and this, naturally, took my mind and parts of my body back to Anshan and Fu. Were Chinese women the same as Chinese meals, in that as soon as you've had one, you feel like another? In the West MSG gets the blame in the food and maybe it's something similar with the women. They have no discernible body odour or taste – when clean – but there is something about them that brings on 'yellow fever'.

My theory is that, unlike Western women, most Chinese women have retained their femininity, even though they have attained a legal facade of equality. Too many women in the West, not satisfied with being equal to men, actually want to *be* men, act like men or worse, emasculate men. The Western World is in danger of becoming a sterile, androgynous wasteland with only mythical movie star images to remind us of how it was and should be. Back in the seventies, when women's lib was very much in vogue, an ageing trade-union colleague of mine had it in a nutshell: 'It's a lot of bollocks, Russ. Why on earth should women want or need equality when they've always had superiority?' Think about it. Don't get me wrong, I'm not a male chauvinist in any shape or form and see nothing wrong with 'girls on top'. I just believe that women should be women.

The afternoon progressed and at around four o'clock I noticed activity across the other side of the lobby at Charlie's Bar. They were opening and a board was displayed which said, 'Happy hour from 4.00 until 7.00. Two drinks for the price of one.' I thought, "Why not? Two or three won't do me any harm."

Famous last words. Not as famous as 'What does this button do?' or 'So, you're a cannibal are you?' or 'Of course the power's off.' or 'What duck?' but not bad.

Into Charlie's I went. Beer, but which beer? Heineken, Tiger, Reeb (beer backwards), Diebels, Kilkenny and Caffreys. Kilkenny and Caffreys? Since my first visit, two months before, the hotel, God bless them, had added the two Irish beers to their cellar – more than £4 a pint, but good value in happy hour and I was on expenses anyway. Go for it. I took up what was to become 'my seat' on the corner of the bar and settled in. On my previous visit to Charlie's, two months earlier, I'd decided which was the best place to sit, to see everything that was going on. A nameplate was never affixed to the bar, but it became 'Russell's chair' for all the time I was to live in Shanghai.

The bar was almost empty, apart from the staff and a couple of other Westerners, who were, like me, taking advantage of happy hour. The waitresses quizzed me as to who I was, where I was from, how long... etc, and were very sweet and attentive until their stock of English ran out. I was to get to know them all very well and they me.

I wasn't left to my own devices for long. A short, tubby, grey-haired, cigar-smoking individual came in and headed in my direction. On seeing me, he hesitated slightly before deciding to occupy the chair next to me. I was obviously in 'his seat'. He ordered a beer – German accent. "Oh, shit" I thought. He opened a conversation with me in a somewhat strange way. He began with, "You German?"

"No. I'm from England. You're German?"

"Fuck, no. I am Austrian. I hate fucking Germans."

I told him that I wasn't keen on them either, which seemed to please him. He introduced himself as Freddie, an electrical engineer, and told me he had been in Shanghai for more than a year, so he knew his way around. He proceeded to give me the low-down on places to go, women, the hotel, women, people to meet, women and a lot more. It seemed he was having a good time in Shanghai.

We sat and talked as the place slowly filled up. Just before seven, two men entered, one very large with a big, hooked, bald-eagle nose and the other bearded, long-haired and wearing sandals – It was January. Freddie shouted them over and introduced them. "Russell, I'd like you to meet Big Ron and Dennis."

The usual friendly greetings were exchanged and the standard questions asked and answered. Both were Americans and seemed like a couple of decent guys. Surprisingly, Big Ron already knew something about me. "Old Geoff told me you wuz on the way. Don't see much o' him lately since his wife got here. What a bitch."

I was to find out about Geoff's wife, Di, for myself - Ron was right. What a bitch. Big Ron's size and manner made him somewhat intimidating, but he was popular with the staff and they all came over to say hello. He was to become a good and close friend while I was in Shanghai.

The other, Dennis, was very laid-back and 'Californiaish.' His age, early fifties, and his appearance told me that he might have had a good time in the sixties. This was confirmed as I got to know him better: "I think I had a good time back then. Only problem is I can't remember most of it." They ordered their drinks – an Absolut vodka and cranberry juice and a CC (Canadian Club) with water on the side and Freddie commented, "Why always 'water on the side,' Ron?"

"I like my liquor and I will not adulterate it, but shit, I miss my Daddy's moonshine."

The drinks arrived and there was immediate uproar. The barmaid was relatively new and had *seen* Dennis's drink but never actually made it before, so, remembering what colour it was, she had used Campari instead of cranberry juice because it was red. It took another two attempts before she got it right, by which time half a bottle of Absolut had been poured down the drain. Dennis was happy, but the bar manager, who arrived just in time to see the last, successful attempt, was definitely not.

Big Ron shook his head ruefully and said, "These dumb fuckin' girls. If their brains wuz Semtex they ain't enough to blow their goddam noses." Followed with, "If you shone a light in their eyes it'd be like you done it to deer or a rabbit. They ain't got nuthin' back there." I had just received my first samples of the wisdom of Big Ron. There would be more.

The 'ladies' began to enter and take up their positions shortly after Ron and Dennis arrived and made it their business to get us to notice them. They were particularly interested in me – new meat and a new prospect – so I got a lot of attention. Ron had a low opinion of most of them. "These bitches? One thousand rmb to fuck 'em? They can kiss my ass till Sunday afore I'd pay 'em that. Shit, man, I can buy a white woman for less."

Time passed quickly with my new, entertaining acquaintances and eight o'clock came and went unnoticed. At about 8.30 a familiar figure wandered into the bar – Geoff. He spotted me, made his way over and opened with, "Got here safe then? You weren't in your room, so I thought you might be in here. Just as well I came to look for you." He cast an evil grin towards Ron and carried on, "I had a feeling you might fall in with the wrong sort and that I'd have to rescue you." He refused a drink and continued, "We're all having an early night cos we're off back to site at six thirty in the morning. Problems. See you at breakfast at six. I'll fill you in on everything then." Then he left, casting a v-sign back at a laughing and jeering Ron and Dennis.

My first evening in Shanghai was ending, so I had another beer, decided against food, said goodnight and headed for bed. What would the morning bring?

The morning came early because of the time disorientation of jetlag and I was awake and ready to go at 3.30. I messed around and killed time until just before six and then made my way to the Club Lounge on the floor below. Geoff was there along with a white-haired individual, whom he introduced as Rab Stewart.

Rab was a mill engineer from one of the company's mills at Perth in Scotland. It had been recently shut down, so Rab had been given the opportunity to help start up the operation in Shanghai with me. He was to be my sidekick and he and the other two in the team had arrived in Shanghai two weeks before me, to run through things and make a snag (fuck-up) list of things that needed to be sorted out. I knew him by reputation, which was good, and this was borne out, as I found him to be a good man and, very quickly, a good friend. His being Scottish wasn't a problem. I can understand Scottish people, being from the North of England and of Scottish descent myself – not that I broadcast the latter too much. I became invaluable to Rab as a translator, both for the Chinese and English people – true.

I enquired where the other two members of the team were, Andrew Hodgkinson and Richard Chang, electrical engineer and electronic/computer engineer respectively. I knew them both: Andrew was an old friend from the North and I'd known him since he had been a shy young apprentice working for his father Arthur's electrical and mechanical engineering company. Richard was Singapore Chinese and worked for the company that supplied all my company's process control computer systems – not the best of engineers, but he could speak Chinese.

The team seemed to be well structured and sound, but Geoff informed me that the company, in its wisdom, had put them in a different, less expensive hotel (alarm bells rang immediately. penny pinching?) and we were to pick them up on the way. We ate breakfast, a good breakfast, and were preparing to go when Geoff gave me some advice. "Go to the toilet now if you need a shit."

"Huh?"

"Yeah, the 'facilities' on site are still fairly basic and commando, so better go now, if you need." I took heed and did the necessary, then off we went through the quiet dawn streets of Shanghai, picking up Andrew and Richard on the way.

Andrew was pleased to see me and I him. Something or someone familiar and trusted is always comforting in a strange new place. He slapped me on the shoulder and said, "Welcome to the land of lunatics, Russ. Good to see you."

Rab casually asked, "How was breakfast this morning, Andy?"

"Humph. Just the fucking same. Cold and no toast - again."

Andrew and Richard were staying in a four-star Chinese hotel and while the rooms were OK, some things weren't – breakfast in particular. It seemed that Andrew had an ongoing battle regarding toast. The hotel had an automatic conveyor belt toaster – put it in at one end white and it comes out the other end hot and browned. However, on first trying it out, Andrew received white, cold bread at the hot brown end. Andrew thought he'd better tell them, but they already knew and said, "I'm sorry, sir, but it's broken."

"Oh."

Next morning he tried again with the same result – untoasted toast – and was told again, "I'm sorry, sir, but it's still broken."

"Oh."

This continued until Andrew enquired as to why they put it out every morning if they knew it was broken and he was told, "We always put the toaster out at breakfast, sir." ie they had been told that the toaster had to be put out every morning, so that's what they did. The fact that the thing was fucked didn't matter to them. They were following orders. This is normal in China and orders, even stupid ones, are followed because the boss says so. Questioning orders is dangerous and can get you the sack. 'Tall poppy syndrome' was and still is prevalent in China.

We continued to the site, with the boys filling me in on the way. It became apparent that the 'problems' that Geoff had hinted at the night before centred on Richard. Richard was a 'lab-rat' and hadn't done a lot of site work. The main reason for choosing him had been his Chinese language ability. Mechanically, everything was fairly sound, but control wise there were problems.

It looked like a job for me. One of my fortes was in getting impractical, theoretical, bench boffins to understand the point of what they were doing and the priorities. Richard was sorting things out and then experimenting and tweaking. What was needed was something that worked for now, so that testing and proving the mechanical process could be done first. Shaving seconds off here and there, experimenting with sequences and improving response times could come later. He was pissing everybody off and I was the only one who had the authority to stop him. It took me two days, but he got the message. The implied threat to phone his boss, another old friend, and ask for a 'team player' to replace him might have had something to do with it.

I'd visited the site four months before, in August, and there had still been a lot to do – too much, I thought, to get it all done on schedule. I was wrong. There it was, one hundred and twenty feet high, white, shining and new, with the company logo in full view. All the alarming bamboo scaffolding had gone and most of the building site rubbish. Henry was his usual, urbane, cynical, laid-back, self and welcomed me to the 'madhouse' with a smile.

He apologised for not meeting up with me the night before and explained, confidentially, that he had been checking up on some interesting things he'd heard about our partner, Mao. It seemed that the man was on the verge of bankruptcy and was trying to use his 49% share of the Venture as security to raise some cash. Bad enough, but the added problem was that he was trying to borrow the money from another feed company in Hangzhou – a major competitor. Shit. And this was only four months away from the grand opening. Henry had headed him off at the pass with the help of the Shanghai local government. Mr Mao was now 'under investigation,' an investigation that was to result in his eventual imprisonment three years later. A report was on its way to the UK, to be pooh-poohed and ignored – again. All it achieved was to drive another nail into Henry's Chinese coffin and hasten his repatriation. NIH – not invented here.

The first day was a lost day because of jetlag and an

excess of alcohol, but I did get an initial feel for where we were with things, what still needed to be done and, most importantly, I met everybody. It was all a bit of a blur, as it always is at the start, with too many Xiaos, too many Wangs, too many people.

Henry took me aside and warned me about one of the staff. "Be careful of Ava Huang [one of the translators]. She doesn't look like it, but she bangs like a shithouse door in a gale. She's predatory, dangerous and vindictive if you refuse her. One of the earlier boys knocked her back and the next thing that happened was a quick trip home and no return ticket, when Dennis (the CEO) found out about some of the strokes he'd been pulling to get things done faster here. Ava was his translator and she was the only one who knew everything he'd done. If she says she wants to visit you in your room, make an excuse or have someone else there as chaperone."

"How did Dennis find out?"

Henry gave me a raised eyebrow look before saying, "Ava is Dennis's translator when he visits. How do you think he found out?"

Useful information for the future; Ava became a good avenue for getting unofficial information onto Dennis's desk or directly into his ear. I took a good look at her; bat-faced, poor teeth, slightly chubby, sausage legs and stumpy hands with chewed fingernails. As we say in Cumbria, 'Ward'a thowt?' (Who would have thought?)

I never did – honest – apart from the time, two years later, when she, playfully, took my dick out in the back of a minibus on the way home from a company night out. We were both very drunk and, as we were the last two passengers, she'd decided to explore. I let her and did some exploring of my own - nice tits, but a shaved, bristly pussy. Hate them. She was well into a very professional blowjob when the driver started talking to her. She stopped, as a well-mannered girl should, but carried on with her hand and had a conversation with the driver at the same time. She wasn't too happy with the mess on her black dress, but it probably wasn't the first time, or the last, that she had to deal with a biological stain. I hadn't heard of Monica Lewinski at that time, but thankfully my work duties had changed considerably by that time, so it was easy to avoid any entanglement beyond the annoying phone calls. I didn't have a brilliant relationship with Dennis at the best of times and this would have brought on the worst of times for sure.

Almost forgot – Ava's Chinese name was Huang Wei and pronounced 'Whong Way'. Inappropriate, as she could obviously do some things the 'Wight Way.'

Where was I? Mmm. I was at the end of my first day at work, Friday as it happened, in Shanghai. Not a bad day either and it got better when the consensus, wish, desire, need, demand of the team was for a weekend off. They'd worked through the previous two, so it was due to them. I needed to do some work of my own anyway and sort out a plan for the next week. Fuck it. There would be plenty of time on Sunday night. Shanghai was waiting.

CHAPTER FOUR

SHANGHAI NIGHTS

Arriving back in Shanghai from Minhang after my first day's work, I was puzzled why Andrew and Richard didn't get out of the minibus as we passed their hotel, so I said, "You guys going somewhere else?"

Andrew smacked his hands together and said, "It's Friday night and we're gonna hev a few scoops an' a ratch." That was 'Carlisle speak' for 'some beers and a look around.' I discovered that everyone's absence from Charlie's on the day I arrived wasn't the norm.

We hit Charlie's at around 6.30 and washed the day away with the first beer and a communal "What the fuck are we doing here?" The next few relaxed us and before we knew it, it was eight o'clock and the place began to fill up. Andrew looked around, rubbed his hands together and said, "Maybe some plunge tonight as well."

"Plunge?"

"You know, women, sex an' that."

I proceeded to tell Andrew what I'd gleaned from my visit to the bar the previous night regarding the 'going rate' and he had second thoughts. "Fuck. I'll do without."

We all decided to stick to beer and food. We were all very smelly anyway – feed milling does that to you. Occupational hazard. A booth was chosen and food was ordered from one of the four hotel restaurants – can't remember which – and we were set for the night. It was a time for bonding. Andrew and I had known each other for years and had shared more than a few beers – I'd shared a lot more with his father and uncle, Jewish John - better known as 'How much?' – so we were off to a flying start with the others following in our wake.

We had many such nights in the month that Andrew and Richard were with us and Andrew became more effusive, outrageous and flamboyant as the time went by. All missed him when he left. Richard, sadly, never even made a ripple on the pond of memory and came and went as if he'd never been. I can't, honestly, even recall what he looked like – very strange for me. Maybe Andrew was too much larger than life for him to be noticed. I'll come back to Andrew and the others later.

We decided we should have a touristy weekend, and my expectations that by the time I got there they would have the place sussed out were dashed. They had been working solidly for two weeks, so they were as lost as I was. Geoff knew his way about, but he was saddled with his wife, so he wasn't a lot of use to us except when we ate. Even then it would have been preferable not to be in Di's company. She found something to complain about everywhere we went – the food, the service, the place and so on. She was a pain in the arse and we, of necessity and for peace of mind's sake, avoided her as much as we could without being rude. – The Englishman's curse upon himself. It sounds bad and anti-social, but the last thing you needed after shit all day was shit all night.

We were going do the sights as per the tourists' guide and I knew, from what I'd already seen, that it would all be very impressive and spectacular. Not, however, being one of the best tourists in the world, I knew one weekend would be enough for me. The others could do as they pleased. I'd already been struck by the contrasts that were everywhere to see - opulence and abject poverty side by side, with skyscrapers towering over shantytowns. Also, at the time, 25% of the world's tower cranes were in China and 75% of those were in Shanghai, so in some areas the city resembled a huge, rambling construction site.

Many of the places we hit over the first weekend and the following couple of weeks became my regular haunts. There were others, of course, that I discovered later, after I knew my way about rather better. There were also many others, I know, that I never got to in all the time I was there and many more that I probably didn't even know of. Shanghai is so BIG that it is impossible to go everywhere and new places were springing up all the time. By the same token, places were closing all the time, like cells dying and reproducing, and it's probable that many of the places I used to frequent exist no more. I'm sure that it must be possible to go out every night of the year in Shanghai, always finding a place that is bouncing, and never go to the same place twice. Somebody should try it, but not me.

However, I always, always came back to Charlie's, probably because I lived in the hotel for almost six months and everybody knew me. I suppose I was like Norm in 'Cheers,' with my regular place at the bar – 'it's nice to go where everybody knows your name.'

I was back in Shanghai recently after a gap of five years and, for old time's sake, I paid a visit to the Crowne Plaza. It was much the same, though the people, of course, had changed. Not all of them, though, and as I sat and drank coffee in the lobby feeling the ghosts of memory pass by, around and through me, a voice called out, "Russell, it's nice to see you again." It was the Food and Beverages Manager, Steven Choi. It was a good feeling and we sat and reminisced for an hour before he was called away.

Anyway, I'll attempt to give a rundown of some of the places I frequented and the activities therein. Some of them, I'm sure, will crop up again and again as I wander through the telling of my time spent in Shanghai.

My first Saturday there arrived along with a major hangover, so the morning was spent quietly, consuming large amounts of coffee and orange juice in the Club Lounge. Rab and I, suitably refreshed and restored, wandered down to the lobby at around 11.30 and found Andrew and Richard there – waiting none too patiently. Andrew was raring to go. "Where then? I've heard there's a good Irish pub somewhere. It's called O'Malley's." I made some enquiries at reception, got the address and off we went.

O'Malley's is, or was, close to the American Embassy

on Urumqi Lu - 'Wulumuchi Lu' it still says on the street sign - on the south side of the Hua Hai Lu, one of the main streets in Shanghai. South of Hua Hai Lu is, or was, the French sector of Shanghai, and the architecture reflects this in its French colonial style. (The French are GONE. Yeah.) It's a pleasant area to walk around, a change from the rest of Shanghai and very similar to much of Hanoi, where I was to live three years later.

O'Malley's was in an old French villa and had a beer garden surrounded by high walls. This, effectively, gave isolation from the rest of Shanghai and, coupled with the British pub style interior, it was a peaceful Western haven away from the frenetic atmosphere outside. Not always peaceful, as there was live Irish music at the weekends and a rowdy, vociferous, multi-national, crowd of partisan supporters during the big screen televising of rugby matches. I should probably mention here that O'Malley's was the centre for Rugby Union in Shanghai and even had a 'team'.

I should also mention that, in my humble opinion, the greatest and best rugby player, outside the scrum, that ever 'played the game' was an Irishman, Mike Gibson. - The equivalent of a Pele, Nicklaus, Babe Ruth etc. And, of course, Barry John is a very close second.

I love the game, follow it and support it, but O'Malley's rugby team was more of a commercial venture than anything else. Enquiries about how to 'get a game' were never answered directly. 'Giv's yer fown number' was as far as I ever got. The 'shirts' were the thing. After I had been there for a while, one year maybe, I was witness to a conversation about rugby shirts – O'Malley's rugby shirts—between a 'Dublin' member of the staff and an American. "What about the quality of these uniforms? 800 rmb seems a mite expensive." Uniforms? Fucking uniforms? Philistine Americans.

The 'Dublin' member of staff smiled and said, " Lisn, I'm wearin' wun now an eye'm tellin' yer now dat if yer can rip it aff mi back yer can have it fur nut'n."

I was waiting for the American to ask about the guarantee and warranty, but I was distracted by a speeding snail and never heard the reply (sorry, Jason).

The only things to remind you that you were in China were the Chinese waitresses and the fact that you were using rmb instead of pounds. Guinness, Kilkenny, Irish stew and an authentic variety of pub food were available. Yes, a haven. Pricey at £4.50 for a pint of Guinness, but OK.

We spent a pleasant afternoon there, talking about work and getting to know each other better. It's very true that when you are away in a foreign country you make friends quicker because of the circumstances and conditions that you share. I'd heard this before, but now I know it to be true. It's also true that these friends are the key to survival, along with laughter. If you can't or don't laugh at the impossible and frustrating things that happen or situations you find yourself in you will go nuts. Laughter was and still is the key. If you don't laugh, you cry and die.

A decision to 'make a move' was made, but where to? We didn't know anywhere, so we stuck to the well-beaten tourist path – the Hard Rock Café. Getting there was easy, though rather convoluted. The taxi driver knew where it was, but seeing we were 'new' he managed to rip us off for about three times the fare. No problem – it gave us an opportunity to see more of Shanghai. Andrew, being the bulkiest, sat beside the driver and after a short distance began to engage him in one-sided conversation. "D'you know how Carlisle got on, pal?" (His father was a Director of Carlisle United Football Club) The driver grinned and nodded at him in response, so Andrew continued. "I see Tranmere had a good result last week." The driver responded as before, but with a broader grin. Andrew then pulled a packet of 'emergency supply' ginger nut biscuits from his pocket, offered one to the driver and asked, "You want a ginger nut, pal?'

The driver took one with a laugh and a shake of his head and said, "Shenjing bing." I found out later that it meant 'crazy.'

The Hard Rock was located in the Shanghai Centre Complex on Nanjing Lu, along with Tony Roma's – best ribs in town – the Long Bar, various other rip-off restaurants and designer boutiques and the five-star Ritz Carlton Hotel (where visiting heads of state stay. I've become somewhat blasé about heads of state since living in Hanoi, where they seem to have a different one every week. Mugabe, Castro, Clinton...) As expected it was not cheap and, therefore, out of reach of the vast majority of Shanghai's population, so it was best visited on an expense account.

The Company (notice the big C? – always) in its wisdom had given me a 'no limit' American Express card. For as long as it lasted I was the King of Shanghai. Dangerous? Of course. Fuck it. Never mind, the food, the live music, the atmosphere and the scenery were good. There was a bar, of course, as well as a restaurant and some of the 'scenery' in the bar looked very familiar and some even smiled at me in recognition. Shit. I'd only been in Shanghai for two nights and I was already 'known'. It was clear that the Hard Rock was part of the regular rounds for the hookers, or 'business women', as they preferred to be called. We stayed long enough to eat, take in the scenery – making mental notes for future reference – and listen to some music until we decided that it was too noisy to have any conversation. Another move.

We made our way across the complex and up an escalator to the Long Bar – big, big mistake. Look, I have nothing against Americans, but why do some of them insist on including everybody in a bar in their conversations? What's wrong with a subdued, private conversation? Oscar Wilde had it right when on his return, he was asked about his visit to the United States: "Far too many wide-open spaces surrounded by teeth." One drink and out, even though the place was heaving with females. I did revisit in future, but not too often. Time was moving on – 10.30 – so not knowing where else to go, we headed back to Charlie's.

In Charlie's the band was in full swing and again, there were some familiar faces and shapes – oh, the shapes. The band was Philippine, which was the norm back then. They weren't bad really and I came to know them very well. Bands usually stayed with the hotel for six months at a time, unless they fucked up and were kicked out or, on the other hand, were asked to stay on because they were better than average or cheap. The only problem was that after a while, they all became repetitive and, like a long-owned CD, you knew what was coming next. I hadn't reached that stage – yet – but some of the clientele had, and were ignoring them completely, so the band decided to 'mix it up' a bit.

After yet another "Hey, than' you ver much" followed by silence when they finished a number, the lead singer shouted, "Hey, anybody want to sing?"

There were a couple of 'takers' who did so-so jobs of performing their party pieces. Then he shouted at our table, "How about you guys?" Andrew, the bastard, began to applaud and point at me, going for yet another wind-up.

I'll never know why – alcohol probably - but I stood up and made my way to the stage. What to sing? I'd heard the band singing 'Desperado', an Eagles song, so… from the stage I looked back to the table to see wide-eyed amazement on all the boys' faces. I sang the song and received the loudest applause of the night. Back at the table I received Andrew's seal of approval. "Fuck. You were the business. Well done. Didn't know you could sing. Fuck. A star is born."

Not quite, but I became a regular performer, friend of the band and of all the subsequent bands. A slightly higher profile, local fame and notoriety didn't do me any harm in other quarters either. Around midnight we decided to call it a day and with arrangements made to 'do it all again tomorrow', we said goodnight. An interesting day ended? Not yet. I was just drifting off into sleep when my phone rang. "Mmm. Yeah?"

"Alo. You want have some companeeee?"

"Who are you?"

"I am Cindeee and you are Russa. I see you Hard Rock and sing in Charlie's. I smile with you. Remember?"

No recollection, but "Oh, yes."

"I will come?"

A pause, a decision and then, "OK". Click.

As she rang off I thought I should have asked how she got my room number, but I found out much later that the hookers slipped the bar staff money for the information.

Less than five minutes later she was there. Not a very memorable night, apart from her helping me to shower and making sure somewhere was clean. At least that's what she said the shower was for, but why she used her mouth to do the cleaning was puzzling. Not that I complained or anything.

She was the standard Chinese package that I was to get to know very well – small, silky haired, olive skinned, small-breasted with tiny, strong hands. She was also so small that I had some concern that I might dislocate her hip joints or something, but she had a preference for doggie style, so my fears were allayed, her reason being, "I like it go long way in." We slept afterwards and woke around eight for a repeat performance – standard missionary position this time.

The next thing that happened was more than a bit disconcerting. I'd taken a shower and was having a shave when she joined me in the bathroom. She sat down on the toilet and began to have a shit at the same time as holding a conversation with me. A conversation that, by the nature of things, was punctuated by grunts, groans, straining noises, anal reverberations and splashes. "You make love - NNNNG. - very good."

"Er…Thank you." Struggling for something more appropriate to say

"What" VVVVT. "will you do - OOOOHH. - today? AHH." Splash.

"Sightseeing."

"Maybe I will see - EEEEEHH. - you tonight. - AAAAAAHH. - Yes?" Sploosh.

"OK. Maybe."

VVVVVVT. "I will go now."

I was dumbfounded. (Looked for a more appropriate word but can't find one – disgusfounded is not, yet, in the dictionary.) Even as a long-time married man I had never been in that situation before except, of course, with my children when they were very small. 'Interesting and different' is how Henry described China. He was a master of understatement. She left shortly after with a wave and a wiggle of her button of an arse – lovely arse. I immediately, mentally, forgave her – I could have forgiven that arse anything – almost. At least I was forewarned for next time. I joined Rab for breakfast, still laughing, but I couldn't tell him why.

It was Sunday. Should I have gone to church? Maybe I should have done what Hernando Cortez and the other conquistadors did and had all my future sins forgiven before I left my native shores. Too late. Not that I'm a Catholic anyway, but what I'd done already would have been difficult to cover with a paternoster and ten hail Marys.

In the event, we had a day looking around the touristy bits of Shanghai: the Bund and the amazing view across the river of the Pearl Tower (third tallest tower in the world) and the Jinmao Building (fourth tallest building in the world); Yuyuan Gardens and Tea House; People's Square and Museum; Jade Buddha Temple, etc etc. Done and finished. Not quite 'finished', but enough for me for the time being. As I said, I'm not, in any way, a good sightseeing tourist and, in any case, I prefer the beauty of nature rather than the doings of mankind, and there's very little 'natural nature' in and around Shanghai. I also prefer to see places of interest in an incidental way rather than make special trips and excursions to visit them. Obviously, this took up most of the day and early evening, so by the time we got back to the hotel we were thinking about food, having only eaten, forgive us, some lunchtime KFC (More than forty KFCs in Shanghai back then. God knows how many now.)

Geoff and Di were waiting for us and it seemed that Geoff wanted to take us somewhere. He said, "Thought you all might like to go to the Tandoor maybe?"

"OK, why not?" I said.

The others only smiled and said nothing. I found out soon that Geoff *always* went to the Tandoor, one of the few Indian restaurants in Shanghai at the time. The route to the Tandoor, on Maoming Nan Lu, took us along the Hua Hai Lu, and I became a slack-jawed country boy.

What a sight. The street was illuminated with neon advertising arches every fifty yards or so and the effect was like Blackpool gone crazy. After I had been in Shanghai for a while I got used to it and enjoyed the amazed looks on visitors' faces when they saw it for the first time. Even so, it was still worth seeing again and again, as was much of Shanghai at night. Taxi rides on any of the overhead roads were particularly good for seeing it all. I would recommend a trip around the Inner Ring Road at night to any tourist. Night visits to Nanjing Lu and Yuyuan Gardens are also well worth the price. The Tandoor was also worth it, even though it was very, very expensive. George paid anyway, so I was saved the bother of feeling guilty. It would be my turn next, however.

There was also a very, very beautiful tall Chinese waitress in full Indian dress. I thought, at first, that she even had a bindi on her forehead, Indian woman style, but on closer inspection it was actually a perfectly placed, natural mole – probably one of the reasons she got the job. Her appearance, and particularly her bare-midriff costume, were eye-catching as, in those days, it was only a 'bad woman' who exposed any part of her body in public.

Even pictures and hoardings advertising lingerie only had Western women on them. It's changed now, but not everywhere. Change, in all things, is slowly spreading from the east coast – very slowly - and it may never get to some places. Suffice it to say, I am sure that Geoff didn't go there only for the food.

We were having a very relaxed evening - and then Di began to perform. We all thought that the food was good – on the eye-watering side of hot without taking the skin off. She, however, complained that it was too bland and that the service was poor AND that there was a draught. She then proceeded to belittle Andrew's bargaining skill when he mentioned some of the things he had bought during the day. In all cases it was along the lines of "I can buy it cheaper than that and in a nice box."

Andrew, believe me, is a gentleman and took it with stoicism, but he whispered to me, "That's it. The gloves are off next time."

We returned to the hotel and thankfully, Di didn't join us in Charlie's. Geoff went to the room with her, but was back downstairs after about five minutes, beaming, "Told her we had to have a meeting before tomorrow. Get me a beer."

"How long is Di staying, Geoff?" we enquired

"Only two more weeks, thank Christ. She's driving me up the fucking wall." We all silently agreed with him.

We had a few beers and decided we'd better get some sleep. We were on the way out as Cindy came in. She made for me and wrapped herself around me before saying, "Russa, you OK? Miss you. Where go now?"

I explained that we were all going to bed – it was eleven o'clock – and that we had to get up at six, and reassured her, "I'm here for a long time."

"OK. See you tomorrow maybe? I be here" she pouted.

"OK. Sure. Bye-bye."

The others had waited for me in the lobby and Andrew was first to speak. "How long have you been here, you fucker?"

"Mmm - what do you mean?" I answered innocently.

"Only two days and you're into it already. Fuck. You fucking dog."

My protestations of innocence were useless and, to be truthful, transparent. And so to bed. Sleep? Not immediately, as Cindy called to try and persuade me that her company would be good for me. I was strong and declined, telling her again that I was going to be in Shanghai for a long time and, again, that I had to work early in the morning. I didn't blame her for trying, though and it is true that the creaking hinge is the one that gets oiled. She was well oiled.

The morning arrived all too soon and I made my way to the breakfast lounge to find Rab and Geoff already there. Rab was a 'morning person' and had already eaten, so he was beginning to chat up and wind up the waitresses. They were all lovely – 'Mr Nasha drinks wodaka tonic, etc' – and their English seemed to be very good. Seemed. However, it became clear very quickly that their language was limited to what they had been schooled in by the hotel. eg, one of them passed by the table and Rab caught her eye and leered, "You're looking very lovely this morning." She hesitated, smiled and then replied, "Help yourself."

We laughed and then, hurriedly, got one of the more experienced girls to explain the implications of her response, as she was more than slightly bemused by it all. She needn't have worried as Rab was a good man, better than me, and behaved himself in Shanghai.

Breakfast negotiated, we made the trek to the site and another frustrating week had begun. Frustration is something that you get used to, or don't, when you work in China. Things get done, but they get done in a different, much slower, way than in the West. You either cope with it and accept it or leave, as trying to change it is an even more frustrating and fruitless task.

Frustration has its own seat at every meeting you hold or attend, with disbelief and anger waiting outside the door to join in if they are needed, which is frequently. I hadn't smoked for twenty-three years, but I had started again within a month of going to China. All right, they are cheap, but frustration was the major reason.

Cigarettes, alcohol and laughter were what kept us all sane in the early days, and even afterwards I found that a 'wasted' evening was essential for restoring perspective and sanity – preferably spent with someone of like mind and situation who wasn't a loud American, Australian, French or German. I'll delve into my ongoing learning of 'the ways' as I go along with the tale and things come to mind. I don't want to write too much about 'work' because it is, quite frankly, boring, and only has a bearing on my life in China because it's what took me there.

Things settled into a pattern of work, play, work, play, which was fine at first, but I began to feel uneasy, for some reason. I was becoming bored. One of the problems about living and working as we were was that we were always together and work was our main topic of conversation. It was work, drink, dinner, drink, talk and sleep. I needed to escape. I did have a distraction in Cindy, but needed something more. Stupid maybe, but I decided to branch out on my own and do my own thing. When the others decided to call it a night I went through the motions of retiring, but would then go back downstairs to see what was going on, either in the hotel bar or in the immediate locality. It worked. Apart from going to new places and getting to know Shanghai better, it expanded my circle of friends and acquaintances, which is always good. It almost killed me, though, and I had to catch up on sleep on the way to and from work and at weekends.

For the first week or so I kept the others in ignorance, even though they were puzzled as to why I fell asleep so easily. They eventually began to smell a rat when we ventured into, for them, new places and I was welcomed like a long-lost friend. 'Russa, Russa, nice to see you again' sort of gave the game away.

I began to spend a lot of time with Big Ron and he helped, more than anyone, in my education about China and Shanghai. He was also very colourful and kept me entertained with his views and observations – all delivered in his own inimitable style. Here are a few that I remember. There were many more.

Home? "I wuz born an' raised on a little island no bigger than this here bar [Charlie's] with my five brothers and two sisters." Ron had escaped his 'white trash' beginnings through education, Military Academy and the US Air force.

Vietnam? "I broke a plane in Vietnam, Russell, and went down in the jungle. Fuck, it wuz hot an' I wuz up to my ass in VC. I 'most took one little fucker's head off with a cheese wire afore I got out." Ron had been an F16 pilot in Vietnam and had a cockpit as his screensaver.

African American/negros? "See that boy? Ain't he just blacker'n a well digger's ass?" Or, "We have a law down our way that says spics (Mexicans) an' niggers cain't marry. Their kids would be too lazy to steal."

"How did you come to work in China, Ron?"

"Well, my job interview went like this: 'How well do you consider that you get on with Asians, Mr Parkes?' I answered, 'Well, Sir, I spent most o' my time in 'Nam tryin' to kill them an' they spent most o' their time tryin' to kill me, so I guess you could say we wuz pretty close.' I got the job."

"How was your day?"

"Just another day of frustration an' balls ache in China."

"Working relationships?"

"I tell him, 'When I kick yo ass you flick that switch an' when I whup you upside the head you push that button, you mother fucker.' It works."

"You're looking very tired."

"Russell, I am goin' to bed sem-eye soon."

"What about marriage?"

"Hell, I wuz married, but she wanted me to live with her all the time."

"What do you think of Andrew?"

"That man is a top hand." The ultimate accolade.

"Traffic?"

"I find that a coupla smacks upside the head resolves most problems."

"I'm doing some work in Anshan."

"Oh, fuck, Russell, you don't wanna go there. Listen, you got my phone and fax numbers an' my e-mail. If you go up there an' need a place to come back to, my place is yours. Those little fuckers up there fight back sometimes. Hell, don't go there."

There were other gems and pearls that came out, of course, which I will drop in as and when I remember them. Ron was, in many ways, a strange character who was both feared and loved in equal proportions. He didn't suffer fools or 'assholes' and if he didn't like you, you knew it. For me, though, he was a kind, generous, big-hearted man who lived life to the full. His exterior was daunting and intimidating, but inside he was a very different character.

Among the other things he did for me was to show me the local 'sights'. Within easy reach of the Crowne Plaza, a walk or a short taxi ride, were many places to 'relax' and meet people. They ranged from the seedy to the sophisticated, but they all had the important things in common – alcohol and women.

First on the list, because it was closest, was the Step Bar just across the road from the hotel. It was a handy place to go after Charlie's wrapped up for the night, if you didn't feel like going to bed. It wasn't a 'bad' place and first impressions were wrong. All the girls were there to do was keep you company and get you to spend money on drinks. Some did go freelance after hours, but while they were working all they did was talk. Annie, the boss and an eventual good friend, made sure that everything was kept above board and was quick to weed out any 'bad girls'. I liked the Step. It was good to have somewhere to go that was safe and relaxing – by which I mean that all you needed to do there was drink and talk without having to fighting off predatory females all the time. You might get conned into buying one of the girls an exorbitantly priced drink now and again, but it was worth it, as they were good, distracting company as well as being good to look at. No touching, well not too much, and any customer who got too friendly was told to cool it or leave.

If you did feel in need of something to touch, grope or fondle, there was another place close to the hotel called Freshers, where touching, groping and fondling were almost obligatory. It was, to be honest, very seedy and very down and dirty and it wasn't unusual to see customers getting a blowjob or 'hand relief'. I never partook myself, though I know it was a regular port of call for many who wanted something quick and uncomplicated. Very off-putting when you are having a drink anyway and you always had to be careful where you sat down or put your hands. Sticky.

If, on the other hand, you wanted to go somewhere noisy, there were a myriad of discos and clubs, which were usually swarming with equal proportions of Chinese women and foreign men. Good places to go to clear the eardrums or anything else that needed clearing. I can't and won't mention them all, but there were two that were frequent, late night ports of call – Judy's 2 and Didis. They were always heaving, sweaty and loud, with a better than average sample of local 'talent'.

Judy's was on Maoming Nan Lu and only got going after midnight. One of its specialties was 'Tequila Time'. This involved the barmaids dancing on the bar, pouring tequila into any mouths stupid enough, for the duration of one song. I never did it. Had it been 'Vodka Time' I might have considered it, but tequila, no. Ron used to take it on sometimes, but he always picked a small barmaid, so that with him being so tall, she couldn't get the bottle too far away from his mouth.

Didis was similar, but different. It was very down market and if you stood in one place too long you became glued to the floor. I couldn't tell you what colour the carpet used to be. The one thing they had in common was the women. My slide into 'yellow fever' was out of control and speeding up.

They all looked much the same – black hair, brown eyes, small breasts, bums like boys and very, very, very feminine. Ohhh. They homed in as you entered whichever establishment and the approach was usually standard – 'What's your name? Where you from? You have lady? You want lady?' etc. etc. They were a bit like hotel staff in that their language was limited to what they did. Here's a conversation I had with one of them:

"You want lady?"

"No. I'm trying to give them up."

"Don't unerstan'."

"Ladies are all right, but you can't beat the real thing."

"Don't unerstan.' You want lady or not?" Puzzled.

"Not tonight. I've got a headache."

"If you sick, go hoptal."

The next step was a puzzled retreat and conversation with friends about the 'strange foreigner.'

I was amazed at how quickly I had become known by the girls – the bush bush telegraph – and I received nods, waves and smiles of recognition, when I walked into anywhere. They gradually began to realise that I could not be enticed and would only move when I wanted. This was good, as it gave me the opportunity to try and find out more about them than how they performed.

Most of them had sad tales to tell about broken homes, incestuous fathers and brothers and no prospects for the future. Slowly my perspectives began to change, and what would have been unacceptable in the soft, welfare state life of Britain became acceptable and the norm. There is no safety net in China and most Asian countries, so people do what they have to do to thrive and survive. The goal of most was to try and find a rich foreigner on a white charger to rescue them and take them away from it all. Life.

Most of Western Europe and North America have no idea, nor do they want to have any idea. Even most of those who live and work in China have little or no real understanding, and seem to be waiting for China to catch up rather than meet it where it is. It gets even worse if you venture away from the relatively cosmopolitan areas into the real China and see how little people have and how little they seem to need. Maybe it's because they know no better – as my grandfather used to say, "If you've only ever seen a calf you don't know how big a cow is."

A quick word about my grandfather. He died when I was twenty-one and I wish I could have spent more time with him. My brother and my sister did, but by the time I was old enough to be able to communicate with him at a reasonable level, he was an old, old man. I share his name and, everyone says, his appearance, and I hope I can be like him as I drift into old age. I think I am like him in other things as well, in that my memory is good and I can remember, in detail, events and conversations that happened years ago. He was full of anecdotes and stories of his life and experiences and it's a great shame that only fragments live on in the memories of others.

His observations and opinions were also very interesting. He had a very low opinion of my uncle, his son-in-law, which was encapsulated in, "If I had a dog half as stupid, I would have it shot." Ouch.

He was alone for many years after my grandmother died in 1940 and lived with my Aunt Ella and the aforesaid uncle. He was alone, but not lonely, as I found out after he died. About two weeks after his funeral I was walking along a street in my hometown when an old woman, Mary, stopped me and began, "Sorry about your Granddad, son. He was a good man." And then, with a wink and a nudge, "He was still a man when he was past seventy." I was, as you would expect, somewhat stuck for an appropriate response. Yes, I hope I'm like him.

Anyway, back to China. Another place I used to visit was The Pauleiner, a German Beer Hall, which served huge steins of beer and German style food – schnitzel, pork knuckle, sausage and things. It was very popular, always busy and, if you wanted a good table, it was essential to book in advance. The Chinese liked it there, but were always knocked over very quickly by the in-house brew – come to think of it, they were knocked over quickly by everything they tried to drink anywhere.

I was there one time for a farewell party for a staff member, Xiao Deng (unfortunately pronounced 'Dung'. Maybe not. She was a little shit a lot of the time). After it was all over I made my way back to the hotel. It was relatively early, so I decided to wander over to the Step Bar for a while. After the usual 'Russa, Russa, how are you?' a large, blonde, German-looking individual engaged me in conversation cum interrogation. He was ultra stereotypical and would have stood out as being German at an SS reunion. It went like this:

Him, "Gut efening. Ver hef you been tonight?"

Me, "The Pauleiner."

Him, "It vas gut, ja?"

Me, "Ja – I mean, yes it was good."

Him, "How vas ze beeeer?"

Me, "OK."

Him, "It vas yust OK? Not gut?"

Me, "Well, yes I suppose it was good."

Him, "Ver gut. Ze nex time you go zer you vill ask for me. I am Volfgang ze brrraumeister."

"Thank God I liked the beer" I thought.

Charlie's, however, was where I spent most of my time and my money. To be fair, a lot of the money was the company's – at the time they weren't too worried about expenditure in China. This was to change after about two years, when the purse strings were drawn tightly and never, thereafter, reopened. Somebody eventually started to worry about the bottomless pit that China seemed to be.

Anyway, Charlie's became my local and I became a very regular 'regular', with the bar staff beginning to pull my drink as I walked through the door and my bill always appearing with my name and room number already on it. In the early days some of the bills were a bit alarming – more than the monthly salary of the bar staff for a one night's session.

I recall one night when I was presented with a bar bill for about $200 after having previously signed one for a similar amount in the restaurant, so I gave it some thought and put Rab's name on the bill to make it look better on my expense sheet. I felt a twinge of guilt and told Rab the next day, but he smiled and informed me that he had signed my name on one of his bills the week before. Bastard.

The staff in Charlie's were entertaining and we had a lot of fun talking to them and attempting to improve their English. One girl in particular, Peggy, was lovely but not very bright. The lights were on, but there was no one home most of the time. She appeared one night wearing a name badge that said 'Jenny.' I asked her why and she looked blankly at me and answered, "I know is not my name, but I couldn'ta finda mine."

She did, however, give me a wonderful welcome on one occasion, after I had returned after a week away in Anshan. "Russa, miss you. Is long time never see youa." was the enthusiastic, smiling greeting. Lovely.

Of the other staff one stands out in memory – Jacqueline. She was built like a brick shithouse and was rechristened 'Winston' by Andrew because of her unfortunate resemblance to a bulldog. She was a character, as well as being a very good barmaid. I walked into a quiet Charlie's one night to find Jacqueline studying a book with a puzzled frown on her face. She saw me and came to the end of the bar and, with a serious look on her face, asked, "Russa, what means 'bowra movamunt'?"

I was puzzled and took the book from her to look for myself. Mystery solved. 'Bowel movement' I explained. Light dawned and she said, "Ah. Take shit. Take shit. Xie, xie."

A few minutes later Dennis entered the bar and Jacqueline, with a big smile on her face, thinking she would use her newly discovered English phrase, asked the question, "Dennis, you have bowra movamunt today?"

Dennis looked puzzled, as I had been, so I explained and after light had dawned he laughed and said, "Yup. I take a dump everyday. If you don't dump you die."

CHAPTER FIVE

MINHANG

I'd better say something about the place where I worked for most of the time I was in Shanghai before I forget. Minhang is a district to the south west of Shanghai and is where my company built its factory. More specifically, the factory was located fairly close to the village of Luhui. I use the term 'village' loosely, as Luhui had a population of around 30,000. Hardly a village by British standards, I know, but it was viewed as such by its massive neighbour Shanghai. For my first two years in China I was to spend most of my time there. It was a real shit-hole, but it's amazing what becomes acceptable and normal through time.

The daily trips to and from Minhang were a pain in the arse – at least forty-five minutes each way. Longer, if your timing was off or if there was a road accident, which was frequently. At first the trips out were interesting and very different, but eventually – after about a month – they became boring and tedious. They became like the rides on the school bus which I took every school day for seven years. Sleep was the best option most of the time after everything had been 'seen.' Everything? There was a lot of 'everything' and it was all still alien, new and different.

Things to intrigue were on view as soon as breakfast was over. One of the lifts in the hotel had a glass back and provided a view out over the city and of some of the 'morning activities'. The building next to the hotel was a recreation centre – sports, ballroom dancing and the like - and had a large open area in front of it. This area was occupied every morning by up to twenty women who performed a variety of aerobic style activities. These ranged from dancing with fans, ribbons, and fake swords to ritualistic Chinese dancing. All the women were over fifty and all performed with smiling faces, elegance and perfect synchronisation. Not too difficult, I suppose, as most things were performed in slow motion.

As the journey to work got under way and progressed you saw more of it, particularly if the route was along Xin Hua Lu. Xin Hua Lu is one of the primary streets in Shanghai, not because it's big and grand, but because it's pleasant, beautiful even, and tree lined. It also has wide pavements and many small park areas, which were always full of 'older' people every morning, engaged in various physical or not so physical activities. Martial art related activities were most popular with the men – tsai chi, kung fu and wu shu – while the women tended to stick to the before mentioned dancing.

There were some things that were very mystifying, like the old man who stood stock-still with eyes closed while flicking the tops of his ears. I was told it was something to do with nerve stimulation - acupuncture? There were also people who didn't even bother with the ear flicking. They, apparently, were emptying their minds, seeking inner peace, oblivion and Nirvana, or maybe trying to put themselves into the necessary state of mind to qualify as taxi drivers. Probably a prerequisite for the job. Who knows?

I asked Lao Zhi at work why they did it. Party edict or something? He said, however, that older people, usually over sixty, did it to stay fit and active. Fit and active? Flicking your ears or sitting motionless? His wife did it and was trying, unsuccessfully, to get him to take part in it. He maintained that watching television was adequate for his needs. Not as big a cop-out as flicking your ears, I thought. (More of Lao Zhi's wisdom later.)

The journey thereafter was through Shanghai at its busiest, until the traffic thinned out when you reached the outer ring road. There was always something to see, whether it was a mob congregated round an accident or someone trying to carry a double wardrobe or a sofa on a bicycle. On one occasion I was witness to the incongruous sight of two men carrying a thirty-foot by nine-inch 'I' beam between two bicycles, totally oblivious to the mayhem they were causing as they made the slow diagonal crossing of a road junction.

Most accidents were caused by bicycles, although the general rule in China was and still is, "if you are the biggest you are to blame", even if it's not your fault. Chinese people seemed to have no or little regard for life, even their own, when they were on the road. Generally, their main concern if they had an accident was how much money they could get from the other guy in compensation. The traffic was chaotic with everybody doing their own thing, regardless of what anyone else was doing. Apparently there were 'rules of the road' and people had to pass a driving test – or, more often, buy the licence. There was, however, no evidence of any order except for which side of the road they were supposed to be driving on, and even that was flouted with alarming frequency. Red lights seemed to be used as a guideline to stop rather than an instruction, and lane discipline was non-existent. The traffic police were observers and didn't get involved unless everything ground to a halt, and even then they seemed to act as referees rather than policemen.

At the time there were not many foreigners who drove in China, the reasons being that if you were doing it correctly you were the odd one out and, maybe the best reason, if you were involved in an accident it was your fault, no matter what the circumstances. It was also your fault if a taxi you were travelling in had an accident. The logic was that if you hadn't been in the taxi in the first place then the taxi wouldn't have been where it was to have the accident. Ergo – your fault.

As progress was made to the outskirts of Shanghai, normal city traffic thinned out to be replaced by heavy transport: trucks, cranes, bulldozes and digging machines of all kinds. Everything in Shanghai was expanding outwards and upwards like a fast-growing fungus, with new roads, bridges and buildings of all types. You could often see old people gazing around in seeming disbelief and wonder, as their neighbourhood was rolled over by the unstoppable, encroaching beast.

Progress? I wonder what they really thought. Probably not much, if their home was one of those in the way and they were re-housed miles away from where they had lived and grown up. It was exactly the same as the Vogon Destructor Fleet in *Hitchhikers' Guide To The Galaxy* – 'Resistance is useless.' I'm just glad it wasn't my home town.

It was all very impressive when it was finished, but not very good to see when it was being built. Most of the buildings, apart from the big ones, were thrown up quickly and covered in tiles to make them look nice, but had a life expectancy of twenty-five years or less. However, the roads, fly-overs and particularly the big bridges, were impressive and grand and, in some cases, mind-blowing. The Nanpu Bridge linking the east and west of Shanghai had a triple spiral exit road at the western end that used to make your head spin if the driver took it too fast. Helter-skelter on a grand scale.

Once past the outskirts and on the outer ring road it was fairly straightforward. Over the Xupu Bridge, turn right and a drive of another twenty minutes to the site.

The road from the bridge to Luhui was new dual carriageway and straight as an arrow. Unfortunately, however, it was not flat. For some reason, every bridge, and there were many, was at a different height to the road, sometimes up to a foot higher. This made sleep very difficult, even though attempts, mainly unsuccessful, had been made to make ramps to level things off. The last bridge before the turn on the factory had a one-foot drop and I christened it the 'alarm clock bridge' for obvious reasons. I postulated that the bridge builders and road builders either didn't like each other or didn't communicate, only to be told that the bridges were built at a higher level because they were heavier and would, eventually, sink to the same level as the roads. Standard construction practice in China? Maybe ground floors eventually end up as cellars. Who knows?

Traffic was sparse for most of the time and varied from three-wheeled, chain-driven tractors to container trucks. Sparse, but still 'interesting'. The rules of the road were given even less heed than in the city and our driver always had to be prepared for something coming at him up the wrong side of the carriageway or for a slow, trundling tractor to exit a side-road after having watched our car approach. Sometimes it even seemed that they waited on purpose just to make our car slam on its anchors and swerve violently. In Britain there would have been confrontation and 'road rage', but this only happened in China if there was contact. Being 'cut up' on the road was a normal and expected part of driving.

Either side of the road was farmland, most of it divided into narrow strips in an almost feudal style. Green vegetables of all types were the main crops, interspersed with larger areas of rice or other cereals. Apart from the appearance, the other difference that struck me was the presence of people working. In Britain it's rare to see people actually working on the land as you drive through it. Mechanisation has done away with the need for them, but in China people still do things manually, bending their backs in cultivating and harvesting everywhere except in the major maize and cereal growing areas. Closer to the factory there were orange groves, which made a pleasant change to the flat, boring expanses. Oranges? A bit of a misnomer, as all the oranges I ever saw or ate from them were green. 'Greens?' Doesn't sound as good or as appetising, does it?

After the wake-up jolt we had arrived, and passed through the gate and into the factory compound. Every morning, as we passed through the gate, the security man rang a bell. After a couple of weeks I asked someone why they rang the bell and received a shrug and a shake of the head. Nobody knew why. Later, I figured out that it was because they had a bell and needed a reason to ring it. Either that or they had been told to do it and not given a reason – a fairly normal state of affairs in China.

We shared the site with our JV partner company, Huinong, owned by Mr. Mao Guiling – a crook of the first order, as some of us always suspected; we were subsequently proved to be correct. Huinong didn't seem to do much except store grain in warehouses and house-like, thatched stacks outside. The grain was part of massive emergency reservoir, which was there as a result of Mao Zedong's fuck-up and subsequent famine in 'The Great Leap Forward,' when around twenty million Chinese died.

For a while, as is normal I suppose, everything was

confusion – faces, language, everything. It took time to figure it all out and it was painful – painful to the extent that I wondered if I had made the right decision. There were many 'What the fuck am I doing heres?' in the early days. The only thing I fully understood was the factory and its equipment, so I focused on that. It worked out, and slowly it began to make sense and the pieces of the Chinese puzzle began to slot into place.

Figuring out the people was the hardest thing. Who was who? What did they do? What were they supposed to do? Who did they work for? There seemed to be a lot of people hanging about doing nothing and, indeed, there were. People wandered into and around the site, seemingly as they pleased. Many were just curious locals, others were hoping to find a job and others were there because they simply had nothing better to do. The situation was made even more confusing by the lack of any order in the way they dressed. They wore whatever clothes they had, no matter what they were doing, ranging from very sharp looking suits to raggedy-arsed jeans.

One day I had my eyes on a guy who'd been wandering around the site for an hour or two. He was wearing an ice-blue suit, black shirt, white tie and patent leather shoes – very sharp. Very suspicious. A spy? A mafia hit man? The latter seemed a possibility, as there was a suspicious bulge in his jacket. Then suddenly he reached inside his jacket and - whipped out a paintbrush and began painting the fire doors.

After a month or so, by which time we had the place

semi-finished and running, we tightened up on who should be there and the number of 'floaters' and vagrants dwindled. Dwindled, but never completely stopped.

I began to get to know people and they me. Geoff and Henry gave me the initial rundowns and I built on the information they gave me until I probably knew them better than anybody. The people in the factory were the first group. Among them was an engineer-cum-fitter called Li. He wasn't very good at his job, but was one of those individuals who thought that he was 'the best'. As such he was dangerous, a bit like a moron who thinks he's a genius, and had to be physically restrained from dismantling high-tech equipment so that he could improve it. Rab kept a close eye on him and always managed to head him off, thank God, when he was intent on some independent, unauthorised exploration and remodelling.

One of the other things about Li was his certainty that we understood everything he said to us in Chinese. He would address us seriously for five or ten minutes and then wait expectantly for a response and become impatient and irritated when he didn't receive one. He also used to listen intently whenever we were in conversation and as a result picked up a few English words and phrases. We found out, one day, that he had picked up a Scottish phrase. Rab, being Scottish, often used to suffix his conversation with the words, 'by the way,' as a normal part of his speech and Li had heard it often – too often.

We were listening to yet another of Li's Chinese monologues and as it ended he tacked on, 'by the way.'

The accent and intonation were spot on – identical to Rab's. Rab gave me an accusing look before saying, "You bastard" and to this day he probably still believes that I set it up.

We didn't have to put up with Li for too long, however, as he went too far with his tampering one day, after a final warning, and was halfway through stripping down a weighing machine because HE thought it wasn't working well enough. Instant dismissal. Bye bye.

There were, of course, many others on site, but unfortunately our mutual lack of language made it difficult to communicate except at a very low level. The ones that could understand and speak some English became good friends and none more than Lao Zhi.

Lao Zhi was the Administration Manager and much more. Every company needs a 'fixer' and Lao Zhi was that man. When you needed something sorted out he always knew a man who 'could' or a man who knew a man who 'could'. He was the man I turned to for help and advice on all things Chinese and he was invaluable to me. He gave me most of my first insights into China and things Chinese.

I recall his comments on an observation I made. I had been in China for about three months when I noticed something – the lack of something. There were no birds. I was walking over to the factory when two cock sparrows hit the ground, fighting, in front of me. They were the first birds I could remember seeing since I had been in China. Strange. Back in the office I mentioned it to Lao Zhi and is response was interesting. "Yes, we were told that birds were bad and ate all the crops and that we had to kill them."

"All the birds?"

"Yes, all."

I thought about it and then asked, "What about insect problems afterwards?"

Lao Zhi half smiled and said, "Mm. Yes, but no one will talk about that, so it didn't happen."

He probably told me more things than were good for him, but he didn't seem to care. Too old to care maybe.

He seemed to know everything that was happening on site and in the immediate surroundings, even though he rarely, if ever, left his office. When 'home time' came he was the 'beach-master' who knew where everyone was and where they would fit into the available transport. We hadn't a clue what was going on for most of the time and it all seemed like chaos. Geoff maintained, "There is a plan, but unfortunately we haven't been told what it is." This seemed to fit in with the way the company operated everywhere.

Lao Zhi, though not directly involved, also had input into the general expenses on site and it seemed, at times, that most of the money came out of his own pocket. This can be a useful attribute, but it led to the one time that we had a quintessential dichotomy (a disagreement). We were organising a party to celebrate Spring Festival 1999 and I was asked to be Chairman of the Organising Committee – not that I was expected to do anything more than say things like 'OK' or 'That's a good idea.' Lao Zhi was on the committee, but not for long: "We must not spend too much money" and then "That is not necessary" and then "The contract drivers cannot come" and then "All right, the drivers can come but their wives cannot." Finally, "We do not need to buy too much food and it is not necessary to buy a small gift for everyone."

This last was the final straw and I gave him his marching orders. He retreated ungraciously, muttering the words, "Too expensive. Too expensive. Not necessary. Not necessary." This apart, he was a good friend and ally during my time in Minhang.

There was another man I spent a lot of time with and who, eventually, became my assistant, Zheng Xi (Xiao Zheng). He was our first control room operator and he drove me nuts for a few weeks until I 'educated' him. A big part of his education involved him helping the labourers sort out his fuck-ups and in him getting very dirty a few times until he understood the consequences of his actions.

As a deskbound computer operator he had difficulty in grasping that his computer was running machinery that had fixed operating speeds and capacities that could not be changed or over-ridden just because he wanted things to go faster. When he realised he wasn't playing a computer game and would have to help clear the mountains of material he had caused or dig out a broken conveyor before it could be repaired, he began to grasp the principles – quickly.

His English was reasonable and he studied hard all the

time. He was, however, a computer buff and his English reflected this – "Russell, could you give me data on what we will do next week?", "I have to design a date with my girlfriend" and so on. He seemed like a shy young boy until I got to know him, when I found my initial impressions were wrong. He approached me one day just before Spring Festival 1999 and said, "Russell, I would like us to eat together over the holiday".

"Fine, Just you and me?"

"If it's all right I will bring one of my girlfriends."

"Girlfriends?"

"Yes, I have two. Xiao Wang and Xiao Li. I like them both and will decide later which one I want to marry." Still waters. He left then, after informing me that he would 'design' a date.

I did as much as I could to modify and improve his language in the two years we were together, though some of it maybe couldn't be described as improvement - "Russell, I have just dropped borrock (bollock)". More colourful maybe?

As my assistant he became closer to me, and I found how great his curiosity and his thirst for knowledge were, particularly with regard to women and the mechanics of sex. After a while he would become a pain in the arse, but he had the sense to realise when this was and would say, "OK, sorry, sorry, I will shut the fuck up now."

He also decided that, as my assistant, he should have an English name. However, he didn't bother to tell me what it was, knowing that I would never use it, as I was too accustomed to using his Chinese name. Anyway, he was talking to someone English on the phone and I caught the end of the conversation. "Yes, that's right. James, as in James Bond." I howled with laughter, much to his annoyance, and he refused to talk to me for the next hour.

He left the company after he had been working with me for about six months, to follow the love of his life as a career – computers. We kept in touch on a regular basis until I left China, and he wept bucketfuls when he came to see me for the last time. I hope he's OK and married to Xiao Wang, Xiao Li or Xiao Somebody by now.

The other people that became good friends were Ye Feng (Frank) who was a translator and my Production Manager understudy, Xiao Tian. Frank was a Chinese Christian and a good, clean living boy. He agonised over my foul language and I, in turn, gave him a lot of shit about his American accent and spelling. He was also very concerned about my soul or the fate of it and shook his head at my excessive drinking and other 'escapades'.

He was puzzled at what he thought were contradictions in me in regard to religion. I have a fairly good knowledge of the Bible, thanks to my mother, and Frank couldn't understand how I knew so much yet didn't go to church and wasn't a practising Christian. I explained that my fall from grace was down to being forced to Sunday school as a boy, a very unchristian local vicar and a love of all the bad things in life. He never gave up with his missionary work on me and even gave me a Chinese Bible when I left China.

I think, though, that I had more influence on him than he did on me and he developed a taste for beer, baijiu and, secretly, women. There were rumours of his having an illicit relationship with Madam Du, our accountant, which he denied with a straight face, so it must have been true.

Madam Du, a dormant or not so dormant volcano. Enigmatic, sometimes demure, butter wouldn't melt, bespectacled, married woman, who had something indefinable about her. There was a sensuality about her in everything she did and just looking at her could sometimes make things start to twitch. Her split skirts and backless tops in summer and her furry collars and high boots in winter. Ooh! She was uncaring about showing her flesh and it was normal for her to unselfconsciously adjust her bra or hoist her skirts to waft cooling air underneath, giving everyone flashes of her crotch. Double Ooh! There was always a half smile on her face, as if to say, 'I know what you're thinking', but she kept silent most of the time.

One day, though, she let slip a question to me and I was taken totally by surprise when she asked, "Russell, have you ever been unfaithful to your wife?"

I paused before my response, "Only if *you* are asking, Madam Du."

That, however, was as far as it ever got. I wondered, though, if she kept her glasses on when she… never mind. Do not screw the staff, Russell.

Where was I? Yes, I was moving on to Xiao Tian. At first he viewed me with a fair degree of suspicion, but he came to respect my experience and knowledge after I demonstrated it a few times. His English was limited, but we had a common bond in the work we did and the exchange of knowledge became two-way, him giving me the benefit of how it all worked in China and me feeding him with the more advanced technologies of the West.

We managed, between us, to set up and run a factory that had the benefits of both, and maybe some of the drawbacks of both. It worked, though, and I even managed to make a semi-western style manager out of him rather than the Chinese warlord that he was.

Chinese middle managers rule with an iron fist and use fear to control. This, of course, stifles subordinate staff, who either become obedient, unthinking slaves or sycophantic arse kissers with designs on the manager's job. I succeeded in getting Xiao Tian to be a tad more arm's length, rather than hands on or whip in hand. It wasn't easy for him to accept, but he finally grasped it when he went on holiday and left me to look after the place. It went like this. He came into my office with Frank and I could tell by the look on his face that it was serious stuff. Frank said, "Xiao Tian has to go away for a week on family business and he wants to know if you will look after the factory."

"Of course, and tell him that when he comes back I will let him know if he's a good manager or not."

Xiao Tian was puzzled and Frank asked what I meant, but I refused to elaborate and told him, "Wait and see."

Xiao Tian returned a week later and popped into my office, again with Frank, to see how things had gone in his absence. I told him, "OK, I only needed to go over there to sort out a couple of small problems. Tell him he's passed the test."

"What test?"

"If I'd been over there all the time it would have meant he's a shit manager, who can't delegate or organise."

Xiao Tian's face lit up as he realised the truth of this. He was a different man after that and our friendship was strengthened.

The more we worked together the more we enjoyed each other's company, and, in spite of language differences, he even began to come to grips with Western humour. Frank was usually involved in the translation of jokes and things I said, but very often the humour was lost on him, while Xiao Tian was doubled over. At these times Frank would look mystified and a little hurt. I remember one. We were having lunch and fish was being eaten and it had a very strong flavour. I made the observation, "Only two things taste like fish, and one is fish."

Xiao Tian asked what I had said and Frank, looking a bit puzzled, translated my words. Xiao Tian had hysterics, but Frank was completely in the dark and pleaded with me to explain. "What? What does it mean? I don't understand. Tell me."

"Sorry, Frank. Married man's joke. You'll have to wait and find out for yourself."

Xiao Tian was another who wept unashamedly when I left China.

Apart from Madam Du there were other females at work worthy of mention, Xiao Ding and Xiao Xu. Both worked in the finance department and both were young, sweet, innocent and lovely. The word cute could have been invented for Xiao Ding, and I'm sure many visitors wondered if she would fit in a suitcase, so they could take her home. Her English was so-so and she used me to practise on whenever she had the opportunity. Often she would slip into the seat next to me on the mini-bus ride home and prattle away.

One day she said, "Russell, I want English boyfriend."

"Oh, yes." my hopes rising.

"Yes. Young English boyfriend." Crushed.

On another day it went like this, "Xiao Ding, who's the new girl?"

"She is Xiao Tan. She have baby."

"Really? You like baby?"

I received a shocked look, so I followed up quickly with a slightly modified question, "Do you think babies are nice?"

"Yes I do." the expression on her face turning to one of relief when she realised I wasn't making an offer.

On yet another occasion she came rushing into my office and shouted something at me that I made her repeat, because I couldn't believe what I thought I'd heard. "Russell, I want you to give me one now." I couldn't believe my luck, but then she followed on with an explanation that dashed my hopes yet again. "You give Ye Feng (Frank) apple and I want one."

The other one I mentioned, Xiao Xu, was tall and athletic and was a sight to see when she was wearing a short skirt. Not as cute as Xiao Ding, but nice, very nice. Some lucky man…

As well as the staff, who were company employees, we had a pool of up to fifty labourers to do all the fetching and carrying. They worked like dogs for virtually nothing and a bowl of rice each day and as long as they exist there will be no major automation installed in most industries in China. They were part of the massive migrant labour force of China – country people who gravitate to the industrialised areas of China in search of a better life. A better life usually meant working for less than three dollars a day and sleeping in a lock-up garage. They were controlled by labour bosses who received the three dollars a day. These bosses then doled out what they thought was enough to the men. They had no rights and no redress and were treated as less than members of society wherever they went.

One of the labourers showed some interest and aptitude in the factory, but when I suggested that we employ him I was met with shock and horror and the answer, "He is not Shanghai people. He is only a labourer."

I was angry, but helpless. Nothing could be done to break him free of his position in the scheme of things. India is not the only country that has a caste system – it exists in China. They are stuck in a social dead-end and a poverty trap with no hope of escape.

I was amazed, also, at what these tiny men would do, without complaint or rest, in 100-plus degree heat. All they had was two barrels of water – one to drink and one to periodically soak their wet towel headdresses (evaporative cooling). The most difficult job they had, after the lift was installed, was unloading barges. This entailed carrying fifty kilogram sacks of anything up a long, narrow, bouncing ramp in all weathers, with an ever-present risk of injury by falling into the river or onto the barge. I tried it once and was lucky not to come to grief. People in the West couldn't or wouldn't do it in this day and age.

My admiration for these people and their stoicism grew during my time in China. Not just the men I saw in Minhang, but everywhere. There was the old woman sitting beside a twenty-foot mountain of old bricks, converting them into hardcore with a small hammer. Then there were the youngsters, weeding the one-acre lawn outside the Anshan International Hotel by hand. These are soul-destroying jobs, but Chinese people just got on with them. I honestly don't know how they coped with the heat as well as they did. I would be running with sweat after the short walk to the factory, but they all looked as if they were working in moderate, cool temperatures and only looked slightly warm after extreme exertion. Maybe it was a genetic thing, but I only know I would have been in big trouble without air conditioning.

Another group of people I should mention, though not part of the company, were the barge people. They worked and lived on the sixty-foot barges that plied up and down the river next to the site, sometimes in trains of five or six. They carried anything and everything there was to carry and always filled their holds regardless of weight. This often resulted in them being more than 50% awash most of the time and in constant danger of becoming submarines. I never saw this happen, but I'm told it that it did – frequently.

The crew of the barges usually consisted of a husband, wife and child, with the husband at the helm and the wife at the bow, using a pole to fend off other barges and assist with turns. The child, if it was young, was tethered with a rope around its waist that was just long enough for it to use the river as a toilet, but not long enough for it to fall in. They all had a small cabin that served as home and their whole life, or most of it, was spent afloat and free. Not a bad life maybe.

I soon realised that, while we were there to implant Western technology, systems and practices in China, there was only so much we could do, and slowly. We thought we were right, of course, but so did the Chinese. The phrase 'But we have always done it this way' was one that I heard frequently and my follow-up question of, 'Well, what are we here for?' was always met with silence. The answer was, 'We want your money', but it was never spoken. Back then and probably still now, many joint ventures were ambushed and taken over by the minority Chinese partner after the investment had been made. Beware.

The five thousand years of Chinese history and fifty years of communism were very, very difficult to overcome. One gave them the 'we know best' attitude and the other had instilled a fear of innovation and change and of making decisions and possible mistakes. If something goes wrong, even if it's a natural disaster, someone has to be responsible and MUST be blamed and censured. Even when there was no mistake made, the tall poppies were cut down, so most people kept their eyes to the ground and stayed safe in their own box.

The attitude is probably summed up best by a situation I encountered early in my time at Minhang. As part of the day-to-day running of the operation there, the testing and assaying of products to ensure quality and adherence to specifications was carried out. The procedures were set in place and agreed. OK? Mmm. We began to encounter a lot of out-of-specification product, and the faulty product began to build up in the warehouse. Everything was checked and double-checked; the process was found to be working fine and the raw materials were of the required nutritional values. Puzzling. A tiny alarm bell, set off by past experience, began to ring, so I decided to check out what was going on in the laboratory. "What have you been doing? Have you been doing re-check testing on out of specification products as you were told to do?"

"Yes."

"So the re-checks confirmed that they were out of specification?"

"Sometimes, but mostly the second test said that they were all right."

"So you released the products as being OK after the re-check?"

"No, we preferred to be safe and believe the original test."

"Why test it twice then, if you don't believe the second test?"

"You told us we had to re-test all products that were out of specification on the first test."

"But if the second test…"

I stopped myself from asking the obvious question and managed to control the outburst before telling them to do a double re-check in future and take 'best out of three'. Logic? Logic means something different in China. Common sense is thrown out of the window in the following of orders or because of 'doing it like we've always done it.'

Here's another example. As part of my job I had to introduce standard Company Operating Procedures into the running of the factory. No problem. Get them translated; give them out; job done. Hmm. Shortly after I had introduced the first batch I was walking past the additives room – the place where all the drugs, supplements and vitamins were added to the feed – and was alarmed to see that there was dust filling the air and the operator was doing a fair impression of a snowman. Apart from the dust making everywhere filthy it was a serious health hazard, so I was very concerned. I thought the extraction system must be broken, so I took a deep breath and went in to see what I could do. I pushed the start button on the extractor and it came to life immediately. Within a minute the air was clear and all was well, but I still needed to find out what the problem had been. I got Zheng Xi from the control room and went back to investigate and get an explanation.

I told him to ask the operator why he hadn't turned the dust extraction system on. Zheng Xi spent a couple of minutes talking to the worried operator before he came back with the answer: "In the new Operating Procedures it doesn't say he had to switch on the extractor, so he didn't."

I was stunned at the stupidity of it, but realised that this was a normal situation for China. If people are told to do something in a certain way, particularly if it's in writing, they will do it and continue to do it even if they know it is wrong. I spent the week after modifying all procedures to make them 'Chinese'.

Another very Chinese way of looking at things was with regard to preventative maintenance. In Britain we try to ensure the continuous running of facilities by doing regular maintenance checks on equipment during non-running time or in quiet periods. Good idea, because, if you don't do this, things have a nasty habit of breaking down when you need them the most. In China, however, it was a bit different.

I was walking through the factory and heard an alarming and potentially costly noise. One of the conveying machines was squealing in protest and I could hear metal grinding on metal – a bearing had collapsed and though the machine was still working, total failure was imminent. I stopped the factory and brought the fitter to the machine, so that we could get it sorted out.

I was amazed at what followed. The fitter had a quick look at the machine and then picked up his tools and began to walk away. I got the translator to stop him and ask what was going on and was informed, "He says it hasn't completely broken yet, so he will repair it when it breaks." There was a very, very brief conversation, as you can imagine, and the fitter did the repair.

I met with this situation again, but in a much more alarming circumstances. I was getting into the car one morning when I noticed a large blister on the wall of one of my tyres. Shit. I called to the driver and he had a look. Change the tyre? He got back in the car and indicated that I should do the same. Going to a garage? No, going to work as usual. I spent a very uncomfortable trip to work and sought out Lao Zhi immediately – he was in charge of the drivers. He spoke to the driver and the answer came back, "The tyre has been like that for a few days and he will change it when it bursts." Fuck!

Staying with transport briefly, we decided that we needed our own delivery truck, so I asked Frank to work out the costs involved so that I could put forward a justification. He produced it and it looked fine until I noticed something, so I pointed out, "Frank, this is only for a five-ton truck. We need a ten-ton truck."

"It's OK. In China five-ton trucks can carry ten tons."

You either accept it or give up and retreat, as many do. Some don't even make it through the door because of the differences. The first encounter or encounters are too much for their 'Western ways' to handle. In the West, as a manager, you make decisions on the spot about things – time is money and tomorrow is too late. We meet people in a business context and decide, based on our needs and what they can supply, to purchase from them, use their services or work together, and we may become friends in the future. In China, however, it is different, very different. You meet Chinese people and discuss a possible business relationship. All points are covered and then you go out and get drunk with them. You meet again and do exactly the same thing – again. This can be repeated four or five times, with no change in position from your first or second meeting. Finally it seems to be done, but there is usually something thrown into the ring as pens are hovering to sign. This 'something' should have been mentioned at the outset and is a 'deal breaker'. You concede this vital point to get 'it' done and the Chinese are happy that they have finished, in their eyes, on top.

Two things are involved here; first, Chinese people will not do business with people they do not know. They have to get to know you and be your friends first; that is what the going out and getting drunk is about. In China business comes from friendship; second. The 'deal breaker' factor is to give them 'good face' and make them look good in the eyes of their superiors and subordinates – 'I am clever'. I got used to it and accepted it, but sometimes frustration boiled over into anger or, as happened once, into another form of release – poetry.

A "lighter" moment, but still born out of the frustrations of living and working in China and a true depiction of how it can be too often.

Zher shi Zhongguo ('This China')

They don't say yes and they don't say no.
They don't want to stay, but they don't want to go.
"We need one more meeting" and you think "Oh no."
Or something far worse. It all seems so slow.

They won't even say maybe or sometime or if,
So you wait in a fury and hold yourself stiff,
Till you think you'll go crazy and jump off a cliff.
Do they do it on purpose to see if you'll miff?

What takes it so long to say what they think?
What the hell's in that tea that they all like to drink?
Maybe I'll try some. It might make the link
And help bring my hopes back out of the sink.

The clock's hands are moving but nothing else will.
You're gripping the chair and ready to kill,
But you'd better calm down. You'll make yourself ill.
Be patient. Be silent, collected and still.

Something is happening. Please, anything, please.
There are smiles on the faces. You feel at your ease.
At last they've agreed to it. Everyone sees.
Problem? What problem? "I love the Chinese."

Then, "Wait one more moment, we'd just like to say
We don't really think we can sign it today.

We think it is best if we have some delay,
So we'll see you next year. Maybe some time in May?"

You sit in the bar with your heart in your shoes.
Get drunk? Go home? Kick the dog? What's to lose?
Up to you. Makes no difference whichever you choose
Because you're still in China and on a short fuse.

Zher shi Zhongguo, "This China", will always be true,
But don't ever think it just happens to you.
There are fifty five thousand in Shanghai who, too,
Get the same daily ballsache whatever they do.

'This China' entered my vocabulary after a taxi ride through Shanghai with a good friend, Lao Xia. He was drinking a can of coke and after he finished he casually wound down the window and threw it out. I laughed and said to him, "If you did that in England you could get into trouble."

He turned towards me, expressionless and said, "This China."

These words stuck with me and became my standard response to any and all things that were unexplainable and mystifying to the Western mind.

I put up with and got used to a lot of things, but I used to get really, really pissed off with the lack of forward planning. Oh, yes, they would plan if it involved making a show of something as they did with the opening ceremony, but for everyday stuff – forget it. The only thing that was sacrosanct was lunch. Everything else was done at the drop of a hat, regardless of consequences.

Example: I had an on site laboratory built in the factory – closer to the bits that mattered and more efficient. I was informed that the building work had been completed and went to have a look. I noticed something and said, "What about the electrics, water and drainage?"

There was silence and then, "We will do that later. No problem."

So, unbelievably, that's what they did and the result was that they hacked channels and knocked holes in new plaster and new walls, causing damage that meant everything had to be re-plastered and rendered. All I could do was shake my head.

I also didn't take long to throw away my 'page a day' diary – useless in China. People would turn up to see you as they wished, with no appointment, and expect to be seen. It didn't matter if you were busy or simply didn't want or need to see them - they would wait and wait and wait. I was continually amazed that anything ever got done.

I was learning all the time, and it wasn't the big things that were hardest to grasp. It was, in truth, more of a combination of learning and unlearning, and there were many things I had to switch off or shelve before I could take the new on board.

After one early mishap, I began to take a deep breath or count to ten before I jumped into situations which I thought needed action. I found one of the electricians asleep in a corner and he was upset when I woke him up. My immediate thought was to sack the lazy bastard and in Britain his feet wouldn't have touched, but… his excuse was that if he was asleep it meant that everything was running with no problems and that his previous boss wasn't unhappy if this situation arose.

Concepts that we take for granted in Britain were alien to the Chinese – a big one was related to demarcation. In Britain now we try to work towards every man having a job, but in China it's more like 'every job should have a man.' My early suggestion that we could get the drivers to do some other work when they weren't driving was met with shock and horror. "They are drivers. That is their job." The fact that they didn't do anything all day if no one needed to go anywhere didn't seem to matter at all. They slept like cats most of the day, after they had arrived at the site and cleaned the car.

I began to accept things as they were – the ridiculous practices and systems and the interdepartmental jealousies. I even made fun of them, but that almost backfired. We had a stock system which involved having someone check on the people that did the checking because the Chinese trust NO ONE. I suggested, tongue in cheek, that we should have someone to check on the checker who checks the checker, and the idea was very close to being adopted.

Looking back on my time in Minhang I can't say that it was a high point in my life with regard to work. It was and probably still is a shithole and I am being very, very charitable. I could never get away from the place fast enough when home time came, but, strangely, most of the Chinese staff lingered after hours and didn't make a rush for the transport home when work was finished. This puzzled me until Lao Zhi enlightened me, "Most of them live in very poor conditions. No air-conditioning and only a small place to live. Sometimes four or five people share two rooms. It is better here."

As time went by and I was invited to people's homes, I was to find his words were true. To quote Henry Pickering yet again, it was 'interesting and different.'

CHAPTER SIX

BANQUETS AND BOOZE

It is difficult to convey how important food is in the lives of the Chinese people. More than just something they do to stay alive, to them it is part of life itself. The buying of it, preparing and cooking it and eating it are done, sometimes, in an almost ritualistic manner. Our involvement with food tends to be as quick and as easy as we can make it, with very few exceptions – Sunday lunch and Christmas maybe – and most of us pay little heed to what we eat as long as it tastes OK. There are, of course, those scrambling at the bottom of the social ladder in China whose everyday priority is making sure that they eat, but most are not like this, although older people still remember the famine in Mao's 'Great Leap Forward'.

Food tends to be bought in small quantities by Chinese people and they have a belief, almost a fetish, in 'freshness'. Most Chinese homes only buy enough food at one time to last about two days and throw away anything that they don't consume in that time. The same goes for Chinese restaurants and even on the streets, where you can buy skewers of barbecued 'something' for virtually nothing. Many foreigners have reservations about food safety in China, but the only times I have been sick because of food have been in hotels that are run on Western lines. True! Freezers and fridges are only now beginning to be used and accepted on Chinese homes and, even so, they tend to be used for drinks rather than anything else.

In the West we think we know Chinese food, but what we see and eat is usually the Westernised version and altered to suit our preferences. There is almost an infinite variety of foods in China with each region, district or city having its own speciality or variations. Each place, naturally, thinks and believes that their food is best and looks down on others. There are universals in rice, noodles and dumplings and there are Chinese people who don't eat or even like rice. The East and the South are the rice areas, with the West and the North being more into wheat and the other cereal staples of noodles, bread and dumplings.

Another common theme is the 'hot pot'. This is a meal that involves you cooking your own food at the table in a bubbling, centrally-positioned pan of either spicy or not so spicy liquid. The tables are usually specially designed with an appropriately sized hole, to accommodate the pan, and a gas ring underneath to provide the ongoing heat. Sichuan is the home of hot pot, but it's cooked everywhere, particularly in the winter. Many Chinese people love it and regard a hot pot meal as special. I think it's all right, but over-rated as, I think, all the food ends up tasting the same. It does vary according to place, but Sichuan is the hottest – skin-removingly hot. Sometimes you get your own individual pot, giving you more control over things, which is good.

I remember eating hot pot in Qingdao, Shandong Province, and having my own small pot. Nothing special about the food, except that the host had tried to impress by providing us all with a large crab each – almost too large to get in the pot. The crabs were big enough and fit enough to be dangerous, so I was careful. I managed to get mine jammed in and the lid back on without any injury, but our Chinese host was not so lucky. He was, to be fair, pissed, but shouldn't have tried to poke the crab in with his fingers. The crab took the opportunity and seized him, which resulted in him running screaming round the table until a waiter cut off the crab's claw. Even then he had to pry open the dead claw with a knife and staunch the blood with a towel.

There was one hot pot place in particular in Shanghai which I used to frequent, the Red Ox, on the Hua Hai Lu. I became a regular visitor to the place, usually after midnight, in the company of Chinese people. Good idea, because all the menus were in Chinese and nobody spoke English. It was a huge place that could hold about six hundred and was always full. It was a bit scary because of the gas pipe arrangements, which involved rubber hoses to all tables, frequent leaks and resulting small - and sometimes not so small - fires. I found out that major fires and explosions are very common in hot pot restaurants and that there is at least one life lost somewhere in China every week. As I said, the Chinese take their food very seriously.

Whatever the type of food or the venue, however, the process was the same wherever you went or whomever you went with. My first experiences were in Anshan, where we were being 'entertained,' so I thought that it was special, but it turned out to be the norm. In China eating is part of the working day and not really free time. The lunchtime banquet and associated drinking are an essential part of business and breaking the ice – a good Chinese banquet could have saved the *Titanic*. It usually began to take shape around 10.30 in the morning with a strategically timed 'visit'. I will recount one or two of the many.

It was 10.30 on a bright Monday morning when some local officials arrived, ostensibly, to inspect the wharf cranes. One made a cursory inspection while his three companions watched him. This is normal in China and no one visits anywhere unaccompanied even when one person is all that is needed. The officials came back to the office after about half an hour and gave us a clean bill of health: "Cranes OK." Then they continued to sit and talk until, at 11.30, everyone stood up. Goodbye? No. Lao Zhi had a word with me, "Russell, we will go to lunch."

"Me too?"

"Of course. You are the most important."

We were expected, and a private room had been prepared in a restaurant in Lu Hui. It began with the ordering of the food, which took about fifteen minutes of discussion and then progressed into the serious business – drinking. There was a brief babble of conversation and nods in my direction and then Lao Zhi informed me, "Russell, they want to drink to your health."

"OK. Beer?"

"No, no. Biajiu and one person at a time."

I was being ambushed. Henry had warned me about this, so I was ready for it. The officials, however, were not. I can drink – a lot – having served a long apprenticeship as a rugby player.

After they had been round the group twice they decided to give up, so I went on the attack and said to Lao Zhi, "Tell them I want to drink to their health now."

Lao Zhi grinned. He was enjoying it. I went around the table twice more and they had had enough. I was glad, because I was starting to feel it. Then Lao Zhi gave me the bad news, "Russell, they have asked the head waitress to drink to your health also."

"Oh. OK."

"Yes. Three times for good luck."

"Oh, shit" I thought. "Baijiu again?"

"No, beer this time."

"OK. Let's get it over with."

The waitress and I did the necessary. Done? Not so. "Russell, now you must drink her health in return. Three times also."

Oh fuck. Halfway through the second glass the head waitress capitulated, but I completed my side of the duty. The rest of the meal was a blur and I can only remember

Lao Zhi saying, as he poured me into the car, "Russell, they were very impressed." God, it was a dirty job, but somebody had to do it.

Two or three banquets a week was normal and each one resulted in a 'lost' afternoon either dozing in the office or going directly home after it was over. I began to get a reputation as a drinker, both with the Chinese staff and visitors. It almost seemed that some of them came just to try me out and see if it was really true. Unfortunately, it was.

Another day arrived and along with it a deputation of local policemen – site security inspection. Being, by this time, experienced, I immediately shelved what I had planned for the afternoon and 'prepared' myself.

We were regular lunchtime visitors to many of the restaurants in Lu Hui by then and I had got to know many of the staff. I was at the stage where I was fending off services other than food, tempting though they were. The restaurant that had been chosen this time was the one with my head waitress and drinking partner, Wu Qing, and she was expecting us. We sat down, as directed, and I enquired why there was an empty seat next to me. Was someone else coming? No. The place was for Wu Qing. She had been detailed off by the police to 'look after' me, and it was clear more than food and drink was involved.

The usual drinking ensued, but it was difficult to concentrate. Wu Qing was 'looking after' me very well, sitting as we were, in a corner. She fed me with one hand and busied her other in massaging somewhere. I was coping with it manfully and giving no indication of what was going on under the table, and I was even managing to carry on conversation reasonably well. It couldn't go on though, and I managed to get her to stop before it got messy, with promises of 'later', so that I could give due attention to what was going on.

I discovered that I had crossed a very big line – a very, very big line for an Englishman. I had been round all the food on the table a couple of times when Lao Zhi turned to me and asked, "Russell, you have eaten dog before?"

"Gulp. No."

How did it taste? It was 'Rrrruff.' Sorry, but I had to say it.

The meal progressed through the necessary stages, the only difference being a long visit to the toilet, with Wu Qing showing me the way. She was not to be denied and was in position before I got the door closed. She was very vocal and appreciative – first white man etc – and spent the rest of the meal sitting beside me with a faraway look in her eyes and a happy smile on her lips. My reputation had grown again. The rest of the company acted as if nothing had happened and I realised that some of the policemen had been absenting themselves with waitresses at regular intervals, for the same reason.

The afternoon progressed and began to go downhill quickly. The three waitresses gave up any pretence of discretion, or maybe they got just got tired of putting all their clothes back on and then taking them off again, so they waited on us braless, with blouses at the ready for quick release – only one button fastened. Everyone except

Lao Zhi, who declined, received some personal attention at one time or another. One of them began to give me her attention, but was slapped away by Wu Qing – I was hers. We had been there for about four hours when we called it a day, our good relationship with the local police ensured. I was taken home semi-comatose in the back of the car. As I said, 'It was a dirty job, but…'

Over my first few months in China I must have eaten everything that it was possible to eat, some of it through a haze of alcohol, thankfully. The eating of turtlehead, as was expected of the guest of honour, was only possible with the accompaniment of baijiu – lots of it. I was tested on many occasions to see if I, really and truly, was the foreigner who could or would eat anything. I did eat everything, though I can't say I liked everything.

As civilised English people our diet is limited to certain things, particularly with regard to meat. The Chinese, however, eat all animals and every part of all animals. This particularly applies to pigs, where every part is consumed with the exception of the bones – from, and including, ears to tail. It's much the same with chickens and it is normal for chicken to be served with head and feet still attached – they are eaten too.

I must say here, however, that I will never understand why they eat the feet. I eat them, but get nothing out of them except a mouthful of small bones and gristle. They love them to the extent that some enterprising individuals in the UK actually export chicken feet from Britain to China.

The other thing that is different in China, regarding chicken and all fowl, is what the Chinese consider to be the best bits. We consider white breast meat to be the prime choice and work down to legs and then wings, whereas the Chinese come from exactly the opposite direction – wings, or even neck or parson's nose, first then legs and then breast, pausing all the while to nibble on feet, head, heart and other internal organs.

Even when something was on the menu that you thought would bear a resemblance to something Western, it was different. There are very few occasions when large pieces of pure meat appear at the table, and when and if they do they always have bones in them. Because of chopsticks most meat is cut into small pieces or even shredded to make it bite sized. If you are after steak, large slices of beef, chicken or anything, forget it. It is a voyage of discovery, and there are many rocks and reefs to founder on. 'What do I do with this?' often entered the mind in the early stages, so you hesitated, waited and observed. Then sometimes you found something in your mouth that you couldn't swallow – bones and things. What to do? Spit it out, either onto the table or onto the floor. Crabs? Do as everybody else did and crunch and spit.

I remember going back to the UK on a short visit and eating crab. I was doing it Chinese style, as I had become accustomed to, and suddenly realised that I was the centre of shocked attention. Oops.

Prawns? Peel the big ones, but pop the small ones into your mouth whole and spit out what you can't or don't want to swallow. Drunken prawns – live prawns -'cooked' in baijiu. No cooking, as such, involved at all, just a steeping in the liquor until they are dead. Sometimes, though, the diners couldn't wait and the sight of still twitching prawns entering mouths was common. It was best seen through alcohol.

Dog, snake, scorpions, monkey brains, sparrows, jellyfish, duck embryos (duck eggs with partially developed ducklings inside) and duck heads, to mention but a few, were all encountered and consumed

The belief that all foods provide certain benefits to health and other things is part of food culture in China. I suppose we are the same to a degree – carrots for eyesight, spinach for strength etc – but in China, everything is good for something; it will keep you cool; it will make you strong; it is good for your stomach; it is good for man, but not for woman.

This last one is interesting. I first encountered it with a dish called 'gentleman's soup' and was informed that women could not or should not eat this. It just tasted like soup, but when I asked what was in it I was in it I found out the reason for the name. Ox penis. OK, but I wish ox penis didn't look so much like ox penis.

My own feelings were that, for me, it would have been more appropriate if female organs had been the key ingredient. I do like to eat them – suitably prepared of course. Mmm. Turtlehead, because of its resemblance to the male 'bell-end', is another food item which is supposed to be an aid to virility, but I feel it would be more appropriate if women ate it – visions of women eating bananas and Cadbury's Flake flash into view. It seemed to have no effect on me – maybe you have to eat a few, or maybe it was the real reason for 'yellow fever'.

Besides the meat there are vegetables – some weird and wonderful ones that we don't see in the West, like lotus root and water hyacinth. They are an essential part of Chinese food, as are rice, noodles and dumplings of all kinds. The Chinese believe in balance in their food and shy away from eating too much of any one food group at one time. They are right. Colour and texture are also given great importance in the overall picture. How it feels in your mouth and how it looks make all the difference.

Apart from the differences in the food itself, there are major differences in etiquette, protocol and how to eat which have to be observed, coped with and accepted. The first thing, naturally, is chopsticks. At first you are fumbling and childlike in your efforts and the subject of amusement, advice and assistance. It takes time and shelving of shyness and embarrassment before you get it half right. Rab even practised alone in his room with peanuts before he felt confident and able to let himself loose on the table. I, on the other hand, just 'went for it' and didn't care when I fucked up. Alcohol was of great assistance in letting go of inhibitions, both when eating and, also, when trying to speak Chinese. I soon reached the stage where I was complimented on my chopstick technique and skill.

The next thing to take in is the way the food is brought

to you. We are accustomed to an ordered progression through a meal in the way it's served, but in China the food generally arrives when it's ready. Cold dishes do come first and fruit comes last, to signify the start and end of the meal, but in between, anything can be placed in front of you at any time. Soup will arrive any time and rice will come on request. In the home large quantities of rice or noodles are consumed throughout meals, to make sure everyone is full, but at banquets requesting and eating rice signifies that you haven't had enough to eat and can be an offence to the host.

Certain dishes have certain significance in Chinese meals. If a fish is presented, the head must be towards the guest of honour or the most important person and he must try it first as he must with all new dishes that arrive. Tough if it's something that you don't fancy.

The progression through a Western meal is baffling to normal Chinese people and I saw this demonstrated in Anshan:

Bob Wilson and I were eating in the 'Western' restaurant in the hotel. Bob had ordered his usual French onion soup and Spaghetti Bolognaise and his spaghetti was duly presented to him. Bob was puzzled and enquired, "Where's the soup?"

"It's not ready yet. Don't you want the noodles?"

"Yes, but I want to eat the soup first. Bring the spaghetti after I've finished the soup."

The waiter retreated with the spaghetti and a puzzled look on his face. He returned a few minutes later with the soup AND the spaghetti. Bob was getting a bit exasperated and said firmly, "Thank you. Take the spaghetti away and bring it back when I have finished the soup, please."

Again the waiter retreated with the spaghetti and with an even more puzzled look on his face. I watched as he hovered outside the kitchen door, the plate of spaghetti still in his hand, unsure and in agitated conversation with other members of staff until, after about a minute, a decision seemed to be made. Bob had his back to all this and was taken completely by surprise when a waitress sprinted over, slammed his spaghetti down on the table and skedaddled before he could object. Bob sighed and shook his head in disbelief. "These fucking people. I give up."

Throughout a Chinese meal you find that drinking is important. We drink wine or whatever in the West when we dine and maybe we will have a toast at some point – usually the start. In China, however, toasting goes on throughout. 'Gambei', down in one, is what it's called and it usually involves baijiu – white spirit. The Chinese call everything stronger than beer, wine and at first it's very confusing when you agree to drink' wine' only to discover baijiu in your glass.

Let's stay with baijiu for a while. It's difficult to describe how it tastes, as it has a taste that is like nothing we drink in the West – the closest similar drink is, maybe, Italian grappa, which is also evil stuff. Baijiu is to China what whisky, vodka and sake are to Scotland, Russia and Japan and it is drunk whenever and wherever there is an occasion that demands it – celebrations, weddings, birthdays and banquets. Whatever it tastes like, however, it is an acquired taste and many Chinese people don't really like it, but they still drink it because tradition demands.

In common with other spirits, it varies in quality, strength and price – from less than £1 a bottle to more than £50 and from 35 to 60% volume. One of the better brands, Moutai, is around $20 and is fairly smooth and leaves you the next day. However, the rough stuff, cigarette lighter fuel grade, can stay with you for two or three days before it finally stops repeating and reminding you what an idiot you were for drinking it.

Whatever strength or quality you drink, it is usually served by the 'shot' during the course of whatever is going on – banquet, wedding or whatever – and it creeps up on you and takes you by surprise. After you've downed a glass you can feel its heat rising back up your body until it hits your head – with Chinese people this means they often turn a delicate shade of pink. This happens irrespective of whether you are drinking good stuff or bad.

Most foreigners find it totally unpalatable and after initial attempts to be sociable, refuse to drink it ever again. I, however, learned how to drink it – too well – and could usually 'see off' most Chinese who tried to put me under. Unlike other spirits, with the possible exception of malt whisky, you can't really mix it with anything to dilute its strength or make it taste better. In malt whisky's case it is sacrilegious to do this, but with baijiu, when you could do with disguising or masking the taste, it doesn't work. The taste of it floods through and blankets whatever you try to add to it.

My ability to drink it without retching or throwing up completely was put to the test in the strangest of places – The far North of Scotland. To tell this, I have to move forward to the summer of 2004:

I was living and working in the Melvich Hotel near Thurso on the North coast of Scotland, having taken a short-term live-in job, so that I could complete my Teaching Diploma before returning to China, after an enforced year's stay in Britain. This period in the tale will be dealt with later. For now, though - one of my jobs at the hotel was barman and what happened regarding baijiu, or Moutai in this case, centres on the bar.

The regulars knew I was heading back to China and were quizzing me about it, when the subject of 'drink' came up. One of them, Hugh McLeod, said. "My brother brought back a bottle o' some evil tastin' shite from China, when he was in Hong Kong last year. 'Mou'-something it's called."

"Moutai. That's the good stuff. £20 a bottle." I said.

"£20 a bottle? Fuck off.. I wouldnae give ye twenty fuckin' pence for it. It's fuckin' undrinkable."

"I can drink it."

"Niver. Naebody could drink thon. I dinnae believe ye. Tell you whit. If ye can drink a double measure o' thon shite, wi-oot throwin' up, I'll buy ye a double malt, of your choice. But, if ye fail, ye will 'buy the bar.' OK?"

A challenge, so I said, "No problem.. Bring it here."

I knew I could do it, so I took partial pity on Hugh, and said he would only have to buy me a double Glenmorangie at around £1 a nip – some of the malts in the bar were £5 or more for a single.

The following night, Hugh came into the bar with the squat, white, stone bottle of Moutai held aloft and proclaimed, "I hereby gi' notice that, if Russell can drink and hold doon a double measure o' this evil Chinese shite, I will buy him a double malt. And, and if he fails or spews up within five minutes o' drinkin' it, he will buy the bar."

There were about a dozen hard drinkers in the bar and they all took a smell of the bottle and a couple of them even took a sip, before they declared. "Fuckin' undrinkable."

The drink was poured and, without ceremony, I downed it in one. There were gasps of amazement and disbelief from the gathered company. "He niver fuckin' well even flinched. He must ha' nae fuckin' taste buds. Fuckin' Jesus."

They watched me closely for about five minutes and one of them even followed me to the toilet to make sure I wasn't sick, before Hugh paid up on his end of the bet, which he did un-begrudgingly. "Yer a better fuckin' man than me. Dae ye actually like thon stuff?"

I laughed and said, "I don't have to like it to be able to drink it."

The bottle of Moutai sat on the top shelf of the bar until I left and was a source of amusement for the regulars, as they tried to get newcomers and idiots to try it and to challenge me. Yes, I can drink baijiu.

I learned to drink it very well and was never 'under the

table' to any Chinese men. I did, however, come very close to losing to a woman. She was Madam Wang, the Dairy Federation President in Chendu, Sichuan Province. God, she could drink. She could do other thing s too, but that's another story.

Anyway, drinking is important, very important and you have to do it or offend. Smoking is also part of eating in China and cigarettes are strewn about during the meal like confetti. Ashtrays are whatever you can use – consumed dishes, the floor, empty glasses and, even, ashtrays. The sight of a duck carcass covered in cigarette ends like a cloved, baked ham still sticks in my mind.

There is, however, one aspect of a Chinese meal that still eludes me – the end. Try as I may I can never work out when it's finished. There tends to be no fidgeting, glancing at watches, asking for the bill or 'I must be goings' to indicate that it's winding up. OK, the food is finished, but nothing happens. Nothing happens until everyone seems to lift on some invisible signal. Maybe it's body language, but I am always taken by surprise.

LANGUAGE AND THINGS

Everything else apart, the biggest and most problematic thing that faced me in China was the language. Unlike most European languages there is no common point of reference, no hook to grab hold of, that enables you to make a 'start' French, Spanish, Italian, Dutch, German and the Nordic languages all have things that are in common with English, but Chinese is totally alien to our ears – as all tonal languages are. Chinese script makes it even more difficult – probably why I found it easier to learn Vietnamese, which is very similar to Chinese in many ways, but has a Romanised script, which was forced on them by the French more than two hundred years ago. Along with teaching the Viets how to make good bread and have a taste for cheese, unlike most South East Asian countries, it was the best thing they did. I suppose even the French, though, have their moments, but there can't be many.

I'm lucky in that I have a good ear, the ability to mimic and to change my accent at will – many others do not (poor Rab) and struggle with it never to succeed. At first all was an unintelligible waterfall of noise with nothing there that was distinguishable. It was the same as trying to decipher the lyrics of a fast moving rock song, where you catch on odd word here and there on the first listening and have to listen again and again to fill in the blanks. Odd words and phrases began, gradually, to stand out and fall into place like a jigsaw puzzle. The only problem is that it was and still is a BIG jigsaw puzzle and you can't spend all your time doing it.

The first things you learn, of course, are greetings and farewells – 'ni hao' and 'zai tian' and the British curse, thank you, 'xie xie'. Strangely, the word 'qing,' which means please, is not one that you hear very often in China. More about that later. Names and numbers are next and you begin to feel you are making progress. That's when you fall flat on your face.

In English a word means what it means, most of the time, no matter how you say it. In Chinese, however, the way you say it, the 'tone', is all-important. There are four tones on vowel sounds – flat, falling, rising and falling-rising – and getting it wrong changes the meaning of the word completely. e.g. the word 'mai' means buy or sell depending on how you say it. Getting it wrong can either cause amusement or be a disaster.

My first 'disaster' was with a name. The company had a Financial Controller called Ada Bi, with the Bi having a 'falling' tone. One day I called out her name, but pronounced Bi with a flat tone only to receive a shocked look. What had I done? Nothing was said, but there were a few smirks from others. A couple of weeks later when we were having a problem in the factory I felt the need to call the electrician a 'stupid cunt' and asked for a translation, so that I could be sure that he understood what I thought of him. The translation was 'xia bi' with 'bi' having a flat tone. Light dawned.

Apart from the pronunciation problems there were the 'howlers' that happen whenever the use of a new language is being attempted. I managed to have everyone in the factory control room doubled up with laughter after they asked me if I could count from 1 to 10 in Chinese. No problem, so why the laughter? I was sure I had done it right. When they had, at last, stopped laughing they explained. Instead of saying 'qi' and 'ba' for 7 and 8 I had said 'ji' and 'ba', and, apparently, 'Jiba' was a very, very rude word for the male sex organ, similar to 'cock' or 'dick'.

I shouldn't forget here that the door swings both ways and for any and every pronunciation or inappropriate vocabulary fuck up I made, there were more coming back the other way - many, many 'howlers', both verbal and written.

Written ones were those that you encountered first. My first 'message' in the hotel was: 'KICK you up at 7.30.' The most common and most amusing written garbage, however, is in translated company literature and brochures: 'unlimited sneerity is the everlasting toad to success' sticks in the mind. The one that is still with me every day, though, is personal.

I was always first into the office and, out of habit, checked the mail as I entered. This day a quick check showed nothing there for me. Later, Lao Zhi came into my office and said, "A letter for you, Russell." He handed it over and was leaving until I stopped him.

"Hey, this isn't my name. How do you know it's for me?"

"The Chinese says so."

I looked again. Of course it was for me. Who else on site had no surname and was called MAVAHILL? I adopted it and still use it in my e-mail address.

As well as the written ones I heard some good ones: 'I need someone to sleep with tonight.' – looking for a hotel room; 'Is there anywhere to eat in this virginity?' – looking for a restaurant; 'I am a good girl. I am still verging.' – sweet young thing proclaiming her purity; 'Are there cloclodiles in Tolonto?' – not real, but a combination of two mispronunciations that I did hear. Other ones that come to mind are: 'Russell, could you please give me a fuck (fork)?' and 'Russell, have you seen my pussy (purse)?' Both of these were from sweet young girls and my answers were, 'Yes' and 'Not yet' respectively. I did, however, eventually see the organ in question in the latter case, but that's another story.

Other problems were in direct translations from one language to the other and you had to be careful. Probably the best examples are in the words 'chicken' and 'yellow', both of which can be used in English in describing fear or cowardice. In Chinese, however, the two words, apart from meaning what they mean, have different connotations. A 'chicken' is a female prostitute – 'duck' being used to denote a male prostitute – and 'yellow' is used in the same way as we use 'blue' as in 'blue movies'. Apart from the potentially disastrous and embarrassing situations this could lead to, there were other nuances of language, which caused major misunderstandings.

One of the first I encountered was in the simple process of asking questions and understanding the real meaning of the apparently simple 'yes' or 'no' answer. If you ask a question in the negative, like 'You didn't have lunch?' of an English person the answer 'yes.' would normally mean, 'Yes, I've had lunch.' and "no." the opposite. The answer 'yes.' in English from someone Chinese would, most often, mean, 'Yes, what you say is correct. I have not had lunch.' It's all to do with the words that the Chinese use for 'yes' and 'no' i.e. 'dui' and 'meiyou'. The real meanings in Chinese are 'correct' and 'not correct' or 'don't have,' respectively. I'm sure that this has and still does cause many problems and misunderstandings both socially and in business when meeting and dealing with Chinese people. It got even worse if someone combined either of the words with body language. The result was often 'Yes' with a shake of the head or 'No' with a nod.

Another word that confused me and still does was 'follow'. When I was asked 'Russell, will you follow me to the factory?' I responded, 'OK, but why can't I go with you?' This response received a puzzled look as, in Chinese, the word 'follow' actually means 'go with'. Very confusing.

Maybe the most dangerous potential misunderstanding surrounds the word 'play'. We usually think of play as something that children do or something to do with sport or a game of some kind. If a female approaches a man in the West and invites him to 'play' with her it usually means sex, but in China this is not the case. True, it can be, but in 99% of cases it is only an invitation to go out and spend time with the person in innocent social activities of any and all kinds. I'm sure that many Western men have received the invitation to 'play' and accepted, full of high expectations, only to be disappointed when they end up sitting drinking coffee somewhere or exploring a place of interest rather than making the beast with two backs and exchanging bodily fluids.

In talking about language I include body language or, rather, the lack of it. I think it must be a deep-seated cultural thing to do with Chinese 'face' and a history of obedience and servitude in the old Imperial system and, more recently, under communism. Most Chinese people give very little away about what's going on inside them except in extreme moments of anger or happiness, so it's difficult to read them. They are self-reliant fortress islands who believe that no one else will help them, so they give nothing away.

They do, however, rely on our body language to help them in understanding what we say, as becomes very apparent when they are talking to you on the phone. I have Chinese friends whose level of understanding seems and probably is very good when they are with me, but goes totally to shit when I speak to them on the phone. I, very early on, got into the habit of double and even triple checking that they had understood what I was saying after I had a couple of disasters, one of which left me stranded in Minhang overnight – not a good experience.

Staying on body language, it is true that women are better at reading it than men. You don't think so? I will give an example – many male readers, I'm sure will say, 'Ah, yes.' - It goes like this:

You and your wife or girlfriend are out for the evening and you enter a bar, restaurant or somewhere. The place is fairly busy and you choose a seat, or rather, your partner chooses. Drinks are obtained and maybe the menu is scrutinised, then your partner says, out of the blue, 'I don't like *her*.' You look to find out who 'her' is and you see the woman. She notices your glance and gives a little smile in response. You look away, but when you sneak another look at her, she is still looking and smiling at you. Oops.

For the rest of the evening you try to avoid looking at her and, for the remainder of the evening, your partner becomes increasingly irritated and frosty. It's fairly obvious that you have done something, but you can't figure out what, so you spend the evening and the silent trip home feeling very confused and uncomfortable.

What did you do? You did nothing. What happened was that as you walked into the place 'her' noticed you and was interested in you. She adjusted her pose, straightened up, pushed her breasts out, crossed her legs, shook her hair… You never noticed a thing, but your partner did. You are innocent and would have been totally oblivious to it all if your partner hadn't made her comment. Sound familiar? I'm sure that, for many, it does.

Staying on body language and women, I find Chinese women very confusing, not counting the obvious occupational body language of some. Chinese women can switch from giggling schoolgirl to mature woman in a flash. You can suddenly find yourself in the company of a sexual predator or a sharp clawed tigress, when you least expect it. Chinese men fare no better and I've been witness to grown men cowering under a tirade from a minute office girl. Xiao Ding, sweet and lovely, stood in for the Warehouse Supervisor for a week and the men were terrified of her and would have done anything she told them. To be fair, though, I would have too.

Anyway, China. Even when face-to-face it was advisable to keep your language as simple as possible and avoid idioms and euphemisms. I have retained this habit and it stands me in good stead. Others, however, never learned this lesson.

One man in particular never grasped this principal – Gordon Knox. Gordon took over from Henry Pickering as General Director for China after Henry was, wrongfully as it turned out, whisked away. Gordon was a nice enough guy, but a pain in the arse and useless. He seemed to think that working until eight or nine at night was virtuous and required in China. I refused to partake in this stupid practice and even pointed out to him that people who worked excessive hours either weren't very good at what they did or had too much work. He never grasped that I was talking about HIM. He lasted longer than he should have because he was appointed directly by Dennis, the CEO, and people like Dennis are never wrong even when it's obvious that they have fucked up.

In addition to being useless Gordon was Belfast Irish with an accent as strong as Reverend Ian Paisley's. Problem. I first ran into it when I came upon a head scratching Fu Yi Gang. Fu was Quality Control Manager and was generally disliked by all the rest of the Chinese staff. This was because he was useless and, mainly, because he was from Guangdong in the South of China. Shanghai people uniformly disapprove of anyone not from Shanghai and regard their city and everything in it as the centre of the universe. I thought Fu was alright, because he had a sense of humour that was close to Western and would often be the only Chinese person in the crowd laughing at our jokes. At first I thought he was kissing our arses, but soon found out that he understood and appreciated most of what we were saying. Anyway, Fu had a problem and he came to see me. He looked worried, shook his head and said sadly, "Russell, Gordon has askeda me-a howa mucha me-az is in the formulations. I have a lookeda and I cannota finda the material me-az anywhere. Cana youa please helpa me-a?"

A difficult one. I pondered for a while and then it came to me. It was 'Belfast speak'. Me-az was maize. Obvious really. Later I was often called upon in meetings to translate what Gordon had said into English before the translator could translate it into Chinese. One day when Gordon was haranguing the troops with an inspirational speech. Real First World War General stuff. "Eye want yew all te know that eye am rayt up there at the sharp eynd with yew."

A baffled translator turned to me and I did the necessary. 'Leading from the front - Front of the ship.' Then I gave some cautionary words to Gordon, which, for some strange reason, he didn't appreciate. "Careful, Gordon. Remember the Titanic."

Gordon, however, thought that there was nothing wrong with his accent and was of the impression that people were just being rude when they said they couldn't understand him. He was also trying to learn Chinese, but his accent, again, was a big problem. He thought that he was getting on fine to the degree that he thought he could manage without a translator in some situations. Pillock. He popped into my office one day and, surprisingly, invited me to have lunch with him. I say surprisingly because he NEVER invited me to lunch. He was after something. I was right. "I want to have a wee chat with you about a few things."

Anyway, off we went to a restaurant in Luhui sans translator – mistake. Gordon knew the words, but his Belfast reproduction of them brought only blank faces in response. At that time I wasn't able to help him out and, much to his chagrin, we had to resort to phone calls back to the office and animal impressions to get what we wanted. Because of all the confusion and delay we never did have the little chat that Gordon was after. Mixed blessings.

I began to learn a lot of work related Chinese out of pure necessity, as well as quite a bit of conversational Mandarin and then I hit a problem. Shanghainese. The Shanghai dialect of Chinese is totally a different language, even though the written form is identical to Mandarin. Shanghainese is used most of the time as the everyday language of the people and only when necessary will they switch to Mandarin. They speak Mandarin unwillingly and use their own dialect to exclude others, particularly people from Beijing, who they hate. They are as rude as the people in North Wales and that is saying something. The result of this was that I had two languages to try and cope with. Had I been in Beijing, which is totally Mandarin speaking, my Chinese would be a lot better, but I found that I had to learn a lot of basic Shanghainese to make life easier in shops and taxis – particularly taxis. More about taxis later.

I found that I could handle tones and pronunciation better than most, which was probably down to my ability as a mimic more than anything else. This sounds fine, but it was a two-edged sword. Because I could say what I knew well, it was assumed that I could speak fluently and understand everything. I have had many one-sided conversations with increasingly angry people who thought that I was being an arrogant foreigner who didn't want to talk to them. I have, however, been complimented many times. Maybe the best compliment I received was on a trip to Anshan. I was out in the city, a rare occasion, when a

Chinese guy in a bar spoke to me in English after he had heard me speaking Chinese – my confidence boosted by alcohol. He asked, "You live in Shanghai, yes?"

"Yes, how do you know?"

"You speak Mandarin with a Shanghai accent." I felt very pleased with myself.

As time went by I even began to invent my own language, which was a mixture of Chinese and good old Anglo Saxon. It was even adopted by some of the Chinese staff that worked closest to me, and phrases like 'meiyo fucking wenti' (no fucking problem) and 'wo buzhi fucking dao' (I don't fucking know) were often heard in the office.

It is true that languages change when they come into extended contact with one another, and I found my own English changing. I began to miss words out. Instead of 'do you want to go to eat?' I found myself saying, 'You want eat?' I think that, given time, the English language will continue to evolve and change even more because of the increasing number of Chinese who are learning and using English. It's happened before, is still happening and it will happen again and again.

I put this to some Chinese friends and they agreed, but they also thought that English would benefit if it were more like Chinese. I agreed with them on grammar, but they had another thought. "English is boring. Not enough words. You need more words, like the Chinese language."

I pondered on this briefly and came back with, "That's maybe why it takes Chinese people so long to say so much about so little." This was not well received.

MEDICINE AND THINGS

Everyone in the civilised world has heard of Chinese medicine and has mixed opinions. I came to China with no knowledge of its entirety and with the opinions of the majority of Westerners. When asked what we know of it, what generally springs to mind are images of tiger claws, rhino horns and bear bile – man's constant holy grails, virility and long-life. We see these and we immediately condemn the rest out of hand. We know, already, the benefits that acupuncture can give, but we still regard it as an oddity, something almost magical – 'Stick a needle in your big toe to cure a headache? Wow.' – and that's as far as we get in understanding it.

We think that we know best, but on the other hand, so do the Chinese. Who is right? We are both right and both wrong at the same time. We have medical science to prove what we say and the Chinese have five thousand years of continually doing what they do. Things are changing and there is now a slow coming together and combination of the two – more so in China than in the West. China is opening up and changing quickly in all things and combining modern science with its traditional knowledge. The West, however, is moving more slowly, with the establishment reluctant to let go of its stranglehold. It's still very much like the 'closed shop' trade union days – 'If you're not a member, you can't work'.

I think that Christianity was responsible, maybe unwittingly, for stamping out traditional medicine in the West and traditional practitioners were persecuted and, in the extreme, burned as witches – a good incentive to stop doing what you are doing. This progressed into colonialism, where Western ways were imposed wherever the flag was planted and traditions, in all things, were discounted and dismissed. It was easy to focus on and condemn the ridiculous everywhere in the world – tiger claws and the like – and dismiss the rest out of hand.

I like to think that I have an open mind, but I was sceptical. My scepticism was fuelled, initially, as I explored a traditional medicine shop in Shanghai and looked at what was on sale. Ox penis tablets, deer antler and extract of oil of tree frog oviduct are the ones I remember, plus the ubiquitous and very expensive ginseng, but there were more. I never did find out what magical powers tree frog oviducts had.

My first contact with Chinese medicine and Chinese doctors came out of dire necessity. I was four days into a horrendous bout of 'the shits' and had tried everything to no avail. My own supply of Imodium had run out and hadn't done any good anyway and I was taking what I was later informed was the Chinese equivalent. Henry, the bastard, had offered a suggestion, "Try Bisto" (gravy powder).

"Bisto? Will it help?"

"No, but it'll thicken it up a bit."

"Bastard."

Dehydration had set in and I was semi-delirious, so I gave in and went to the nearest hospital. I was attended to by a nice old doctor who, to my relief, spoke perfect English. He listened to me, nodded, as doctors do the world over and asked if I had brought or could 'produce' a sample. I informed him, 'no' and 'not at the moment'. I was totally empty. He nodded again, dug in his drawer and produced some medicines before saying, "This is what you have been taking – Chinese Imodium. This is an antibacterial and these are to aid in your recovery."

I looked at them. Yes, Imodium. Yes, antibacterial. Yes, what? There was no information on the small packet of bright yellow pills that he had given me to 'aid in my recovery,' so I raised my eyebrows in query. He answered my unspoken question with a serious look on his face, "It's very important that you take these at the same time as the antibacterial tablets. They are essential to your recovery."

Off I went. I got better. The yellow pills, though, had a slightly alarming side effect. I was back at work and in the toilet when I noticed something. I was pissing bright orange. I shouted to Henry and he came and peered over my shoulder. He laughed and said, "Oh, yes, very colourful. He gave you the little yellow pills then?"

A couple of days later, when I was fully recovered, I was recounting the experience to the rest of the boys and Geoff gave me some advice. "Make sure you take all the little yellow pills."

"Why?"

"Well, if you have any left and you take them back to England you might get locked up. They are banned everywhere else in the world and, apparently, you can't even give them to animals." To this day, I still don't know what they were.

My visit to the hospital had alarmed me more than a little and I hoped and prayed that I would never have to be an in-patient. I understood why Chinese people had a fear of being sick. There are no GPs in China, or very few, so the hospital is visited for everything from a headache upwards. People's first worry was in becoming sicker if they had to go into hospital – sadly there is the same fear in Britain now – and their second was the cost.

In China, if you are really sick and have no money you die. Communism? My first impression had been of an unhygienic, under-funded, chaotic and uncaring asylum. 'Abandon hope all ye who enter here.' It was and still is common practice in Chinese hospitals to stick a needle in anyone who is sick, no matter what is wrong with them. You are then left on a drip on a bed and shunted out when you are done. Anything from a headache to a heart attack received the same treatment. I had been lucky to escape. I may be exaggerating, but others share my opinion and some of the opinions are borne out by experience – bad experience.

An American friend, another Ron – Small Ron - was married to a Chinese woman. She was pregnant, but there was a problem. They couldn't see the baby with a scan and she was diagnosed as having an entopic pregnancy – baby in the fallopian tube. Very serious. As she was being diagnosed in the Chinese hospital she had insisted on visiting, she began to experience severe pains and was told she needed immediate, emergency surgery to save her life. There was no time for Ron to take her to a Western hospital, as they had to do it immediately. Immediately? Immediately, that is, after Ron had rushed out to the bank to get the $400 they required before they would touch her.

They operated on her – major surgery – with only an epidural anaesthetic, which meant she could see everything in the mirrored ceiling. Ron listened to her moans and screams outside the operating theatre and was stunned when the surgeon walked out with a dish in his hand to show him what he had just cut out of his wife. He was further stunned when he had to push the trolley to the ward himself AND put his wife into a bed unassisted. There were no screens around the bed to give any privacy during subsequent, infrequent, cursory and uncaring examinations and the bloody bed sheets remained unchanged for four days, until Ron managed to get her moved to another hospital. The hospital didn't even provide the necessary sanitary towels to help keep her bed clean.

Chinese people are treated no better - worse if anything. If they can't pay, they are given painkillers and sent away to die. The effect has been that Chinese people are terrified of getting a major illness and they panic at the sight of the smallest ailment. Medicine is bought and consumed in large quantities to ensure recovery. Children with running noses are fed antibiotics as if they were sweets and the result is the same – the discoloured and bad teeth that are much in evidence in China and, for that matter, a lot of South East Asia.

I managed to steer clear of anything other than stomach upsets and colds, so I didn't have the need to visit hospital any more – until I began to play squash again. While I was playing one night, something 'popped'. I was winning, by the way. It felt bad and I couldn't even put my foot on the ground without severe pain. I hadn't broken anything, but I knew, from past experience, that I had torn something and torn it badly. I looked forward to a possible two weeks of discomfort and limping. Fuck and shit.

I made it to work the next morning, only to be the butt of everyone's humour – Chinese people are into visual humour and Benny Hill, Mr Bean and Charlie Chaplin go down well. After a morning of discomfort and ridicule I decided that enough was enough, so I made my way back to my apartment.

As I was going in, my next-door neighbour, Mr Huang, saw me and came to my assistance. He was a nice guy and he and his wife were much taken with the kudos of having a foreign friend and neighbour. He had some English and indicated that I should go to hospital. "Yi yuan. Yi yuan. Hoptal go!"

"Bu yao le! Bu yao le!" (I don't want to) was my

response to his advice. He left me reluctantly and I closed my door and flopped onto the sofa. A couple of minutes later there was a knock on the door. Fuck. I hopped over, opened it and found my neighbour and his wife, serious faced and he tried again, "Hoptal go."

They kept at it and I gave in. "OK, hospital go."

I was frog-limped to the hospital and seen by, thankfully, an English-speaking doctor. He examined me carefully before saying, "You have torn your calf muscle – badly. I will give you something to help. You will be fine soon."

"Soon?" I thought "In your fucking dreams, mate."

I looked at what he had given me. Ibuprofen – OK. Liniment – OK. Yunnan Baiyao? The doctor saw the scepticism on my face and said, "It is very important that you take this medicine. You must or it will take a very long time to heal."

I was taken back home and supervised while I took my medicine and received nods of approval for being a good boy. My neighbours had a brief discussion, inspected my medicine and then went home, after making sure that everything I was likely to need was in easy reach. I settled down to watch TV and drink my way into oblivion, so that I could avoid the pain. I began to feel drowsy and the next thing I heard was a loud, urgent knocking on the door. I stumbled to it and discovered my neighbour and his wife again. What did they want? They'd just gone home. I glanced at my watch and realised that six hours had passed. Shit. They had come back to make sure that I took my next batch of medicine. I took it and they left happily.

I slept again and woke at around 7 am. I was feeling great, even allowing for the fact that I had slept on the sofa. I stood up to go to the toilet. I stood up. On both feet. I could walk. It still hurt, but I could walk.

After I sat down on the sofa again, I decided to have a closer look at my medicine. Yunnan Baiyao – 'for the treatment of blood disorders, bruising, muscular damage (my bit), stab wounds, gunshot wounds, cuts, abrasions, plus sore throats, skin infections and women's blood disorders'. No wonder I was getting better. It wouldn't have mattered what was wrong with me. It gave me pause for thought, as I knew from past sporting injuries how bad it felt. Was it the Chinese medicine or had I suddenly developed strange healing powers? I doubt that it was the latter.

As a result of this I began to look more seriously and with a more open mind at what was available and have discussions about it with others – both Western and Chinese. It turned out that most, including longer-term Westerners, were taking some ongoing health or strength giving potion or other. None of my Chinese friends would admit to taking the more exotic and questionable remedies and said that these were for desperate people who would try anything to get a hard on or to make them young again. Very similar to the West. They took both traditional and modern medicines, but believed more strongly in the value of the former. "We have done this for thousands of years, so we know it works." I think it does.

CHAPTER NINE

VISAS

If you spend any time in China you have to know about visas. It's best to find out before you need to know, to avoid surprises and pitfalls, but unfortunately I had to find out for myself, and usually by default. My ongoing saga only helped to confirm my feelings for my company. Everything was a surprise to them, reduced in significance by distance or viewed through rose-tinted glasses. 'There's gold in them thar hills, boys. Go and dig it up.' They had no regard for, or interest in, either the 'Indians' or the 'rattlers' and most transient visitors to the 'new and exciting development' were shielded and protected from the realities of China. As I've said before, 'The Queen thinks that everywhere in the world smells of new paint.'

Anyway, visas are required in China no matter what the reason for your visit or stay, and they have to be extended and/or renewed periodically. Most companies look after things for you, but mine left it up to whoever wanted or needed to do it after they supplied the first one to get you there.

My first experience was in late February or early March 1998. Rab and I were sitting in the office at work when I mentioned that I would need a visa extension. Rab glanced at his passport and his eyebrows shot up. "Fuck. Mine expired three weeks ago."

"Not good" I thought, even though I didn't know, at the time, how much it was 'not good'.

"I'll have to go with you" said Rab.

I arranged for the necessary letters of explanation as to why we needed extensions and Rab and I set off for the Public Security Bureau (PSB) on Wusong Lu. We went alone, without a translator – big, big mistake. As we walked towards the high counter I had a thought and said, "I'll go first, Rab. Yours might take a bit longer to sort out."

They were prophetic words and an understatement. I had no problems, apart from feeling rather intimidated by the frosty-faced, uniformed young woman who dealt with me. "Come back in three days to collect your passport. Next."

Rab sauntered forward, smiling and handed over his documents. The girl glanced at his passport and her frosty-face hit absolute zero. There was an immediate flurry of activity and within two seconds Rab had two more hard faces looking down at him from behind the high desk, as two 'heavies' positioned themselves either side of the young dragon lady. The girl spoke. "You have contravened the Laws and Regulations of The People's Republic of China. You have overstayed the period of your visa and must pay a fine and write a letter of apology and an explanation why you have contravened the Laws and Regulations of The People's Republic of China."

I moved forward to try and give moral support, but she stopped me with a frosty glare and the words, "Stay on the other side of the yellow line. Only one person is allowed to be on this side of the yellow line at a time unless they are a translator."

Rab, by this time, was a bit subdued and, being Scottish, the mention of a 'fine' disturbed him even more. He plucked up courage and said, "How much is the fine?"

The girl had a quick look at his passport and did a mental calculation before answering, "You have overstayed by twenty-three days and the daily fine is 500rmb." Rab's chin hit the floor with an almost audible 'CLANG' before she continued, "However, the maximum fine is 5000rmb, so that is how much you will have to pay."

This was better, but not a lot and he turned to me, stunned and asked, "Have you got any money?"

"Yes, but I don't think that five hundred will do you much good."

Things eased somewhat when he was told that he had to pay the fine when he returned for his passport in three days. However, he was instructed to write his letter there and then. He was given a piece of the usual tissue-like paper that passes for writing paper in China and dismissed. He was in shock, but brightened up when I told him that the company was responsible for the fine – more so because he was a Scot. He studied the blank piece of paper before saying, "What should I put in the letter? Will you gi's a han'?"

We found a vacant desktop and began. I started to dictate and Rab actually began to write what I told him before he realised what I was doing. I thought 'I am a stupid illiterate Jock' would have been a good start, but for some reason, he disagreed. Can't think why. Strange.

Anyway, we concocted a letter with an adequate amount of grovelling in it and presented it to Frosty Face. She gave it a cursory glance before giving him a warning. "Right. Make sure you do not contravene the Laws and Regulations of The People's Republic of China ever again."

Rab thought he would try to use humour in an attempt to relieve the situation. I kicked him in the shins, but too late. "I certainly will not, darling, because I don't particularly want to see your smiling face again."

She was not amused. "This is a very serious matter and if you do it again you may not be granted permission to stay in The People's Republic of China." She stared coldly at us both before looking past and through us and barking, "next".

Off we went, chastened, and we were going through the door when Rab stopped me and said, "I need tae go tae the cludgie" (toilet).

"Problem?"

"No, I just need to swear a bit, somewhere private."

Swearing done, we left and found a taxi. The driver asked where we wanted to go and I turned to a still crestfallen Rab. "Charlie's?"

"Charlie's."

Charlie's it was. A few beers sorted him out, along with me getting confirmation that I was right about the company paying the 5000. Rab mellowed, even though I continued to give him shit, 'Jock kicking' being the national sport that it is and all. I know it's bad form to kick a man when he's down, but let's face it, when else can you do it? Rab took it like a man, shook his head and said, "You wait, my friend, there will come a time."

I laughed. "Never."

Saying 'Never' is dangerous. Spike Milligan's first book was called 'Puckoon' and in the foreword he wrote, 'This damned book almost drove me mad. I will never write another book.' At the beginning of 'Adolf Hitler, My Part In His Downfall' he wrote, 'After I wrote Puckoon I swore I would never write another book. This is it.'

'Never' duly arrived prior to Spring Festival 1999. I needed to extend my visa and avoid the trip to Hong Kong, which I detested, to get a new one. I gave Lao Zhi the nod, obtained the necessary letter of explanation from our new JV partners SAIC and off we went. No problem. In. Up to the desk. Hand everything over. Come back in three days. Pay the money. Job done. Oops. Unsmiling, uniformed official. "You have overstayed the permitted length of stay."

I was puzzled. "No I haven't. My visa is good for another week."

"Not that. On this visa you are only allowed to stay in China for ninety days at a time. After ninety days you must leave China and re-enter."

"Eh?" still puzzled.

He showed me and sure enough I had a six-month visa, but it was a two-entry, ninety days each time. My previous one had been an 'open' visa' with no restrictions. I hadn't looked. Oh fuck. Then he carried on, "There will be a fine. Let me see. Mmm, yes. The maximum 5000rmb."

"OK. Very sorry."

I explained the reason for my oversight, but he really didn't give a shit. Bastard. I thought that was it, apart from paying the fine when I came back and writing my abject letter of apology before I left. No. He wasn't finished and said, "Also, I need your certificate of temporary residence before we can process your visa."

"What certificate of temporary residence?"

"You no longer live in a hotel. When you are in a hotel the hotel registers you, but if you move into an apartment you must register with the local police station within three days. Register and come back here." Dismissed.

I was not happy and walked away with Lao Zhi, muttering and cursing. Nobody had told me about registration or anything. Now I was looking forward to a day of boomeranging around Shanghai getting myself legal. Fuck.

As we were walking away Lao Zhi paused. "Wait a moment. I have just seen someone I know. We may be able to speed things up."

He made his way back to the counter and spoke to a young Chinese official. It was Xiao Xu, the son of one of our business partners. After a few moments Lao Zhi returned smiling. "Come back to the counter, Russell. We can do it all here today."

'Things' began to happen. All was sorted; residency certificate supplied; fine reduced to 3000rmb after a letter of mitigation was faxed from SAIC (our new JV partners); a letter of apology was written and accepted, and all done under the smirking eyes of the previous nasty bastard. I returned three days later to pick up my visa and it was Mr Happy again. His wry smile said everything as he handed over my passport. "Yes, you have friends."

I thought I was done with problems, until – oops again. About six months later I was having a meal with my friend Small Ron when the topic of visas cropped up. He had just returned from Hong Kong after getting a new Z visa, so I told him of my previous experience. "I'm OK now. Everything sorted out."

"That's OK then, as long as you remember to re-register within three days if you leave China and come back."

My heart fell and the wine in my glass turned sour. I'd been 'out' to Hong Kong two months before for a new visa and didn't know about the rules on re-registering. Fuck. Fuck. Fuck. On top of having my phone swiped it rounded off, as Del Boy would have said, 'a blinding weekend.'

Monday morning arrived and the sun was shining. How could it and how dare it? I sought out Lao Zhi and told him abjectly of the new problem. He pursed his lips before saying, "Hmm, let me think." He thought for a while and then stopped and then thought again before saying, "I think we must go to the police station in Gubei close to your apartment." Same thought as me.

Off we went. Lao Zhi liked to escape whenever he could, so he was happy. We arrived at the police station at Gubei and queued for forty-five minutes, and as we neared the desk my heart fell again. The policeman at the counter was none other than my miserable, nasty, officious friend from my previous visa experience. Shit.

False alarm. Wrong police station. Normally I would have been very, very pissed off, but I felt fortunate in having avoided Mr Nasty. Off we went to another police station on 'Something' Lu and were greeted, eventually, by a grumpy, half-asleep policewoman who sleepily said, "You are more than three days over, so it's a Divisional matter and I cannot deal with you here." Her face also said, "I am also not happy that you have woken me up for nothing."

We left and she returned, no doubt, to her slumbers. Lao Zhi scrutinised his watch, decided that time was not on our side and said, "We will have to go another day." As I said, he liked to escape whenever he could.

'Another day' arrived and off we went to the Divisional police Headquarters in Minhang. Lao Zhi had been thinking how to handle the situation, so he suggested, "Better not tell them that you have been registered before. It might be a problem. We will say that you moved into your apartment only two weeks ago. They will not check in any case – I think."

I decided to trust my fate to his wisdom and strangle him slowly if it went tits-up. Arriving at the place, we discovered that it only opened for public business for a very limited time, but, by lucky chance, we had hit the time window. An omen? In we went, with me fixing my face with the look of forlorn repentance that I was becoming very good at portraying. Up to the desk and the two bright-eyed, smiling policewomen. Smiling? Maybe it wouldn't be too bad after all. Lao Zhi spoke to them and probably said something along the lines of, 'This stupid foreigner...' because heads were shaken ruefully and smiles broadened. The bigger one, the boss, turned to me and said words with which I was becoming too familiar. "You have contravened the Laws etc... of The People's etc.... sections 39 and 45 dealing with alien residency. Did you read the entry paper given to you before you re-entered OUR country?"

"No. I used to, but I haven't for a long time now."

She shook her head and continued, "It is wise that you read EVERYTHING that we give you when you enter OUR country. It is for your protection and security [you stupid foreigner]. You will have to pay a fine after you write a letter of apology and explanation as to why you contravened etc etc... I will go and present your letter to my superior and he will decide on the amount of your fine. Write it now [you stupid foreigner]."

I fell back on my ignorance and stupidity and on being 'all alone' in a strange country. She smiled and nodded, but didn't quite say, 'There, there.' I wrote my letter and off she went. She returned after about five minutes with the verdict. "You will be fined [wait for it] 400rmb and

you must carry the record of your contravention of etc...
in your passport in future."

Not too bad, I suppose. We chatted for a while before
we left and I decided that she was very nice, particularly
in her uniform. Good figure and legs too. Behave.

Outside, Lao Zhi advised me to throw away the paper
they had given me. "It could cause problems for you when
- I mean if - anything else goes wrong. We have similar
things for Chinese people from other provinces, but
nobody bothers. Too much paperwork for the police
anyway."

Again I decided to trust his judgement, with the same
reservations as before. Better informed, but no wiser.

CHAPTER TEN

BIG RON REVISITED

I've written about Big Ron, a good friend in Shanghai, before, but now find I have more to say as things he said have come creeping back into memory. He was a large, larger than life character, and a strange mix of redneck bigot and nice guy, who always, always had something to say or an experience to relate about everything. What he came out with usually had a humorous twist to it, no matter what the subject was. When I was in the depths of divorce he was a source of relief and a sympathetic ear, having been through it twice himself. He had a story – of course. It went like this:

"I wuz almost done separatin' myself from 'The Bitch' when everything went to shit. I wuz tryin' to kind o' do it easy and slow. Couldn't tell her an' didn't dare tell her cos she woulda cut my throat, or worse, when I wuz asleep. She wuz a nasty, unforgivin', vindictive Cajun woman. The worst of the worst. The only things she had goin' for her wuz that she fucked like a mink an' coulda sucked the chrome off a trailer hitch. She'd moved to Denver from

New Orleans with me a couple o' years before and we'd bought a house there. Nice place. Anyway, the deal in Denver went sour pretty quick, so I took me a contract in Minneapolis that wuz goin' to last for about three years or more. Good money, but freeze your nuts off in the winter. Cold as Harbin. Fuck. I'd gotten myself another woman in New Orleans a while back an' it wuz lookin' real good. Rich family, didn't screw around an' a real neat figure. Really loved that gal. I told her that me an' 'The Bitch' wuz finished and separated an' that I wuz waitin' for the divorce to come through. Big lie. What I wuz tryin' to do wuz get my things away from Denver before I did anything.

"I used to go down South to see the new woman every couple o' weeks an' would stop over in Denver for a day to get a few of my things out of the house. Like I said, slow. Didn't tell the new woman. Mistake. It wuz goin' well an' I only needed another two or three trips to get it all done when I got careless. I did the usual an' arrived in New Orleans for the weekend with another batch to stash away. Everything OK. Anyway, I goes out for a carton o' Strikes an' when I come back I find her sittin' on the sofa cryin,' with my airline ticket stubs in her hand. Oh shit. She opened up with, 'You went to see HER didn't you, you bastard?'

'Yes I did, but I only picked up some o' my things and left. Honest.'

'Did you fuck her?'

'No I did not!' Lie.

"What I didn't know wuz that she had just phoned

Denver an' she had left the phone on conference, so a voice comes out of the speaker. 'Oh yes you fuckin' well did.'

"That wuz it. I was totally fucked an' tryin' to tell her that it had only been a blowjob only made the hole deeper. No home an' all my shit burned or thrown out. Be careful, my friend."

For a while Ron and I lived in the same hotel, the Crowne Plaza, in Shanghai and spent a lot of time together. Ron had a very good time and a lot of his activities were slightly frowned upon and, at times, barely tolerated by the hotel management. It got to the point where Ron decided it would be best if he found a place of his own. More privacy and less hassle. He moved out into an apartment only ten minutes walk from the hotel, so we still spent a large amount of time together. All seemed to be going well in his new place at first, until he rolled into Charlie's bar early one Saturday night. All was not well, so I asked, "What the fuck's wrong with you tonight?"

"Fuck, fuck, fuck, fuck!" was all that came out.

"What? Tell me."

"Looks like I gotta move. Fuck!"

"Go on. Tell me what you did this time."

"Well, you know that new woman I wuz chasin? The one from Nanjing with the big hooters? Right? Well I finally got her back to my place last night."

"And? No good?"

"Hell no. She wuz fine - at first. Didn't even squeal too much, like they usually do, when I shoved the old hog leg right up her ass for the first time. Took it like a man, in a manner o' speakin', an' she wuz up for anything."

"So what was the problem? Did she want money or something?"

"Hell, no. She'da been clear outa luck there. She wuz fine that way. It wuz when she was givin' me a blowjob that there was a problem."

"No good?"

"No, no. There ain't no such animal as a bad blowjob. It wuz after she was done an' she had her mouth full. The dirty bitch spit it out onto the carpet. The bathroom wuz only a coupla steps away. Dirty bitch. Anyway I wuz so pissed at her that I threw her out right there an' then."

"That's OK then. Finished."

"Not so simple. I threw her out, as she wuz – buck-naked – an' she got caught on the security camera. I wuz up all the rest of the night arguin' with the security guys an' payin' them off. Cost me five thousand rmb and no guarantees that they won't tell the police if I piss them off again. I gotta move out. Fuck!"

It all blew over, however, and Ron stayed where he was, but only because he slipped a regular payment to the security guards, so that they would forget the incident and keep their eyes closed in future. He even managed to get back with the 'Nanjing woman' after they had reached an agreement that she would swallow in future. All's well that ends well.

I met Ron another night in the usual place, Charlie's, and he had an interesting tale to tell. He had been down to Guangzhou on business for a few days and had had a strange experience, which he proceeded to tell me about:

"I goes into a bar down there. It wuz a place I never been to before but it looked OK. Anyway, the place was full o' pussy, so I thought I'd stay a while. Fine lookin' women as well. Classy. They wuz also a heap o' fit lookin' young Chinese guys. Anyway, I'd had me a coupla CCs (Canadian Club) an' wuz settlin' in for the night when a woman come up to me. We talked a while – the usual preamble – then she says 'One thousand rmb. To sleep with you.' I could buy a white woman for that, as you know, so o' course I told her to fuck off, but nicely. She was cute. An' then she says, 'OK then, fifteen hundred.' I was confused and then the penny dropped. She wuz gonna pay me. I wuz so surprised I couldn't speak, so she fucked off. I took a look around an' it hit me. I wuz in a gigolo bar. All the Chinese boys were studs an' all the women were rich, bored Chinese women lookin' for some action. Fuck!

"She come back to try me again, so I took pity on her, let her buy me a drink an' eventually we lit out o' the place an headed back to her apartment. I had a good night."

"She paid you?"

"Hell no. I couldn't do that. Against my beliefs an' all that. You want the address o' the bar?"

TURN DOWN, TURN ON

The title of this piece refers to the 'turn-down ladies' in the Crowne Plaza Hotel, the women whose job it was to give your room a quick early evening check, turn the bed down and leave a chocolate, along with an inspirational message, on your pillow. Every floor in the hotel had its own turn-down lady and if you were there long enough, like me, she became your friend and not just another scurrying, faceless, nameless member of the hotel staff.

The woman on my floor was called Wang Ying and was somewhere in her late thirties. She was married, had a sixteen-year-old daughter and lived close to the hotel. She was reasonably attractive and her figure was still OK, but there was nothing remarkable about her at all. She'd known me long enough to give me shit if my room was in too much of a mess when she checked it at night and we carried on a friendly, joking banter whenever it was too untidy. She was nice to me and there often used to be two chocolates on the pillow and sometimes all my clothes would be put away, even though it wasn't really her job to do it.

Obviously, in her job she'd 'seen it all' and I'd often be semi-naked when she walked into my room after the polite knock. She'd got to the stage where she didn't even apologise if I was lying watching TV in only a pair of underpants or a towel when she walked in. I, in like manner, didn't care, and I suppose to my mind she was almost the same as a hospital nurse. There was never the slightest hint of anything – not even the possibility of anything.

It was early one Friday evening and I was taking a shower, getting ready to go out for the night. I finished showering and walked out of the bathroom, with only a towel over my head and face, drying my hair. A hand gripped me, gave a couple of gentle tugs and I heard 'ni hao' (hello) spoken in time with the tugs. I got a shock, naturally, and lifted the towel. It was a laughing Wang Ying and, after the initial surprise, I laughed as well. We stopped laughing and I realised that she hadn't let go of me. She wasn't looking up at my face any more, but down at what she had in her hand. After a few seconds she looked up at my face slowly and there was a look on her face that said, 'I want. I need.'

My reaction was natural and instant. I drew her close to me and kissed her upturned mouth. She was hungry, her tongue bursting deep into my mouth as her grasp on me changed from holding to urgent tugging. I was rising quickly because of the eroticism of it all and then, suddenly, she became frantic and began trying to take her clothes off with one hand, the other keeping a firm hold of me, whimpering softly in her need. I helped her and, between us, we almost ripped her clothes off in our urgency.

By the time she pulled me down on top of her on the bed, guiding me into her as she did, her eyes were half closed, her eyelids flickering and she was panting like an exhausted dog. I almost came as soon as I was inside her as she rose to take my full length, but I managed to control it long enough for her to have a screaming orgasm, which she tried to muffle with a pillow. Her climax triggered me and I came long and deep inside her. It had only taken about twenty seconds at most, but WOW.

We lay quiet, still locked together, for almost a minute, neither of us sure what to do next. Then, slowly, we rolled apart and lay looking at each other, not speaking, trying to figure out how what had happened had happened.

She spoke first. "Before never do."

"Mm?"

"Have husband. Never man. Husband. Husband."

"Oh."

She was quiet for a while then, shaking her head, "Me and husband never long time."

"Ah." I didn't know what to say to her, so I thought it was best to let her lead things.

She was quiet for a while and then spoke again, but this time she was smiling happily, "Never AAAAH before." repeating a quieter version of her scream. Then she hugged herself happily, smiled and then hugged me and said, "Sank you."

She moved her hand down to touch me again and as I

reached to touch her, she took my hand and guided it to her breasts. They were still firm and round, for her age, and her nipples were large and dark and stiffened at my touch. Then she moved my hand down her body, opening her thighs for me as she shifted onto her back. She lay with her eyes half closed and her arms over her head displaying the profuse, untrimmed, deep, black pits of her arms that matched the black delta further down her body. She was inviting me to do as I pleased, so I carried on touching and teasing her surprisingly maiden-like pussy with my fingers and working on her breasts with my mouth. She must have had nipples three quarters of an inch long and they were hard and erect. Ohhh. She started to breathe faster and her eyes began to roll. She was ready again – We were both ready. Then, suddenly, she went rigid – shocked. "No. Work. Have work. Aiya."

She jumped up and hurriedly started to put her clothes on, only to discover that her bra strap was broken and the elastic in her knickers had snapped. We both laughed and she laughed even more as she pointed to the stream of semen running down the inside of her leg. "Long time no have. Long time no have. Very much. Wash quick."

She disappeared into the bathroom with her clothes and reappeared five minutes later looking presentable. She had made a quick inspection in the mirror and said, "I go work now."

She came back to the bed and gave me a quick kiss on the cheek followed by a long, lingering one on the mouth. As she moved away she made a grab for me and gave me a couple of quick tugs, in time with 'zai jian' (goodbye) and laughed as she picked up her work bits and pieces and headed for the door.

I lay for a couple of minutes, thinking about the ramifications of what had happened, and then there was a knock on the door. I opened it and it was a smiling Wang Ying. What did she want now?

"Sorry sir." She handed me two chocolates and a 'pillow message'. She turned and went to carry on with her 'turn down' duties as I slowly closed the door.

I ate the chocolates as I watched the TV and thought about what had just happened. It couldn't have taken more than ten to fifteen minutes in total, but in my mind it seemed to be much, much longer. The 'time' had worried me at first because there were security cameras all over the hotel and most of them had little to do with security. Staff monitoring, big brother style, was what they were really all about. Fifteen minutes, at the most, shouldn't be a problem. I began to relax a bit, not that I was worried for me. I didn't want Wang Ying to have any problems, as life was hard enough for bottom level Chinese. I idly opened the 'pillow message' as I was thinking and looked down at it. No. Not possible. Her English wasn't good enough. It said, "IF NOT YOU, THEN WHO?"

I left the hotel about two weeks later and moved into an apartment, so Wang Ying and I snatched only two or three more 'moments'. It was sad, really, as the first time was special and memorable. The other times were still good, but perhaps it would have been better, and definitely, more romantic, if the first time had been the only time.

PS: I had occasion to go back to the hotel, obviously, many times because Charlie's was my local and all foreign visitors to the company stayed there. However, for some reason I never bumped into Wang Ying until six months later, when I went to meet someone there. He was an absolute arsehole from the 'Head Office Finance Department', as he liked to introduce himself. His name was Neil Something and he had been with us for about a week. I was volunteered to chaperone him for a night. He was a typical cost-of-everything-value-of-nothing accountant, plus I suspected that he was a bit 'light on his feet'.

I was to meet him in Charlie's at six, and he was late. I phoned his room, but the phone was engaged, so I decided to go and get him. Up I went and knocked on the door. "Sorry, Russell, I was on the phone to my boy... er girlfriend" he replied. I was right.

As we walked back towards the lift a figure was coming towards us. It was Wang Ying. How to handle this? Wang Ying did it for me. She stopped and clasped her hands. "Ni hao" she said, in time with a double bow.

We both laughed and then had what conversation we could with our limited language. She was fine and happy. We said goodbye and she repeated the quasi-ritual with, "Zai jian" before going on her way. I was never to see her again.

As we walked on to the lifts Neil Something, who had been quiet throughout my exchange with Wang Ying, broke the silence. "What was that 'ni hao' 'zai jian' thing? Private joke?"

"Yeah, something like that, but even if I told you, YOU wouldn't understand."

GEOFF

Geoff Smithson was the on-site engineer during the construction of the factory in Shanghai and was sixty-two when I met him, but he had the energy and drive of a man thirty years younger. He was an aggressive, tenacious bulldog of a man and good to have in your corner. Conversely, I imagine, he would have been a bad man to have against you. Fortunately, I never had to find this out.

He had been away from the UK for most of his working life and had worked on all continents. The breadth of his knowledge was amazing, covering everything from surveying and building through mechanical and electrical to electronic and computerised process control. This last was surprising, as many older engineers shied away from the more recent developments in computerisation. Geoff, however, had the lot, probably because he'd been in too many situations where he had no one else to turn to – "If not you, then who?"

He smoked like a chimney, could drink like a fish and seemed to eat almost nothing. I can never recall seeing him eat a full meal in all the time we worked together – six months. As a result he was wiry, gaunt and cadaverous and never looked healthy. This was misleading and he would sometimes still be going strong when the rest of us were falling over, with sleep seeming to be something that he only got involved in because everybody else needed to do it. What kept him going? I don't know, but it could have been a combination of his undefeated character, determination and an acerbic, rasping sense of humour.

He also had an explosive temper, to which he gave vent at least twice a day at the frustrations of China. His explosions were probably what saved him from a heart attack or bursting a blood vessel, and were legendary amongst the Chinese. However, the explosions were mainly for his own benefit, to release pressure and let off steam, as most people who knew him took no notice. "Oh, Geoff is angry – again." If I, on the other hand, was angry about something, they used to scurry about trying to look busy and keep out of the way until I calmed down. I'll relate a couple of examples of Geoff being less than happy – two of the more amusing ones.

Commissioning a factory (or any installation) involves many things. Everything has to be checked, proved, calibrated and double or even triple checked before final hand-over and signing off can be done. The process is repetitive, laborious and tedious as well as being frustrating when things, as they always, always do, go wrong or break. Small niggling problems take on major proportions in your mind, but eventually all is well and you look back and wonder why you got so wound up about it all.

Among the many problems we had was one in particular that occupied us all for two long days. It was a small automatic weighing machine – small, but essential. If it didn't work correctly, then it didn't matter if everything else did. We were past hair-pulling stage with the machine, to the degree that we would sit thinking for ten or fifteen minutes before trying something else – again.

Unfortunately, we usually sat on the mounds of limestone that we had been running through the machine as a test material. Limestone is cheap, but it's also dusty and sticky, particularly when the temperature is above 30C, which it was. We all looked like snowmen and noses, eyes and mouths were encrusted with the stuff. Everyone was very, very pissed off and tempers were frayed, when humour, again, lent a hand.

From nowhere, it seemed, a song surfaced and we all began to sing and to laugh. Apologies to Glen Campbell, but I think he has nothing to fear from our parody of 'Rhinestone Cowboy' – 'Limestone Cowboy.' After we stopped laughing we decided to 'have another go,' so Geoff turned to the puzzled labourers, who had witnessed our manic phase, and said, "Two tonnes of limestone. Number six floor. Chop, chop."

The labourers were not happy at the prospect, and I didn't blame them, of carrying 50kg bags of limestone up six floors – the lift was way down on the commissioning list. It was hot, the bags were almost as heavy as they were and sometimes heavier, and they'd already carried five tonnes up there only two hours before. There was a huddle and much jabbering until Geoff lost his cool and said, "Listen, you fuckers, if you don't start right now I'll make it five tonnes."

There was another huddle and more jabbering, which pushed Geoff over the edge. The neck began to bulge, eyes to pop and steam to escape and he screamed at them, "OK, FUCKING TEN TONNES."

The labourers took the hint and disappeared, still jabbering. Geoff turned, still blazing, to find us all collapsed and helpless with laughter. "Bastards! You're no fucking help at all. Bastards!" He had no choice but to join in the laughter and the spontaneous chorus of 'Limestone Cowboy'. Once again laughter was the key, and remained the key.

Time moved on, and we got to the stage where finishing off the surroundings of the factory was good idea. Geoff and I made a trip to a local contractor to discuss what needed to be done and agreed a price, date and time-scale for the work, which was considerable. As we left, Geoff fired a parting shot, "And don't just send two men with a wheel-barrow and a shovel each. If you do, there will be trouble."

The day arrived and at 10 am, as I expected, (cynical? Me?) so did two men with a shovel each and a wheelbarrow. Geoff watched them from the control room window as they sat and smoked, his agitation growing. The men sat for an hour and then wandered off to have lunch – the most important activity for all Chinese workers.

After lunch, around 2 pm, they began to scratch about unenthusiastically in a corner of the one acre site. Geoff kept an eye on them and after scrutinising his watch, yet again, said, "Those two fuckers had better start making noises like a bulldozer by three o'clock or there will be big trouble."

Three o'clock arrived to find Geoff striding across the site to saw the nuts off the two hapless workmen. Just as he was about to swoop, an antique bulldozer trundled through the gate. The cavalry had arrived in the nick of time. John Ford lives. All was well for approximately half an hour, until we discovered that the bulldozer driver was a learner, who had his own ideas about what levelling and clearing a site meant. In that short time he had managed to fill in the newly-dug and staked foundations of the new toilet block, demolish a workmen's hut and drive over clearly marked no-go areas, thus fracturing the mains water pipe.

It took two of us to restrain Geoff and disarm him. The shovel wouldn't have fitted in the place he wanted to shove it anyway. The driver didn't hang around for the fitting and disappeared, never to return.

Looking back, it's amazing that we ever got it all done in time. Geoff, when not losing it, tended to be philosophical about it all. He knew from experience that it would all come together in the end. He became more relaxed as we neared the end, more so because Di had gone back to the UK. We began to see more of the relaxed Geoff and he liked to relax – a lot.

He was as randy and as horny as a billy goat and nothing was safe. He liked a place called the Golden Violin, which was about ten minutes' walk from the hotel, and was a regular visitor. The place, however, never 'did it' for me and I found it a bit too cattle-marketish for my taste. High rolling Japanese businessmen frequented it and, as a result, most of the women were very young and barely legal. Also, they were subservient to the point of being doormats and never raised any objection, no matter what perverted indignity was inflicted on them by the deviant Japanese. Different strokes.

When Geoff was not in pursuit of pussy he was entertaining, and he had a wealth of stories from everywhere. Again, there are too many to tell, but one sticks out in the memory. We had been talking about the apparent lack of street crime, against foreigners at least, in Shanghai. As I've said before, this is true and I can honestly say that I have never felt unsafe or threatened in any city in China when I have been out and about alone at any time, night or day. Draconian punishments could be the reason, but whatever the reason is, China is safe.

Anyway, Geoff recalled a 'gentle mugging' that had been inflicted on him in Kenya. It was early morning and Geoff was making his way from the hotel to a site on the outskirts of Nairobi. As he walked along the road in the bright morning sun a shadow suddenly loomed over him, blocking out the sunlight. It was a two-metre tall Swahili warrior, with a machete tucked in his belt. The words, "Good morning, Bwana" were uttered in a deep, Darth Vader voice.

Geoff stopped, being a well-mannered man, not to mention the fact that that 'warrior' was blocking his onward path, before giving the nervous, apprehensive, response, "Er, good morning."

"It is a fine, bright morning, Bwana."

"Yes it is, isn't it?"

"Yes, Bwana, it is a fine morning and I have not yet had breakfast and I am very hungry."

"Oh?"

"Yes, Bwana, it would be a great shame on this fine morning if I had to beat you and take your money, so that I can buy my breakfast."

"Yes it would be a shame wouldn't it?"

"What shall we do, Bwana, about this problem?"

"How much is breakfast?"

They parted with Geoff's skin and wallet intact and a happy, soon to be fed, Swahili. Very civilised really.

I was sad to see Geoff leave and we had a monster farewell party for him, which, unfortunately, I can't remember too much about. I do know that I woke up with two women in bed with me and that the hotel was very pissed off when all the staff from the Step Bar came to the club lounge for breakfast - at Geoff's invitation, I hasten to add.

Geoff went to start up a cane-crushing factory for British Sugar in Guangxi and kept in touch for a while – mainly to moan about the shitty place he had landed in. Sugar factories are the worst. I called him one day to see how things were. "How's it going, Geoff?"

"Well, yesterday it was fine, but today it's gone to shit."

"What happened?"

"Well, yesterday I had three engineers. Today I have none. One's dead, another's in intensive care and the other's fucked off."

"Christ. What happened?"

"Not sure, but it has something to do with baijiu and homemade guns. I'll probably never know. The only thing I do know is that the one who's fucked off is a dead man when the police catch him."

It's fair to say that Geoff's life was colourful.

CHAPTER THIRTEEN

LIFE AND LIVING

I really wish I'd listened to what my mother told me. Unfortunately, I don't know what it was, because I didn't listen. Too late again.

'Into every life a little rain must fall.' This is true and anyone who hasn't experienced a little 'rain,' doesn't fully understand or know about life. If you never experience the bad then you don't recognise the good when it happens. That being said, too much rain is not good and, as an old friend once said, 'There's a difference between having a crap and ripping your arsehole open.' Too much rain and you will drown. Some things in life are best avoided, if possible, and very high on the list are broken marriage and divorce. I do not recommend this experience, even though it may be unavoidable.

As I've already said, I had been married for twenty-five years when I went to China and within three months I knew in my heart that it was over. I had been discontented with my life and uncertain about many things for about ten years, but thought it was normal. I knew many men who felt the same as me, so I thought it was just part of the overall patchwork quilt of life. I had been in the rut of family for a long time and thought that there were no alternatives. Don't get me wrong, I think my children are the best part of my life and, so far, my greatest achievement, and I wouldn't change anything. However, as time moves on you find that the things that gave your life meaning and purpose for so long are vanishing before your eyes. Something needs to take their place – a new focus. I wasn't prepared to begin to grow old and die just yet. My wife, on the other hand, seemed to be looking forward to it. Maybe her being six years older than me had something to do with it and she was further down the slippery slope than me. Maybe.

As time drifted by in China I found that the pictures of 'home' were beginning to blur and fade, to the point that they didn't seem real any more. At the time, August 1998, I wrote the following, which sums up how I was feeling:

A warning - a personal viewpoint in a very low moment.

China or maybe just Shanghai changes you. The place, the people, the distance. Detachment. The longer you are here alone, the more real this dream world becomes and the more it transposes the reality that you left behind. Distance and time make the pictures in your head start to blur and fade. Initially you are caught up in the excitement and difference of it all and the phone calls home tell it all to the ones who did not get invited to the party. An edge begins to enter the conversations, as you try not to become a 'Shanghai bore' or sound too enthusiastic.

The phone calls home become a routine - something you have to do. On occasion conversation stops, as you struggle to find something different to say or ask about.

You make a decision, maybe not consciously, to live your life here as best you can or go crazy thinking about what you left at home. In doing this you begin to lose interest in things that happen six thousand miles away. What can you do about them anyway? 'The lawnmower is broken.' 'The car won't start.' Do you care? Do you want to care? Will you ever care again? Does anybody else care? Ignored? Forgotten?

The two weeks' 'holiday?' at home every two months doesn't help. After the jet lag you spend what time is not devoted to preparing to come back to China fixing things, seeing the bank manager, mowing the lawn, cutting the hedge etc. There is almost a sense of relief when you get back onto the plane and escape to your new reality, leaving behind what has become a stressful environment.

'Bring your family over,' they say. Not that easy. 'What do I do about my mother? I can't leave her and she won't go in a home.' and – even more important, 'What about the dog?' Then there's 'What about the house? We can't leave it empty for the winter.' and 'I'll have to give up my job.' Trying to sort it out on the phone doesn't help.

You start to wonder about the future. What are you going to go back to? Your life will never be as it was - is it ever? Is it worth going back? Is there a point of no return, after which it isn't possible to go back or is it linked to a fear that what you have experienced will make it impossible to 'fit in' again, as was and is the experience of many ex colonials. If you do go back will you spend the rest of your life boring people to death and wishing you were still in China?'

My wife blamed China completely, plus my relationship with a Chinese woman, and will never be convinced otherwise. She was wrong. All China did was speed up the coming of the end. The divorce was acrimonious, of course, and most of it was my fault. Not true. It was ALL my fault. I took the coward's way out and did it all from China, which my daughter has never forgiven me for and probably never will. I can't blame her. The sadness I feel now is not so much for the break-up of the marriage, but for the lost and damaged relationship with my children.

Doing it from China kept me focused on it, without any pressure from family and friends, and probably speeded things up. She was restricted to invective and anger over the telephone, but she managed to save enough up for when we eventually did meet and took great delight in presenting me with a shoebox containing my 'things' from our twenty-five years together. Nice touch.

My wife refused to divorce me, so I petitioned her, which she wasn't happy about. Mental cruelty were the grounds for divorce and they were somewhat trumped up, but as my solicitor said, "Surely there must be something in your twenty-five years of marriage that you're not happy about."

There was. My wife's annoyance at my unwillingness to make love to her in our latter years and her accusation, tongue in cheek, that I must be turning 'gay' was sufficient for the judge. Gay. Me?

It all got done by late December 1999 and is behind me now, but the pain of it all is still there and I still regret the way it happened and the effect on my children. Where they are concerned it doesn't take much scratching to open the wound and make the blood flow again. I doubt whether it will ever change. Again, I wrote something at the time that demonstrates how I was feeling:

Black moments occur - not too often thank God - and this one was precipitated for reasons which should be obvious to anyone who knows me or has had similar experiences in their lives.

Regrets, Guilt, Remorse And The Future

Who am I? Where am I? What have I done?
I've shattered the hearts of everyone
Who always loved and believed in me.
Even when it was plain to see
I was wrong, so wrong, so very wrong
They'd stand beside me to keep me strong.

I've done it now for good or for bad.
Too late to think about what I had
Or to even think of turning it back
To that time when I chose the track.
Too late to explain or hope to regain
Things as they were before all this pain.

My wonderful girl, my stupendous son
Can't understand why I've done what I've done.
I can hold them no more, but even so,
They'll stay in my heart wherever I go.
I'll hold them there for all my life long.
Fixed like the words of my favourite song.

She. I've broken her heart, that I know.
She'll never believe that I just had to go.
It wasn't as sudden or quick like she thinks.
Everyone else saw the cracks in the links
Of the chain that bound us for so many good years
Now gone and lost, all drowned in the tears.

"It's never too late." So they say. Says who?
Someone who's too late with too much to do?
It's always too late when the damage is done
To the lives and the people and you are the one
Who stuck in the knife or fired the gun
That brought on the darkness and put out their sun.

Tomorrow, tomorrow. That's where I must look
To make any sense of the path that I took.
Tomorrow is clouded with maybe and if
Sometimes in my mind like a jump from a cliff.
I'm falling and falling not scared of the drop
And who knows what I will find when I stop.

Tomorrow, tomorrow, a new life in my mind
And try to forget what I left behind.
What will it all hold, my chosen new life?
New questions, old answers, more problems, more strife?
"You're a fool. You're a fool." The voice in my head.
Too late. I must go where my heart has led.

Enough. Move on or die. While everything was going to shit with my family life I was doing 'other things'. Some of these things, as you would expect, were things other than work. My fall into 'yellow fever' continued unabated, slowing slightly when I encountered the person who was blamed for my losing my way. Not so. She was a symptom, not the disease.

I met Amy. She was a receptionist in a drug company and she and her friends used to visit Charlie's now and then. At first she used to talk to me to practise her English, but we gradually drifted closer until we ended up in bed together. She was twenty-six, or said she was, when we met, but I could never believe anything she said. I have never known anyone who could lie so well and so consistently. Everything she said was bullshit, but she had a very good memory – essential for good liars – and very rarely made mistakes or tripped herself up. She was tall and slim, but had a good body and was very easy on the eye. Good in bed too, apart from her reluctance to go the whole hog with her mouth. She only once, by mistake, went the full distance and then she reacted as if I'd physically abused her. "Never do that again. Hate it. Hate you."

She calmed down after a while, but 'it' never happened again. She did make me an offer, though. "If you need this I can find a woman who likes to do it. You want?" I told her it wasn't a problem and not to worry about it, but she carried on. "Only thing. If I find a woman, I have to be there when she suck you. Don't want you touch her and she can't take off clothes or do anything else. Only suck."

I never did take her up on her offer, but it sounded interesting. This apart, she was very keen, so we spent a lot of time horizontal and in other positions – never with company. We moved close and then drifted apart, as I tired of her continuous lies, deceptions and possessiveness. It got so bad that even a glance or a hello to another female would cause a blazing row – too much. She even suspected that I was carrying on with my 'ayi', the Chinese for maid. The fact that the woman was sixty, fat and had a face like a robber's dog made no difference. Her reasoning was, "She is woman and you alone with her sometime."

My ayi, Guo Ying, was a wonderful woman and took her responsibility, looking after me, very seriously. She washed, ironed, shopped, cooked and cleaned, as well as giving me Chinese cookery lessons. If I washed a dish, made a bed or did anything, it was a capital offence, and the result was a finger-wagging lecture. She was very honest and would produce receipts for everything she bought and would refuse to keep even small amounts of change. On top of it all, her salary was only six hundred rmb a month, but she was happy with it. I think, too, that she watched over me in her own way and worried about me.

She never liked Amy and was happy when our relationship ended. Amy, in typical Chinese fashion, had treated her as less than human for most of the time and was always trying to get me to sack her. No chance. Guo Ying wept inconsolably when I left and gave her everything I didn't want or need from the apartment. I hope she is well.

My life in China gradually became 'normal' and things that had, at first, shocked and amazed me became part of everyday life. My everyday life began each day with an early morning wait for my car outside my apartment on Ronghua Dong Lu, later to be at Mandarin City, and during this wait I used to watch the city begin to stir and come back to life.

The first things on the move were the waste collectors. They sorted through all and any garbage to recover anything that could be sold for recycling. Some specialised in paper waste, others in plastic and others in everything. There was even a scruffy little man who collected waste cooking oil from all the restaurants on the street. He had really made it, and had a bicycle and trailer to carry everything. Others only had barrows or plastic bags to load and stuff with recyclable crap. The worst sights were at public garbage dumps. Every area had its own dump and they looked like lock-up garages without doors. This was stuffed with garbage of all kinds from the surrounding community and hordes of scrabbling, desperate sorters would descend after dark to get what they could.

Most of the people doing this were Shanghainese poor

and what they did was regarded as being a step above begging, but not much of a step above. Shanghai people, even the poor ones, are proud though, and begging is beneath most of them.

Another 'service' worth mentioning was at public toilets. Some of the public toilets in Shanghai had no running water or sewerage facilities, so what was left there was deposited into drums of all kinds. These were emptied every morning and the collected waste taken to – wait for it – fruit and vegetable farms. There was and still is a good reason for washing ALL fruit and vegetables in China before you eat them or cook them.

Staying with the bottom of the social ladder – the very bottom – I'll move onto beggars. Beggars are a feature and a fact in every country in the world and so it is with China. Everyone is looked after in a communist society? Hmm. Almost all the beggars in Shanghai are country people who have come into the city for a better life. A better life? Getting your arse kicked every day and sleeping rough? How bad could it have been in the country?

Beggars where I lived used to begin to come out of the woodwork in the early evening and seemed to know when I would be arriving home. Most nights I would be mobbed by six or seven small children, with the 'Fagin' in the background egging them on. It was likely that some of these small children had been kidnapped and sold to their masters. This is true and is common in China. The lucky ones are just shoved onto the street, but others are purposely crippled or mutilated to give them an 'edge.' This is also common in India.

When I first became aware of this in China, something else raised its head in my mind. You see very few people with birth defects in China and most physical deformities are the result of injury or disease. No birth defects, or has the one child policy had a spin off into infant euthanasia? No one would answer. Be that as it may, there are some pitiful sights; a man with no lower jaw; another with both arms off at the elbows - how did he go to the toilet? I saw yet another with neither legs nor arms.

Many, it's true, are used by their families, or someone, as a source of income, as must have been the case with the beggars I saw at the LingYi Buddhist shrine in Hangzhou. On the way out of the place, crippled and mutilated beggars were spaced about every twenty yards or so. None of them could move, so someone had put them there and someone would collect them. Who? Family or employer? Sadly it was often the same thing.

At the other end of the scale are the rich, and they are becoming richer, with the gap between themselves and the poor widening every day. Ripe for revolution? Again? The richer Chinese people want and pursue all the trappings of wealth – the house, the car, the latest model mobile phone etc etc, while the other end of the social scale are happy just to get enough to eat.

There are contrasts everywhere in the world, but they seem to be more marked in China. As an example: I had a haircut and Lao Zhi asked me how much it cost. His mouth fell open when I said, "75rmb." His haircuts only cost him 4. Even the hookers covered the range, from

30rmb 'hairdresser' girls to $200 princesses in the Long Bar. It was much the same with housing. A small, but growing, number of Chinese have Western-style homes, but the rest live in cramped conditions with, sometimes, four or five people sharing two rooms with beds doubling as sofas and food eaten on the floor. Things are improving, though, with old housing being demolished and new being built all the time. Unfortunately most of the time the new stuff was built miles away from where the old stuff was demolished.

As far as most of my Chinese friends were concerned I was richer than rich, even though my salary was low when compared with other ex-pats, particularly the Americans. Big Ron's words on the subject were, "I told 'em I wouldn't work in China for less than $100,000 plus benefits."

The trick was to try and live Chinese on a Western salary, which I did as much as I could. It was also a good idea to get Chinese friends to make purchases, as foreigners did and still do get ripped off most of the time.

I remember visiting a vegetable market with Ava and my driver, Jonathan and, when Ava saw that I was going to walk round with them instead of waiting in the car, she expressed her concern and gave me the instruction, "Try and look as if you are not with us, or the prices will go up."

I know this is true because I've seen two 'Rolex' watches sold on the street for 40rmb and 150rmb respectively – the first one to a Chinese man and the second to a foreigner, less than a minute later.

On that topic; I bought an 'Omega' watch on the street

in Shanghai, for 100rmb and on a subsequent visit to Britain I was in a jeweller's shop in Carmarthen, South Wales, buying I forget what. The jeweller had his eye on the watch, so I gave it to him to have a look. His eyes went wide and he warned me, "Ah. I hope you don't want me to change the battery."

"Why?"

"Well, if you did, I would have to tell the police." He indicated a small notice that was stuck on the wall beside the counter before he continued, "If you don't mind me asking, how much did you pay for it?"

I made a quick mental calculation and said, "Around £6.50."

His eyes widened and he said, "Well, I know it's a fake, but it's a nice watch. You would pay about £70 or £80 for a watch like this in Britain."

The Chinese are good at copying and back then, were unashamed about it. I've visited milling machinery factories and seen Western equipment on the shop floor being copied bolt for bolt. I had a friend who worked for a European machinery supplier. He went to check on a machine he'd supplied to a Chinese company and found another two beside it, identical in every detail apart from the manufacturer's nameplate.

They copy everything and they are good at it, to the extent that sales of brands like Rolex and Louis Vuitton have declined because you can no longer tell the difference. Nothing is safe, not even cigarettes.

The main concern for the rest of the world seems to be

in entertainment-related copying. DVDs of new Hollywood movies appear on the streets within a week or two of release and nobody cares, so what chance music CDs? The only thing the police seem to bother about is porn – yellow movies, as they are known in China. Female nudity is very much frowned upon and, apart from the regular politically motivated censorship, is the main reason some satellite movie channels go off the air – mainly Japanese channels. Good job they didn't get German or Dutch channels.

Copying is a way of life in China and everything that can be copied or pirated is. Perhaps the best one I heard was about an HMV executive in Hong Kong, who was asked how the company's new outlet in Chendu was doing. He asked, "What new outlet?"

I also went into what I thought was a KFC, in Hangzhou. Everything was the same as KFC in every detail, and had I not looked back at the restaurant after I left, I would have been no wiser. Not KFC, but CFC. 'Chinese Fried Chicken.'

Anyway, living Chinese. I did become 'native' in many ways and food was one of them, to the extent that too much Western food gave me problems. I made frequent checks on skin colour, but could detect no yellowing. Maybe it was only happening internally. At work I seemed to be fitting in very well and many admitted to forgetting that I was English – compliment?

I began to get used to things not happening when they should or when I expected. The staff also got used to me and began qualifying things when they spoke to me – 'I'll only be five minutes Chinese time.' That meant half an hour., whereas 'five minutes Western time' meant 'five minutes'.

I also got used to things happening when I didn't expect them. Prior to the opening ceremony an expensive granite plinth was constructed for flagpoles – flags of China, Britain and The Company. The day before the opening ceremony there were still no flagpoles in position and enquiries as to when they would be put in place and by whom were met with shrugs and blank faces. I started to get pissed off and asked, "Is it a secret or is the fact that it's a secret a secret?" I still got no response other than more shrugs.

As you would expect, on the night before the opening ceremony, I was very late finishing work and I left about 8.30. Still no flagpoles. Fuck it! The next morning I went to work early and was there by seven and I found? Flagpoles with flags flying. I asked questions, but again got only shrugs and blank faces. I never did find out what had gone on. Maybe it was the 'flagpole fairies'. It was more likely to have been a fuck-up by someone whose job it was to get it done, who had forgotten and been afraid to admit it. Afraid to 'lose face.'

In the West we tend to think of 'face' as a Japanese thing, ritual suicide etc, but it is equally important to the Chinese and runs their lives. It often leads them into deep shit, as it makes them lie to keep people happy. One lie leads to another and so on. They try to please and say yes all the time rather than admit that the answer should be no.

'Face' or loss of it was used as part of the draconian disciplinary procedures at work, and other places, in China. In addition to the 'reward and punishment,' with emphasis on 'punishment,' there is something called 'public self criticism.' This involves whoever's nuts are in the wringer standing up in front of his workmates and confessing his sins and shortcomings and asking for forgiveness - 'mea culpa' Chinese style. Believe me, this, for Chinese people, is like walking naked in the street, and many leave their employment rather than go through it. I was amazed when I first saw it take place and the effect it had on the individual going through it. He changed from being a chirpy, enthusiastic young boy to a bowed-headed shuffler for the rest of the time he was with the company, which wasn't long. This sort of thing, added to the total lack of consideration given to the lives and personal considerations of workers, makes working life something that has to be endured rather than enjoyed.

Working hours tend to be whatever and whenever the company decides. 'You will work all night', or 'You will work on Sunday' is common and accepted as being normal. Try it in Britain. The problem that this can give the Chinese, when working with us, is that they think that we will accept the same lack of thought and communication in our working lives. They come unstuck in a big way and it takes one or two refusals before they realise that we will not be fucked about. Work is important, but so is life and the Chinese are still a long way from the concept of 'working to live' rather than 'living to work.'

I staged my own mini rebellion on this issue when I became the involved with a crazy Chinese sales manager, Chen Fei. Chen Fei was a lovely man, but even by Chinese standards, he couldn't run a bath, let alone a sales team. He was in a world of his own and seemed to think information was passed by thought transference rather than by written or spoken word. He would arrange meetings and trips away, change the times without telling anyone and then be upset because nobody turned up.

His best one with me was an impromptu visit to a local pig-breeding organisation. He popped his head into my office and asked, "Russell, if you are free now could you come with us to visit Laoyang company? It would be very useful to us."

I said OK, as I needed to make an assessment of a small feed mill they ran. It was another 'can you give us some money to improve our factory?' situation and I was only slightly involved in Chen's part of it. All he wanted me for was my 'white face' to add credibility to our side of the table. My real involvement was in making an assessment of their small feed mill, and this was a good opportunity to have a look and tell them how crap it was. Chen had, to my surprise, organised a translator to accompany me. Forethought. Unusual. The translator was Sei Ling from our Rep Office in Shanghai – yes, it's pronounced 'Sailing' and I'm certain she got totally brassed off with the standard reaction to 'Hello. I am Sei Ling.' She was a nice girl and a very good translator, but ugly, with a complexion that was like a relief map of the Rockies. Sad.

Anyway, off we went and I made a discovery. Apparently, the meeting had been arranged for at least two weeks and everyone involved knew I was going apart from me. I began to have some niggling doubts, and I was right. The meeting was full of things about 'live weight gain,' 'feed conversion rates,' 'levels of back fat,' 'breeding rates per sow', etc. Riveting stuff. I understood it all in a 'passive smoker' sort of way, but I wasn't, in truth, very interested. My mind was off somewhere else when Chen Fei leaned over to me and whispered, "I need to know what you will say in your speech, so that I don't repeat what you say or contradict you."

"What fucking speech?"

Chen looked surprised and said, "Your speech about improvements to pig genetics in China."

I'm a production and operations person, who knows enough about domesticated farm animals to know that I don't know enough about domesticated farm animals to get technical. Even if I'd been forewarned, I wouldn't have been able to handle it well enough. I got angry – rapidly. I held it down, turned to Sei Ling and hissed, "Come on we've got a feed mill to look at." and we walked out, leaving an open mouthed Chen Fei.

Sei Ling was smiling to herself, so I enquired, "What's amusing you?"

"I thought it was strange when you didn't send me a copy of your speech, or call me about it before I saw you today. Chen Fei didn't tell you about it, did he?" and she shook her head. "Always the same."

We made our tour of the mill and joined up with Chen and the others for the trip back. Chen was quiet for most of the way and then said, "I thought I'd told you, Russell, but why didn't you speak anyway?"

I forget what my exact response was, but it was short, to the point and made Sei Ling bury her head in her dictionary for a while. Good old Anglo-Saxon.

Not everyone was as bad as Chen, but you always had to be prepared for the unexpected. Meetings were a minefield, and you could almost guarantee that what was on the agenda, if there was one, would only be a small part of what was discussed. Hiding behind a translator was useful, as it gave you more time to think and the Chinese used to do this too, even when their level of English was good. The good thing, however, was that it taught you to think on your feet, which I'd always been good at anyway.

This was probably due to my early days as a trade union official, when I often had to handle, manage and placate angry meetings of, sometimes, semi-literate men whose unreasonable demands had been refused: "What do you mean, they can't pay because they're making no money? We don't care. We want more."

In China, though, you are never sure what waits round the corner, what will land on your desk or walk through the door. Sometimes I missed the predictability of Britain, but not very often. Boring and soul destroying. In Britain when things were falling apart at work, as they can do in a production environment, I wished for everything to be on an even keel, but after normality had been restored I used to find myself wanting 'something' to happen. Normality is boring. It's much more fun fighting alligators than draining the swamp.

Outside of work, my life settled into a pattern and I became, as much as I could, part of things. I seemed to spend very little time with foreigners, apart from Big Ron, and became a regular visitor to the homes of Chinese friends.

Shanghai never sleeps or, rather, never sleeps all at the same time. In some places, if it hadn't been dark you wouldn't have been able to tell if it was night time. Restaurants and shops were open and full of bright-eyed and bushy-tailed people – not going to or just finished work.

Summer 1999 came upon us and I got used to the sight of men and women wandering about in nightclothes at any time of day. It's not a bad idea, given the heat of summertime Shanghai. Thank God for air-conditioning. I began to sweat at the beginning of April, but the Chinese don't divest any of their clothing, up to five layers, until much later. I asked Lao Zhi why and got a very Chinese response. "It is not yet officially summer, so it is not wise."

'Officially', if the 'official' temperature rises above 37C, some factories have to close and workers get special concessions. The result is that it never 'officially' gets hotter than 37C.

There seemed to be something about wearing nighties and pyjamas that relaxed them more and changed their attitudes to certain things. Women would hoist up tops to waft cooling air over their breasts or to make inspections of their nipples, seemingly oblivious to anyone's gaze. To be fair, though, it was mostly older women and they would have been best left covered. Some of them, though… ooh. Even if women didn't wear night attire they became better to look at – split skirts, crop tops and the like. Very nice. I began to notice something more and more, particularly if I happened to see a normal-sized white woman walking in the street. Chinese women really do have bums like boys, making me wonder how they ever had babies. Difficult. They obviously do, but it must be a struggle for some of them and, I believe, many countrywomen die in childbirth, with the problem getting worse as better nutrition increases birth weights.

The more time I spent with Chinese people, the more my understanding of everything increased, with one exception. The one thing that confused me and still does is age. When you ask a Chinese person how old they are, the answer you get can be misleading. The answer requires an explanation. Because of the way Chinese reckon age it is possible for someone to be two years old the day after they are born. As soon as you are born you are one, and as soon as the New Year starts you are two. Therefore, if you are born on New Year's Eve, you are two on New Year's Day. I pointed out that this was illogical and was shouted down, but came back with, "OK then, if you buy a car in 1990, in 2000 it's ten years old. Right?"

"Right."

"So, if you were born in 1974 and it's 1998, that means you are twenty four. Right?"

"No. Not the same. Not the same."

I always gave up with mutterings about 'fucking Chinese logic.' This almost always resulted in questions about why I had come to China and stayed, if China was so bad. If I was up for it I would then detail some of China's faults and shortcomings and say we were here to help them. I would then wait for the tirade about foreign exploitation and colonisers that always followed.

The past is never far below the surface in China, as I found out many times. The Chinese, rightly, hate the Japanese for their wartime atrocities, but they keep older memories alive too. I was in a taxi with Amy going along the Bund and I commented about the architect, "This was designed by the British."

"Yes, and built with the blood of Chinese workers." Ouch.

On another occasion Rab and I visited the Shanghai History Museum. It lays out the History of Shanghai chronologically as you walk through, and as you walk, you become aware of the bold printed references to 'Foreign Exploitation,' 'Atrocities,' 'Gunboats' and 'Colonialism.' By the time you reach the exit you are more than half expecting to have to run a gauntlet of whips and baseball bats.

Another thing that confused me was the Chinese family. I was aware of the one-child policy, so I was surprised when I heard the terms 'brother and sister.' I posed the obvious question and was told that, as most young people do not have any brothers or sisters they use these words to describe cousins.

The one-child policy was necessary, I suppose, but has led to problems – the Little Emperor syndrome. The single chick is doted upon and given everything it wants, whenever it wants, and this has resulted in a generation of selfish, rude and increasingly fat offspring. Many diminutive Chinese parents haul around a cuckoo-like, roly-poly spoilt brat.

The rule does not apply everywhere in China or, as usual, if you are rich. Outside the main areas of population, people tend to do what they want – farmers and ethnic minorities etc. Also, people are allowed to have another child if they have a baby girl, but the opposite doesn't apply. Of course there's equality of the sexes in China. They have also changed the policy in Xi Zang (Tibet) as an inducement to get people to go and live there and to swamp the ethnic population.

I could carry on writing endlessly about the differences and the contrasts, but I have more to tell about other things. Maybe later.

HANGZHOU

After a short while in Shanghai I began to feel the need to get out of the place. Somewhere quieter, less frenetic, less crowded and with less of everything was beckoning, but where? Amy made the suggestion, "You can go Hangzhou. Small country place. My mother is teacher there. Very quiet."

It sounded like just what I was looking for, so we decided to go the following weekend. Friday night arrived and I had my first encounter with Chinese railway stations and train travel – see 'Taxis, Trains and Things'. Interesting. The journey took about one and a half hours and, as we were coming close to the end of it, I became puzzled. We had reached the outskirts of somewhere – a city – and I asked where we were. She replied, "Almost there."

I looked out of the train again at what seemed to be, by Western standards, a fairly large place. Lots of tall buildings, flyovers, tower-cranes and things as far as the eye could see, which wasn't too far in the fading light. I was still puzzled, so I said, "You said Hangzhou was a small country place."

"It is. Only about five million. Very small."

Only? I suppose that when you come from Shanghai, everywhere else IS small. It looked like just another big city and I thought, "Oh well, at least it'll be a change from Shanghai" and resigned myself to it. First impressions were not good, but every city looks bad when you approach it in a train, as railway lines always seem to enter via the arsehole. This is true wherever you are in the world.

By the time we got off the train night had fallen and we made our way, by taxi, to the hotel – the Hua Hai, which, I had been told, was close to somewhere called 'West Lake.' We checked in, had a meal and went to bed around 11 pm. What would the weekend bring?

In the morning I pulled back the curtains and looked out. Wow! The view was spectacular. There was West Lake and the mountains behind – beautiful. Amy had made a good choice. Venturing outside, it got better. Anyone you saw moving quickly or in a state of agitation was probably not from Hangzhou. It was all very relaxed and easygoing and peaceful, either walking by the lake or taking a boat trip on it. In a way it reminded me of the town of Keswick in England's Lake District National Park, only on a larger scale plus pagodas. No ducks or swans swimming on the lake either – eaten probably. The Chinese will only go so far, and the stomach is always given priority consideration.

Everything was on a smaller scale than Shanghai and 'quieter'. There were a lot of high rise buildings, but not too close to the lake, showing that the Chinese had had the good sense to preserve the major attraction to the city.

Hangzhou is one of the main tourist attractions in China for Chinese people and more and more are coming as travel gets easier, so it's best avoided at National Holiday times. Even then, it's still better than Shanghai and it's cheaper, though prices are climbing.

As I saw more and more of the place and its surroundings, I could understand why Marco Polo thought Hangzhou was the most beautiful place he had ever seen. Maybe I wouldn't go that far, but it is beautiful, even allowing for the tower-cranes. A Chinese proverb says, 'In heaven there is paradise. On earth there is Hangzhou and Suzhou.'

There are many things to see around the lake area; the half-mile long Broken Bridge across the lake to a small island; the Six Harmonies Pagoda; the Lingyi Temple, and much more. In the daytime it's beautiful, but at night everything takes on a new perspective, as floodlights are turned on. Apart from the lake itself, I was most impressed with the Lingyi Temple. It was a short taxi ride along the north shore of the lake, not too far from the Shangri-la Hotel (great place to stay) and is located in the centre of acres of tea fields.

When I got there I expected most of the people there to be tourists, but I was wrong. The vast majority of the Chinese people there were there to worship and pray. At the time I was surprised, as I thought that most religions had been suppressed in China. Buddhism, however, holds a special place in China and was wisely left alone during the heavy days of communism. Apart from the five shrines, the place has thousands of statues and carvings of all the aspects of Buddha, the most impressive being a sixty-foot long reclining effigy of the Bodhisattva, Quan Yin.

Moving around in Hangzhou was easy because everything you needed to see or do was fairly central, if your hotel was close to the lake, which mine always were. My favourite hotel was the Shangri-la, which had a magnificent view of West Lake. It was set in its own heavily wooded grounds and was a long, low building that blended into the landscape. Secluded, peaceful and relaxing. It was also only a short taxi or bicycle rickshaw ride from the centre of the city.

The only bad thing about it was a bar called 'Desperados'. It was the most expensive bar I was ever in - in China. Sixty rmb for vodka and tonic and it was a single. 'Desperados' was a very apt name.

Outside, however, taxis were cheaper, and even though the taxi drivers were still useless and stupid, they had fewer options to make mistakes or rip you off. A lot of the time, though, I used bicycle rickshaws. I was in no hurry. The men who drove the rickshaws were interesting. They were always pipe-cleaner thin individuals, but with speed skater legs. Very often, after the heart-bursting push up the hill to the Shangri-la, they would crash out for fifteen minutes to recover. I always gave them a tip.

At night Hangzhou is very 'studenty' with discos, bars and cafes along the lakeside. There is also a very strong French presence, which doesn't manage to spoil the place too much. It could be worse and they could be in Shanghai.

A lot of the student population was from Africa – Namibia – and they provided additional entertainment in the discos. How can they dance so good? I met a lot of 'Chicos' and 'Stompies' during my visits – all of them coal black, with flashing white teeth and a low tolerance for alcohol.

The night time was a good opportunity to hit the street markets, and even allowing for the 'foreigner factor', you didn't get ripped off too badly. Again, everything was a lot cheaper than Shanghai and you could save the cost of travel and hotel, if you were looking for a lot of Chinese souvenirs – 'antique' Ming vases, silk and the rest. The evenings were usually rounded off with a visit to one of the discos.

My favourite one was a place just across the road from the Hua Hai Hotel and had the dire name of the LA Disco. It was a lot better than the name sounded and played a good mix of music – not too techno. The clientele tended to be the usual blend of foreigners and Chinese – Chinese women, of course. The women tended to less sophisticated than their counterparts in Shanghai, with longer hair and darker skins – country girls. They were also less persistent and could be brushed off a lot more easily. Still very, very nice, though.

After only a few visits I became regarded as a regular and the boss, Charlie, would greet me, buy the first drinks and sort out a good table for me. 'Russa, Russa, how are you?' Then fingers would be snapped and a good table made available – usually a booth. He was from Shanghai and we knew some of the same people in low places, eg

Lao Xia. It seemed that everyone knew my friend Lao Xia.

The activities in the place were as you would expect and, because of the music mix, I often got involved in giving rock and roll exhibitions and lessons. Amy wasn't happy about this as it got me too much attention from the 'wrong' people, ie women, so I kept these activities for the times when I was on lone visits, which became more frequent as time passed and Amy and I saw less of each other.

The disco also specialised in 'tableaux', and the one I remember most was a representation of the *Titanic*. The bow of the vessel had been built protruding from the stage and a Chinese 'Rose and Jack' performed a tasteful ballet routine on the structure. No iceberg, so all ended happily.

I had an interesting encounter in the LA Disco one night, which added to my store of things Chinese. I was in the toilet, doing what you do, when somebody shouted at me. I turned and behind me was on open cubicle, with a young Chinese boy in it. He was perched on top of the Western-style toilet in a squat position, trousers round his ankles, with his little acorn of a dick hanging in full view. He it was that had shouted at me, and he smiled and beckoned me towards him. My immediate thoughts were what you would expect, and I was naturally reluctant to go anywhere near him. Then he made a gesture that indicated what he wanted me to do – close the door for him. He had gone into the toilet for a crap, got himself in position and then the door had swung open. I closed the door, but I was still puzzled. I thought, "What the fuck?"

Then it dawned on me. He was accustomed to using

Chinese toilets, which are the same as many you encounter in France - you have to use them in a downhill-racer position. If you go into Western style toilets in hotels and other places in China you will see many broken toilet seats – Chinese people tend to stand on them rather than sit on them. They do it because they are not accustomed to taking a dump any other way or, they say, because it's more hygienic. They could be right.

I ventured out of Hangzhou sometimes and found that I liked what I saw. I liked Zhejiang Province and I still do. I made a couple of trips to Ningbo, further round the corner, and found that I enjoyed it. It was much the same as Hangzhou in many ways, but seemed to be developing faster because of its port. The good thing about it was its proximity to the sea, just like home, and a lot of my time there was spent either looking at it or up to my knees in it. I never stayed there overnight, though it was in the plan to do so, at some time. Back then, travelling was an inhibition, as the road system was still being developed and flights to Ningbo weren't designed for weekend travel.

One of my best trips out was in an October holiday, when it was HOT and Hangzhou was heaving with people. Someone had told me about a cave complex called Yao Lin Dong, about two hours south of the city, so off I went. I don't particularly like caves, but the prospect of spending time where the temperature was less than 100F seemed good. It was good. The caves were immense and very impressive. They were also not too commercialised, and on the two-hour walk through them I saw only two plastic dinosaurs. I couldn't believe that they weren't more publicized, but there are many things in China that never get onto the tourist map.

The trip there and back was also very good, through relatively unspoilt Chinese countryside, with water buffalo and people working in the fields and on the mountainsides, as they had done for centuries. Threshing rice by hand – backbreaking.

On the way back my hired driver, Xiao Lu, stopped off at a small place called Chang Ko. It was his home village and he wanted to introduce me to his family. It was 'real China' with crooked little streets and a village pond, which was used as water supply, laundry, fishing hole and pig wallow. It probably served as a toilet as well and I saw two small boys using it as such, trying to see who could piss highest and furthest. Children are the same everywhere.

The smiling, dirty, shoeless children hadn't seen many 'laowai' and egged each other on to touch me and talk to me. They were much taken with the hairs on my arms and managed to relieve me of a few before Xiao Lu dragged me in to see his family. The house and furniture were simple and basic, but the people were lovely and their kindness was overwhelming. The best food and drink was brought out and it was impossible to refuse. They were simple, uncomplicated country people whose priorities in life were family and living life as they had done for generations. Not a bad life at all – working in the fields or the garden, making sure you kept the pigs out of the house and making sure that everyone in the family was looked after.

Xiao Lu's grandmother was the Matriarch of the family. She was a sprightly, serene and smiling old woman of eighty something – Xiao Lu wasn't sure – and her white, waist-length hair still shone with health. She seemed to exude an aura of calm and goodness and was, obviously, revered by all the family. She gazed at me for about five minutes after I entered the house and then walked over to me and stood directly in front of me. She was tiny, and when I stood up I dwarfed her. She indicated that I should sit down and then she put one hand on my shoulder and the other on my cheek. What was going on? She peered deep into my eyes and I became aware that everyone else in the room had stopped talking – even the small children. After what seemed an age she took her hands from me, smiled and said, "Hao" (good) and went back to her chair. There was an audible sigh in the room, as everyone, including me, seemed to start breathing again. I raised my eyebrows in enquiry at Xiao Lu. "She says you OK. She know inside people" was his explanation.

Everyone else relaxed and the hospitality continued. I wondered what would have happened if she had said 'buhao' (bad). Not to worry. Whatever the test had been, I seemed to have passed it.

Things are different in the country in China and as our visit progressed I became aware that I was the object sly glances and giggling from the women. Xiao Lu shook his head and put me in the picture. "Is OK. I tell them no."

"No to what?"

"They say you look very strong and would make strong baby, but I say no."

"No to what?" I repeated.

"Mm. They think strong baby is good and can work very good. They ask if you want wife here."

"Wife? Me? Which woman?"

"The girl there." and he pointed towards a very young girl.

"She's very young. Fourteen maybe?"

"Fifteen, but she is 'woman'. They say old man and very young girl make baby very clever."

I looked at the young girl and she was smiling coyly at me. She thought it was a good idea. Fuck! I would have killed her or dislocated something. I indicated that I was flattered, but said I could not stay in China - lie. I received a further shock when the response came back that I could still 'make' baby. It was getting hairy.

How to get out of this without causing offence? The girl looked lovely and very nubile, but... Xiao Lu sensed my discomfort and came to my rescue. He spoke to them and they expressed disappointment, but still kept smiling at me, so I asked him, "What did you tell them?"

He smiled and said, "I tell them you have something cut in England and can't make baby any more. They know bout this."

Vasectomy. I had been rescued. Afterwards I wasn't sure if I was happy about it or not. Maybe it was for the best.

The visit carried on and I must have stayed there for about four hours, with most of the village wandering in at some point to have a look at me and shake my hand. When we left it seemed as if the whole population escorted us to the car, with Xiao Lu's grandmother in the lead. At the car she took both of my hands and stood for a while gazing at the ground before looking up into my eyes. She smiled and gave me a pat on the cheek before turning to go back to her house, chuckling and muttering to herself. The rest of the village stood and waved us off, with my young prospective wife looking at me wistfully. Once again China had been 'interesting and different.'

I escaped to Hangzhou as often as I could during my time in China, but towards the end it became difficult, as I began to travel more to other places. I went back there when I could, however, and always returned to Shanghai with a tinge of regret, but always consoled myself with the thought, 'I can always go back, can't I?'

TAXIS, TRAINS AND THINGS

Wherever you go in the World, some of the problems and annoyances tend to be the same. One topic that is close to the top of everyone's list is taxis and taxi drivers. After you get wherever it is that you are going and leave the airport, your first encounter, and often your first instance of being ripped off, is with taxis. Bangkok, Cairo, Mumbai, Hanoi or Shanghai – it doesn't matter. You are new, and therefore fair game. To be fair, it has improved over the eight or nine years since my arrival, but when I arrived in 1997 it was bad. I've already covered my first taxi ride elsewhere and will continue from there.

My first impression that taxi drivers were dishonest lunatics did not change and, indeed, was compounded. I quickly worked out that qualification to be a taxi driver relied upon medical evidence of a lobotomy and an abject failure of a mental age five intelligence test. If you did happened to come across one who knew where he was going and didn't try to rip you off, it was a case of the exception proving the rule. It was, more than likely, a moonlighting schoolteacher or office worker.

Finding a taxi was never a problem, except around Spring Festival, but getting where you wanted to go thereafter could be something of a lottery. Accustomed as we are in Britain to having a taxi driver say, 'Yes, guv' and taking us where we want to go by the fastest route, it was hard to believe that a taxi driver didn't know where the railway station or the Hilton hotel was. A delay after giving verbal or written instructions, followed by an 'OK', were a good signal for you to get out and find another taxi.

The same applied if you reached the first road junction on the trip, only to be asked, 'youguai, zouguai?' (right or left)This was another firm indicator that you should tell him to 'ting' (stop) and get out and look for another taxi.

The best one, though, was the winding down of the window to ask a fellow imbecile where such and such a place was. If this happened and was followed by a 'U' turn, because he was going the wrong way, your alternatives were to either tell him to stop or to point to the meter and say, 'fapioa' (receipt).This would scare him because if you contacted his company to complain about him not knowing where to go, they would dock his pay. Either that or flog him, castrate him or cut off a redundant extremity – his head for instance. All punishments for work-related misdemeanours tend to be draconian, eg 50rmb (£3.50) for forgetting to turn off an air-con – about 20% of a weekly salary.

Knowing some Chinese was useful, but it could be a two-edged sword. Sometimes the taxi driver would be very happy and try to help you with pronunciation and new vocabulary and you would part as friends. Sometimes, however, because you could speak some Chinese, the driver would assume that you were fluent, understood everything and could answer everything. A one-sided conversation would follow, with the taxi driver becoming more and more annoyed, muttering, making 'tut' noises, casting his eyes to heaven, shaking his head and probably thinking that you were just another 'arrogant foreigner'. He hated you and, by sod's law, you would only have a 100rmb note to pay for the less than 20rmb fare. This would lead to more muttering and a rummage around for change before he handed you a mixture of small notes and coins. You could always get the last blow in, though, by asking him for a 'fapiao'.

As I said, some Chinese language was useful, but in Shanghai you needed two languages – Mandarin and Shanghainese. Sometimes your instructions of 'you' or 'zou' were met with a blank faced 'shenma?' (what?) You then had to resort to sign language or Shanghainese 'xiaozuwai or dazuwai' to get your message across. Using Shanghainese impressed them and scared them a bit, so you had an immediate upper hand – if you needed it, or even if you didn't need it. If Shanghainese didn't work you knew you had a problem, because the driver was probably a country boy who didn't know his arse from his elbow, so it was time to unload.

Even native Shanghai drivers had problems, though, as the map of Shanghai changed and grew every day. The changes were done and made without any consideration for people, with roads blocked off and directions changed without any notice. It was called progress. At times I even felt sorry for taxi drivers and what they had to cope with every day. Not too sorry, though. They thought that they could get away with murder and were always upset when you caught them out – except the women. They thought that they could make it right with a laugh or a sweet smile. It worked on me most of the time.

There was one time in particular. I was on my way home from the Shangri-La Hotel in Pudong (East Bank) and grabbed a taxi. The driver was a woman, and a pretty woman. She was very friendly and quizzed me all the way about everything; where I was from; if I was married or had a girlfriend; how long I'd been in China and so on. We arrived at my apartment and I had a problem. Not enough money to pay the 60rmb fare. I indicated that she should wait while I went up to my apartment to get some more cash, but she laughed, said, "bu, bu" (no, no) and got out of the taxi to go with me.

"OK" I thought. "She doesn't trust me."

We went up and into my apartment on the sixth floor and, when we went inside, she gazed around open mouthed at, what must have been to her my lavish home. While I was sorting out the money, she made a quick tour of inspection before plonking down on the sofa and switching on the TV. I made motions to give her the money, but she laughed and patted the sofa next to her. Hmm. I sat down beside her and she took my hand and placed it on her thigh, at the same time as putting her hand on my thigh and working slowly towards my crotch. Then she turned towards me and opened her legs while unzipping me. After she had unleashed the beast and had a look at it she murmured, 'Wodemaiye!' (my god) but continued bringing me to full size. I began to work on her, but she didn't need much work. She was running like a tap and ready.

She shifted position and took me in her mouth briefly, but stopped and shook her head. She stood up and took my hand, indicating that we should take a shower. She was right. It was after midnight and it had been a long, hot and sweaty day. I probably didn't taste too good and neither, I suppose, would she have. Fishy and salty. We showered, and while still in there she resumed her attention on me. We made it back to the sofa and she knelt on it, with her back arched and her hands braced on the back of it. She was just the right height and waiting, and I never keep a lady waiting.

I was gentle at first, but after making sure she could cope – I didn't want to hurt her. Not too much anyway – I went for it. In less than a minute she was a boneless, twitching heap and full. After she came round from sexual coma she lay for a while, rubbing her stomach, smiling all the while and saying, "Hen da. Hen hao. Wo xi wan." (Very big. Very good. I like.)

We slowed down and 'played' for a while before we made ourselves sweat again.

Her name, it turned out, was Wu Ling Fang and she was thirty-three. She was married and had an eight-year-old son, who lived with her mother. I asked about her husband and she made a dismissive gesture and said, 'Hangzhou'. Her body was still good and her small breasts were firm, with her nipples showing the effects of breast feeding – big and black. Ahh. She had a tidy, bikini-line caesarean scar, which indicated that there must have been some money somewhere; the standard practice in the East is to make a vertical slash, which leaves a very unsightly big scar. If you want a neat one it costs. Her pubic hair was black and silky – almost as fine as the short black hair on her head – but long enough to plait, which I did for a few minutes until she decided that I should part it instead.

She said she'd never had a foreigner before, but I didn't totally believe her, as she had coped with the extra inches without a problem. All she had done was give a little yelp and a gasp when I had first buried myself in her. Normal. She stayed with me until around four in the morning and then decided that she should go back to work. I was worn out anyway, by that time, and drained after a second blowjob.

I walked her back down to her taxi and then got a surprise. She'd left the meter running. We both laughed as I handed over the money – 250rmb. 'Waiting time' is cheap. She gave me her mobile phone number in case I needed her again, which I did on a couple of occasions. Eventually, however, I had to distance myself, as she seemed intent on moving in. Never mind, plenty more fish.

That's about it for taxis, apart from an intriguing notice that was displayed in many – 'don't forget to carry your thing.'

Next on the list of transport experiences is trains. The train service in China is the cheapest way to go anywhere, so it's popular. The trains run frequently and they run on time. Being British, this last seems contrary to the laws of nature. Trains are always late, aren't they? Not in China. I usually used the train on my regular trips to Hangzhou and at first, the train journey was further adventure.

It began with getting a ticket. You can get a hotel to get you a ticket or buy one at the post office, but if you really want to have some fun, buy one at the station. Maybe I should say try to buy. Back then there was a single ticket booth, which only opened for a limited time. The result was a heaving, fighting, sweating pyramid queue, more like a logjam than anything else. If you didn't want to queue, however, you could buy a ticket on the black market. Yes, there were ticket touts at railway stations, who would sell you a ticket at anything up to 50% more than face value, but you had to haggle.

Getting on the train was fairly easy, once you were through the gate – Chinese 'queues' again, as each carriage had a hostess to point you in the right direction. The Chinese, however, used to ignore them completely and piled on wherever they wanted, seeming to prefer to struggle through the confined space of the train to find the right carriage. Once you had found your seat the first thing you usually did was throw somebody out of it. The trains were always overbooked, with the latecomers getting a standing ticket, so they sat in any available seat, hoping the rightful occupants wouldn't turn up or wouldn't be able to find the correct carriage.

The next thing you did was sweat profusely, as the air conditioning never came on until the train was in motion. None of the Chinese seemed to sweat – must be genetic. After sitting down you could look around and take stock. Too many people. Too many bags. Too much of everything. Absolute chaos.

As the train got under way, everything settled down and other things started to happen. Chinese people love to eat and the small tables were soon covered with mounds of snacks, bread, instant noodles, tea flasks and fruit. Instant noodles? How were they…? Then you would see the alarming sight of a small woman swaying under the weight of a huge kettle of boiling water as she struggled up the gangway. It was her job to supply the hot water the passengers needed for their noodles and tea flasks. When everyone's initial needs were supplied things settled down and moved on, and as a lone foreigner you became the centre of attraction for attempted conversation and samples of food etc. Nice.

The view from the train was always interesting and it improved, as you got closer to Hangzhou – hills and mountains. I found that I had missed the hills and mountains of Wales. When you arrived at Hangzhou or wherever, getting off the train was the same as getting on, but in reverse – another logjam, with the added dimension of fighting off people trying to sell you tourist maps or return tickets or drag you off to a hotel. I've already dealt with Hangzhou elsewhere.

There are always surprises in China, and I had a big

one on my second train journey to Hangzhou. Well, what I should say is that what started on the train led to a surprise. I was sitting in an aisle seat and there was a woman sitting opposite me. She was nice. She was in her thirties – thirty-six, it turned out – elegant, very well dressed and beautiful with her hair piled up loosely on top of her head in an attempt to stay cool.

We had been making fleeting eye contact for about twenty minutes and each time our eyes had met she had looked away, with a half smile on her face. She was lovely and knew it. I watched her as she dampened a small towel with water from a bottle and, eyes closed, squeezed it out onto the nape of her neck. She continued, shifting to her throat, and the water trickled down onto the valley of her breasts. Summer of forty-two. I was mesmerised. How to talk to her? I was thinking of ways to make verbal contact when something broke the ice. She began to clear her nose and throat loudly and, when she'd done the 'clearing,' deposited the 'product' carefully into a tissue. If she'd hitched up her skirt and scratched her pussy it couldn't have surprised me more. The look on my face must have said it all and she smiled, gave a small laugh and said, in fairly good English, "Sorry. Maybe we do strange thing in China. Not same as…?"

"England." I offered. "No problem. I'm getting used to many things that are different in China."

This was true and my first reaction of disgust when seeing man or woman deposit sputum, wherever and whenever they felt the need, had mellowed to only mild distaste. I'd also got used to the sight of men, even women, relieving themselves in public. There was a strange dichotomy in this, when the Chinese taboo on public nudity was considered.

Anyway, the ice had been broken, never to freeze over again. Her name was Lu Mei and she had a clothes shop in Hangzhou. She was doing OK and was opening another store in Shanghai, hence the reason for her trip. We chatted away pleasantly for the rest of the journey and, as the train was pulling into Hangzhou she asked me, "Can I invite you have dinner?" I gave this a positive response and she followed on with, "Good. I have friend, who never meet foreigner and he will very happy eat with you."

My immediate thoughts were, "He? Fuck. Another 'can you use chopsticks, do you like Chinese food?' night."

I had been trying to figure out how to get her into somewhere, so that I could get into her. The mention of a friend dashed any hopes I had in this direction. Shit. Too late and I resigned myself to eating with her and her boyfriend. She wrote the address of the restaurant on a slip of paper and we agreed a time – 6.30. She then said, "I very looking forward eating you." Prophetic?

I helped her with her bags and the fight through the crowd after we got off the train, said, "See you at 6.30" and watched her swaying hips disappear. What an arse. What a shame I was only going to be able to look at it.

The evening came and I made my way to the restaurant and found Lu Mei waiting for me - alone. My hopes were dashed, however, by her explanation: "My friend is on way. Come soon."

Shit. We talked for about five minutes and then her friend arrived. A woman. And she was a beautiful woman. He? Lu Mei introduced her. "This Xiao Ming. He don't speak English much. He have shop close me. He model before. He beautiful, yes?"

'He' was. Lu Mei had made a typical Chinese mistake and used 'he' instead of 'she' – in Chinese there is one word, 'ta', used for he, she and it, and they often get confused when translating into English. For once, I didn't mind.

I was then quizzed mercilessly about everything and became the subject of much giggling, whispering and saucy little smiles. What was going on?

The evening progressed and I did my own quizzing. They were both divorced and lived alone and neither had a permanent boyfriend. My mind went into overdrive. My supercharger kicked in as we were about to leave and I asked, "Do you want to go somewhere else?"

They had a quick, giggling exchange and Lu Mei said, "No. We both tired. Want go bed. You want follow us my home?" ('Follow' means 'go with'.) I indicated that I 'want' and off we went. In Lu Mei's home, which was very nice, they disappeared into the bathroom together and I could hear them giggling and laughing like schoolgirls. When they came out they were wearing a bathrobe each and had let their hair down. Wow. Both had long hair, but Xiao Ming's reached to her waist. They sat down either side of me and Lu Mei switched on the TV and DVD player. Blue (yellow) movie time. It was two Chinese girls and a Negro. He was enormous. We watched the performance and they moved closer to me and began to undress me. They were happy with what they found. Xiao Ming said something in Chinese, which Lu Mei translated as, "She say she happy you not big as the black man. If too big, hurt and can't all inside. You enough."

They slipped out of their bathrobes and I saw that Lu Mei was still wearing knickers, so I moved to take them off. She stopped me, saying, "Can't. Have red water."

"Red water? Oh, blood." Her period.

"Is OK. Can with Xiao Ming. Will watch and help."

What a night. Lu Mei did more helping than watching and shared her helping equally between us. Xiao Ming didn't seem to mind at all and even positioned herself so that Lu Mei could get at her with her mouth and tongue. It obviously wasn't their first time in a threesome. It was my first, but not the last.

Lu Mei wasn't 100% happy though, and the second time things reached point of release she pulled me away from Xiao Ming and took me in her mouth after saying, "I want drink you". After she had drained what was left of me she turned to a still spread-eagled Xiao Ming and gave her the same attention, with Xiao Ming moaning and holding her head firmly in position. Dirty girls. We needed a rest or rather, I did, so we slept.

A familiar feeling awakened me. Xiao Ming was still asleep, but Lu Mei was busy bringing me back to life. I didn't object. When she had, very quickly, succeeded in getting me back in condition, she stopped and looked at the result of her labours. She came to a decision, looked at me and said, "I want. Don't care red water."

She stripped off completely and mounted me, taking my full length in one thrust. She gave a gasp, "Oooh. Good feeling. Like big. Hurt, but don't care. Give me."

I gave her and we slept again. I awoke around seven to find them both tearing around the apartment. Lu Mei explained, "We have to open shops. Late." They left me to look after myself, after making sure that we would meet again that night at my hotel.

I spent most of the morning in Lu Mei's bed before going back to the Shangri-la Hotel and a relaxing afternoon and early evening spent drinking beer and watching the world go by. To be honest I wasn't fit for much else. I recovered by the time the 'girls' joined me at seven and we ate, talked and did it all again before I had to go back to Shanghai the next morning.

I 'saw' them both again, but never together. Lu Mei used to come and stay with me on her frequent visits to Shanghai and Xiao Ming would come and stay with me sometimes when I visited Hangzhou. It was a shame about her lack of English, as she was the better of the two in every way – willing, uninhibited, innovative and very fit, as well as being very beautiful. Such hair. There was never any real relationship with either, though. It was all about lust, need and yellow fever.

That's about it for trains. Life is full of surprises – everywhere.

There are other modes of transport in China, of course, but I had limited experience of them, with the exception of airplanes. At one time Chinese internal flights used to drop out of the skies like falling leaves, but things have improved and are still improving. Gradually the quality and reliability of the planes is improving, as are the airports – even Beijing. (I've written elsewhere about my airport experiences.) The quality of the food, however, seems to be staying the same – uniformly bad, in line with most economy airlines in the world. It has to get better, surely.

I tried to avoid using buses and ferries, after trying them each only once. The buses, back then, were little better than cattle trucks, into which as many people were crammed as possible. They had no air-conditioning, not many seats and were designed, as I said, to get as many people in as possible, which they did. I'm sure you could have slept standing up without falling over. Midsummer on a crowded bus must have been horrendous, and winter was bad enough.

Ferries were very similar. Cram as many in as you can. Life jackets? Lifeboats? Forget it. I only had one ferry trip, to Chongming Island, and was nervous all the way. Like many of the passengers, I made sure I was drunk for the return trip. I made a quick check on the name of the ferry, but it was in Chinese, so I couldn't tell if it was called 'Titanic' or 'Lusitania'. I breathed a heavy sigh of relief as we re-docked in Shanghai and headed for the nearest bar. If first prize were a free trip on a Chinese ferry then the second prize would have to be two trips.

THE 'WAYS'

('The ways' is my term for the Chinese word and phenomenon called 'guanxi.' which basically means 'relationships.' It's a bit like the old boys network in the UK, but stronger and deeply entrenched in Chinese tradition and culture. It is how things get done and, often if there is a lack of it, why things don't get done. At the time of writing, Chinese people did not regard it or refer to it as corruption, but...)

I was going to include this part of the ramblings in with work-related bits, but on second thoughts decided it would be better on its own. Much of it has nothing to do with work, more to do with how to do things and get things when you live in China. Things have to be done in a certain way in China. These are 'things' that you never see on television or hear or read about in anything official. Also, sometimes, what we consider to be straightforward, everyday activities in the West end up as long, convoluted procedures that can frustrate you, drive you nuts or make you shake your head in disbelief. It's probably best encapsulated in what follows.

As part of living in China I had to have money – of course. At first the company Amex catered for all my needs. All my financial needs, that is, in Shanghai and the other places that the West had reached. In the rest of China, however, and even in off the beaten track areas of Shanghai and Beijing, strange plastic was viewed with suspicion and often, refusal. Also, ATMs were at a premium back then and many of the ones that were available only accepted Chinese cards. Cash was best in most places and it was better if you didn't have to exchange anything except dollars. Even then you would get ripped off if you did it anywhere except a bank.

I remember exchanging a £20 note in the Anshan International Hotel. The girl held it up open mouthed and her eyes filled with wonder. What was this strange piece of paper? Was it really money? She rushed away to consult someone with superior knowledge before completing the transaction and managed to get it wrong twice before handing me my rmb. It has improved, but I would still advise using cash, especially in Hong Kong. This, however, is for a different reason, which I'll come to later.

Much of the reluctance to do anything different is down to the way things work in China. I call it 'blame culture'. Everything is somebody's fault and everyone is terrified of doing anything outside the norm and possibly making a mistake. If a cashier accepts a forged bank note they have to pay for it from their own pocket, so getting someone to accept a strange credit card or a foreign banknote, other than dollars, is difficult.

Even 'swiping' a card again, if the first attempt fails, makes them twitch, as I found out one day. I was one of the few who had a company Amex and I often used it to pay hotel bills for short-term company visitors. I was doing this one day in the Crowne Plaza and chatting away with the hotel staff as usual, when there was a problem. The card was refused first time and I immediately changed from being 'Russell' to a very frosty 'Sir' until the card was accepted second time.

Anyway, my circumstances changed when I accepted a longer-term stay in China. I needed a bank account that would accept transfers of funds from the UK, so that part of my salary could be sent to me as well as reimbursement of expenses. Bank of China was the only option and, even then, pounds had to be converted to US dollars before being transferred. No problem. Money was duly sent to me every month on the dot - $1500 – and I could draw it out either from an ATM in rmb or over the counter in either rmb or dollars.

'Over the counter' was interesting. Every time I withdrew money my passport had to be handed over for checking and photocopying, even if I drew money out twice in the same day. I also had to enter my pin number about six times during the course of the transaction. In China everyone is a 'cheat, a liar and a scoundrel' or treated as one. Once you get used to it it's all right and you came to expect it and accept it.

I was going through the usual rigmarole one day and was leaving the counter, when I glanced at my updated passbook. I got a shock. A $10,000 shock. Money had been transferred into my account the previous day, and instead of the expected normal $1500 there was $10,000. I returned to the counter and got them to check the paperwork, but the quick scrutiny indicated that the amount was correct. I was mystified. Tax rebate? Bonus? Mistake? The last one seemed the most likely. My company managed to fuck up everything at one time or another during my stay in China, so a mistake was probable. What to do, though? Keep quiet? Tell them?

I decided to keep half quiet and phoned Gary, General Manager/Director for all of China, in Anshan, to see if he knew anything I didn't. He thought for a moment and then said, "No, nothing that I know of going on with bonuses or anything. How much is it?" I told him and his response was typical. "Shame it's only that much. If it had been a couple of million, we could have considered doing a runner. Keep quiet and act innocent if they get in touch with you about it. They're sure to notice it sooner or later."

They did notice it or, rather, somebody else did. At work next morning there was a fax waiting for me: 'Russell, we've sent you the wrong amount of money. Please get in touch as soon as possible.' Later in the day I phoned the UK to find out what the fuck-up was, who had made it and what they wanted me to do about it. I was told, by the panicking fucker-up, that what she had done was use Hong Kong dollars exchange rate instead of US. The mistake had only come to light because she had made the same mistake, in reverse, for a British Sugar employee in Hong Kong. He, naturally, wasn't happy and had screamed about it. He was easy to make happy, but it was different with me.

The girl on the other end of the phone was distraught over her fuck up and said, "Russell, we need you to return it." I thought for a moment and then told her that I, as the fuck-uppee, could do very little to help her. I said, "Short of me withdrawing it from the bank and bringing it to you or taking it to Hong Kong, there is no way I can get it back to you. Have you ever tried to transfer money out of China? Impossible."

The female on the other end was even more distraught and seemed very close to tears until I came up with the obvious solution. "OK then, for the next six months or so don't send me any money to China. How about that?"

She was very relieved and, I'm sure, would have had my babies had she been able to.

So there I was with a wad of unexpected cash in my account. Sure, it had to last for a while, but it was there. Then I had an idea how to gain from it. Change it. Outside all the major branches of the Bank of China, there are usually two or three seedy-looking black market moneychangers. I'd used them once or twice when the bank had been busy and found that they gave better than official bank rates – not a great deal better, but better, and I'd been told that the rates improved for larger amounts. The reason for these guys existing, at the time, was that Chinese nationals could not easily get their hands on foreign currency, which made it difficult for anyone who was going outside China on business or on holiday. It has changed since then, but is still very complicated for them.

Anyway, I enquired what kind of rate I would get on 10K and was very happy when I found out that it was one above the official rate. I sorted it out with my chosen man and he hurried off to get sufficient funds to cover the deal. When he came back I went into the bank to withdraw the money and was somewhat surprised when he came in with me and stood at my shoulder as I made the withdrawal. I thought it was maybe to save time in counting it again, but when I headed for the door he stopped me, indicating that we should recount it using the customers' counting machine in the bank. I shrugged and said, "OK, if you want." but thinking, "Fucking untrusting Chinese".

After we had put it through the machine and he had randomly checked a few of the notes he smiled and said "OK". Then he took his money out of a bag and began putting it through the same machine. By this time I was starting to get rather nervous. We were, after all, under the noses of the bank staff and what we were doing was illegal. Then, slowly, light began to dawn.

We completed the full deal under the scrutiny of the bank staff – withdrawal, counting, exchange and re-deposit – and nobody seemed to care or turned a hair. It was, what you might call, 'unofficial official' and the Bank Manager probably got commission from it, as well as all other black market dealings. China. Still, I shouldn't complain. It's the quickest and easiest $1200 dollars I've ever made.

Similar things pervaded all parts of life in China and

maybe always will. Finding 'the way' was essential to get most things done quickly, if at all. Insurmountable and impenetrable barriers could be overcome and pierced by knowing who to contact or how to go about things. Frowning faces and shaking heads could be turned to the positive by knowing 'the ways'. Problems could be made to evaporate by knowing the right things to do or say and the right people to see. It's all condemned publicly as 'corruption', but without it China would never have got off the ground in its quest to join the rest of the world. Conversely, without it, no Western organisations would have gained a foothold here. Trying to do it all completely by the rules would only have resulted in everybody picking up their marbles and going home.

My first steps into this subculture were interesting and enlightening and were the result of actions by our partner Mr Mao. Mr Mao made his play to take over the joint venture about a month after the Grand Opening Ceremony. He demanded total control or his money back, much to the surprise of the ostriches on high. We, and particularly Henry, had seen it coming, but had been ignored. A new partner was found, but the situation was far from good. We were on Mao's land and using his labour force – far from good. Minor inconveniences began to occur on a regular basis; no water in the office block for three days; gates chained shut and security guard missing. Bolt cutters are very useful, however, and smelly toilets are fairly normal in China.

His final throw was to withdraw his labour force, giving

us the generous notice of two working days to find an alternative. Rapid action was required, so I obtained quotations from two other labour team 'organisers' and made a simple and quick decision. The cheapest. Crisis over? Unfortunately, no. I received an unexpected angry visitor the next day. It was the unsuccessful boss of one of the labour team, Xiao or 'Boss' Dai, with a bevy of 'minders'. He was not happy and he made it clear that it was my fault. He was upset because I had not given him time to 'negotiate' and discuss his quotation, and even after I explained the urgency of the situation, he insisted that I had acted unfairly and not given him 'respect'. Also, he said that the team that I had chosen were not a local team and, as a result, the local community was unhappy. I told him I was sorry, but the decision had been made and it was too late to change anything. He grinned and spoke to Lao Zhi, who then translated, "It's never too late in China. You may find it difficult to operate on Monday morning, if the local people block the factory gate." (We were talking on Friday afternoon.)

I suggested that we could always ask the police for assistance and he smiled again. "They are local police and they are also my friends." He left us then and we waited for what would unfold on Monday morning.

Monday morning arrived and I waited, with some apprehension, to see what would greet me when I arrived at work. All was quiet; the new labour team were in place and there were no pickets at the gates. Storm in a teacup. What had all the fuss been about?

I had barely sat down in my office, however, when things took on a Sicilian twist. Xiao Dai arrived with another grim looking gentleman – the boss of the successful labour team. It turned out that they were old friends, virtually brothers in fact, and had come to a decision over the weekend. The successful guy had decided that he didn't really want the work anyway and that life would be easier if his friend's team took over the contract. Of course this would mean that we had to pay Xiao Dai's price. There is a very crude term to describe this, but 'stitched up' will suffice.

Anyway, the banquet that followed put things right and Xiao Dai and I became friends. I managed to stay clear of his offers of gifts and services, though some of them were hard to refuse.

One in particular was tempting. At the end of our banquet there was a 'show', which involved a naked female dancing on the table. She was fit. She was also a contortionist and could put her legs and body in amazing places. It's the one and only time I've seen a woman lick her own pussy or screw herself with a cucumber, using her feet to hold the vegetable in question. Very fit, and she made it very clear that she was willing to do whatever I wanted. Xiao Dai laughed, slapped me on the back and gave me to understand that I had his respect and admiration for my, as he saw it, strength. He conveyed this through Lao Zhi, who passed on, "He thinks you are a good 'laowai' (foreigner) and you are now his friend and brother. You must be very careful, Russell. He is a bad man."

He *was* a bad man, but he was useful – following the Godfather principle of 'keep your friends close, but keep your enemies closer' is a good idea.

We used Xiao Dai to help us with a problem we encountered about two months later. Things were running smoothly – always a bad sign. It couldn't last and it didn't. Frank, Ye Feng, came into the office in a panic. I calmed him down and eventually he told me, "The police are stopping all our trucks from leaving the site. They say we are overloaded."

I was puzzled. 'Overloading' was normal in China and we were friendly with the police. What had pissed them off? I said this to Frank, but he shook his head and said, "It's not the village police. It's the traffic police. They heard that we had entertained the local police and think we've ignored them. They are angry."

The answer was obvious, but how to organise it quickly and get things back to normal before the business went to shit? Frank and even Lao Zhi, didn't know how to sort it out quickly and we were heading for deep shit when Xiao Dai popped his head into my office. Lao Zhi was with him, as usual, to translate. He had decided to pay me a visit and had brought a gift – a bottle of Moutai (very good and very expensive baijiu). Lao Zhi had a quick word with him and explained our 'problem.' Then Xiao Dai made a phone call. He spoke to someone for about five minutes and then smiled and said, "OK" and the problem was over as quick as that.

A discussion between Frank, Lao Zhi and Xiao Dai

followed and then I was told, "There will be a banquet tonight. Xiao Dai will organise everything and help to entertain the traffic police."

Xiao Dai then insisted that we sample his bottle of Moutai, in the spirit of friendship and brotherhood. I managed to drink as little as possible and even tipped some of Xiao Dai's expensive gift into the bin when he wasn't looking, but I still had too much for nine in the morning, particularly as I would have a heavy night ahead. I made an attempt to get out of the coming evening's activities, but Lao Zhi flattened that idea with, "No, Russell, it is important that you go. They will expect you to be there and will be unhappy if you are not. Also, if you are there it will help to control things."

"Control things?"

"Yes, if you are there they will not order food that is too expensive and if you are there maybe they will not ask for karaoke and girls."

"Fucking great" I thought.

The evening came and I sought out Lao Zhi. When I caught up with him, he was getting in the minibus to go home. He grinned weakly and said, "I have decided that I do not need to go. Frank will go with you. Be careful, Russell, these are bad men. Black community."

"You fucking old coward" I thought, but said nothing.

Frank was shitting himself, so I tried to reassure him. "It'll be OK, Frank. Xiao Dai will be with us anyway."

"That's what I'm worried about. I'm afraid of Xiao Dai. He threatened to have me killed before he got the labour contract."

Poor Frank. Off we went to meet the police; we were to pick up Xiao Dai on the way. Xiao Dai was late and eventually arrived running and out of breath. He got in the car and gasped his apologies to Frank. Frank's eyes went wide. "He's sorry, but he was arbitrating between two rival groups of his friends."

"Arbitrating?"

"Yes, sorting out compensations for damages and injuries."

"Injuries?"

"Yes, he says there was a gang battle in Luhui yesterday and many men have knife wounds and things."

"Things? Bullet wounds?"

"No. They do not use guns. Only knives and clubs."

"Only knives and clubs. That's all right then."

Apparently possession of a gun carries almost as severe a penalty as murder, which means life imprisonment, at least.

Aside here. On a stint in Bolivia as Fisheries Consultant (Amazonian catfish) my friend Edward was in the company of five Mafia types in a La Paz karaoke bar, where a less than melodic guest was giving an ear-torturing performance. Edward passed a comment on the vocalist, "Isn't it always the way? The time you really need your gun is the very time you've left it at home." No sooner were the words out of his mouth than five revolvers were slammed onto the table in front of him.

Anyway, back to China. We went on our way to meet the traffic police and after about five minutes Xiao Dai indicated that we should stop. I looked out of the car, but all I could see was a group of ragged-arsed louts on a street corner. Where were the police? Xiao Dai got out of the car and went over to the group of men. They knew him, of course. Some of the friends he'd been talking about earlier maybe? No. They were the police. Frank looked unhappy, but I tried to reassure him. "It won't be too bad, Frank, and we'll be done by eight o'clock."

He didn't seem to be convinced and in truth, neither was I. In the event, however, it wasn't too bad and went off successfully and smoothly. Part of the reason was because of a lucky choice and a discovery. I was asked to choose what we should all drink and, having drunk expensive, good stuff earlier in the day, I didn't fancy going cheap and nasty, so I decided we should drink red wine. I can drink a lot of red wine, but it's something which, I discovered that night, makes Chinese people fall over very, very quickly. I wish I'd known it sooner, but better late than never.

The evening wrapped up uneventfully and yet another important relationship had been cemented in place. Most of the credit was given to me, but all I'd done was to be the 'white face' again, answer the usual round of inane questions and drink everyone's health – again. Xiao Dai was the real hero of the day. He'd also made it clear that if I, personally, needed anything sorted out I had only to ask. Friends in low places.

Later that evening something else happened that was to make me realise that I had other friends in low places.

I was back in Shanghai by nine and was feeling good, so I decided to drop into Charlie's before going home and see if anyone was there. The place was fairly quiet, but there were two or three Chinese guys I knew, so I joined them. One of them was my friend Lao Xia, who was reputed to be a Kung Fu Master as well as being very high in the Black Community. He was only about five foot four, but had a 'presence.' I've walked down a crowded street with him in the lead and the people have parted like the Red Sea. He was heavy. His English was also excellent as a result of living in Hong Kong for a while. He said that he'd had to get out of Shanghai for a while, back in the seventies, but no other explanation was given and I thought it best not to ask.

As is the way of things, there was nothing in Lao Xia's demeanour that gave away his skills. I only once saw him display them, and that was when he was drunk. He was being goaded to 'do something' by his friends and at last shouted, 'Haode!' and, without any wind up, leapt five feet straight up into the air in a Bruce Lee fighting stance. It was always the silent, small ones that you had to be wary of.

Frank had studied for a while, but given up. 'Too difficult.' He was very impressed, though, when I told him that *I* had a black belt and said, "Really?"

"Yep. Black belt in baseball bat."

I chatted with my friends for a while and after a short time someone else came in who I knew. It was David, the owner of the Step Bar. David was drunk and when he saw me, he came over. He was very drunk and I couldn't understand what he was saying at first, but then I made out, "Where have you been? I haven't seen you for months. Don't you like my bar any more?"

I explained that I'd been busy or out of town and, anyway, I had calmed my lifestyle down. He wouldn't have it and became abusive, to the point where the Chinese guys with me fucked him off and he left the bar, still hurling abuse in both English and Chinese at me. My Chinese friends were not happy. Lao Xia had a word with me. "He can't talk to you like that. Lose your face." I told him it was OK and that David would say sorry when he was sober, if he remembered. Lao Xia and the others still weren't happy and Lao Xia carried on, "No, he can't speak to you like that. We will 'talk' to him. In any case we don't like him. He's from Beijing."

I changed the subject and thought everything would be forgotten, but... two nights later I was in Charlie's again and, again, David came in. He was sober this time and looking very sheepish. He came over to me and asked if I would go and sit at a table with him. I followed him to a table close to the stage, we sat down and then he gave the most abject of apologies for his behaviour. I told him it was forgotten already and that everyone does stupid things when they are drunk. David then ordered a bottle of brandy – XO. Expensive. We proceeded to demolish half of it before he decided he would go.

As he stood up someone caught his eye and he hesitated before turning towards the stage. At the stage he stopped the band in mid-song and took the mike, before making an announcement. The announcement was a public apology, in English, to me, for his unacceptable behaviour.

He finished and was about to give the mike back to the singer when there was a shout from the back of the bar, "Zhongwen!" (Chinese). He then repeated what he had said in Chinese before leaving quickly, with his head hanging low. I was mystified until Lao Xia joined me at the table and explained, "We told him that if he didn't make a public apology, we would close his bar or have the police close it. Beijing bastard."

What they had made David do was very serious stuff and David kept away from Charlie's for months. No face left. He also sacked all of his staff, so that there was no one left who knew what Lao Xia and friends had forced him to do. More friends in low places.

We finished David's brandy and then Lao Xia and his friends left. I sat where I was for a while, until I realised that most of the Chinese in the place were casting glances my way and that I was the subject of their conversations. I can't think why. I moved back to the bar, hoping to make myself less conspicuous. When I got there the guy who I'd chosen to sit next to prodded me on the shoulder. It was an amusing little encounter and began like this, "Hey, what the Jesus H. wuz that awl about?" An American. A drunk American.

I gave him a quick run through of what it was 'awl about,' and he was impressed. "Fuck, man, I bin tryin' to make connections like that for two fuckin yeeears. How the fuck d'you do it?"

I explained that it must have been down to charisma, personality, charm or some such, but he replied, "Bullshit. How much did ya pay 'em?"

After that we settled into a more normal conversation and I found out that he basked under the name of Rocky Naff. True. I didn't believe it either until he gave me his business card. He was East Asian Sales Director for something, but I can't remember what.

I decided that it was time to go, as the brandy was having its effect. I needed sleep and I was on my way to it when he stopped me and said, "Hey, have a drink with me before you go, but none o' that chicken-shit brandy crap. Have a man's drink."

"Why not?" I thought. It would round off the evening.

He shouted the order to Jacqueline behind the bar, "Gimme two double John Daniels on the rocks. Pronto."

"Don't you mean JACK Daniels?" I said.

He shook his head and came out with, "Hey, when you've known the fucker as long as I have, you can call him whatever the fuck you want." It cracked me up at the time and it was with some disappointment that I later found out that he had stolen the line from a movie – Al Pacino in 'The Scent of a Woman'.

Everything you do or need to do in China can be done in many different ways, depending on where you are, whom you know and what you want. Things can be bypassed, ignored, driven through or circumvented, depending on who and what you know. A hefty bank balance is also useful. However, it's a lot easier if you can avoid getting involved in some things.

Disturb a government department at your peril. If you are unprepared or badly informed you will find yourself in a labyrinth that seems to have no way out – until palms have been crossed with silver or you find someone whose self-interest can be served in some way or another. A job for a family member is a favourite method and very useful, if you can find a 'safe' management position, ie one that doesn't have any real power or influence and is well away from the money. Definitely not in the finance or purchasing departments.

On the surface it seems as if things have moved or are moving forward, but when you get closer to it you find that much of it is only a façade. One of the best examples of this is within the so-called Free Trade Zones. I was involved in trying to set up an import warehouse and a possible factory in one of these zones in Pudong – Wei Gao Qiao. There seemed to be, and were, a lot of agencies that specialised in advice and assistance to these ends, but on closer inspection and investigation they were all the same and all controlled by the same government department. They all offered slightly different packages, but the bottom line cost always came out exactly the same. It looked good on the advertising brochures, but had no substance. I met up with about three or four different agents and then we gave it up as a bad job. Far too many hoops and rings to make it practical and this became more obvious when toured the zone and found an occupancy rate of less than 10%.

My brush with the 'zone' did give me one memorable, amusing meeting, though. A Miss Yu, from one of the agencies, came to see me. A very nice girl, but when she gave me her card I almost exploded. Her English name had been given to her by someone very evil – Even Yu. The bastard. How could he or she? I've seen worse – much worse. Hitler Wang, Wicky Wu and one poor boy called Pulley – onanistic tendencies? I also once saw an air hostess with the name Stansted Liu - London's third airport. Maybe there's a Gatwick or a Heathrow somewhere. Probably.

Related to my brush with the Free Trade Zones there was another minefield of frustration – importing something new into China. This exercise gave me what was definitely my most exasperating day in China, and I've had a few. As I've written elsewhere (further on), I was involved in developing the market for a product, Megalac, and we needed to get it into China to supply trial customers. 'Trial.' Typical of China and Chinese companies, it didn't matter that the product had been used successfully and documented as such all over the world for many years. All they would do was smile and say, "We have to make sure it will work in China."

"But your dairy cows have the same genetics as dairy cows everywhere in the world."

"Ah, but this is China."

What they actually meant was that they wanted some free or at a reduced price. OK. The product arrived at Shanghai. Let's get it. Not so fast. We entered a minefield of bureaucracy, which kept us occupied flitting from office to office in Shanghai Port for a full day before we obtained 'release.'

We had a release document, which needed about ten 'chops' (official stamps) on it and each one required money in varying quantities. It began with document checking and continued through inspection, sampling, health checking, customs approval, Port Authority approval, transport company acceptance, shipper's release (to show we paid them) and on and on. We even had to pay 60rmb for an 'official' plastic and reusable sample bottle. The final throw was paying 20rmb for a plastic cable tie to reseal the container and another 50rmb to get out of the port.

The reason for it all was the 'opening' of China. Before Deng Xiao Ping initiated the 'change' the system was one big spider web pain in the arse, but it changed into many spider web pains in the arse. As was the case in Britain with nationalised industries, no one really cared or had to justify their existence. They weren't accountable. Then, suddenly, they were fragmented, becoming individual cost centres that had to justify their existence and show their importance. A Hydra now guarded the gate instead of a Cyclops. I accept that it was new to us and things had to be learned, but it has to change, or foreign companies will pull up their tent pegs. WTO membership has helped, but it's still a pain in the arse.

To the outside world, China tries to project an open face, but the reality is different. They are changing, but it's slow, with old habits dying hard. They are still afraid to show themselves and hide behind their 'face' most of the time. 'If I don't expose anything and I don't get involved in anything, then I am safe and I can't be hurt' is how they are most of the time. The words 'not my business' are very common in everyday life and people keep themselves closed off from others. They exist secretly in their own boxes and don't care or want to know what other people are doing in theirs.

If we meet someone or work alongside them, we find out about them as a matter of course, but in China it can be very different. I asked Zheng Xi, who was working as Control Room Operator at the time, what the name of the new machine operator was. I was stunned by his answer: "I don't know."

"He's worked here beside you for a week and you don't know his name? Didn't you ask him?"

"I don't need to know his name to work with him and his name is his business" was his explanation, and I shook my head in amazement. This, however, is common, and Chinese people keep silent about personal details and don't ask others. One evening I asked a guy, Lao Bai, what his full name was and was told, only half jokingly, "My name is my business. If you want to know it you must pay."

It seems to be very much like the British armed forces, as was explained to me by an electrician in South Wales. His name was Paddy Andrews (strange name for a Welshman) and he had served in Northern Ireland. He was crazy as a shithouse rat and specialised in melted screwdrivers and pyrotechnics. Switching off something with four or five hundred volts running through it before working on it was something he regarded as a waste of time. Anyway, from Paddy I learned some abbreviations that would fit well into China: DFK - don't fucking know. DFC - don't fucking care. NFI - not fucking interested. I also invented one of my own because of Paddy, and when enquiring if the factory could accommodate a late order, customer services staff adopted it. 'Another ten tonnes, Russell? NFC.' No fucking chance. I was, however, a very co-operative and flexible mill manager and 'rabbits out of the hat' were a speciality.

At the opposite end of the scale was – is - something that is regarded as public knowledge. In Britain, what you earn is your business and is usually only known by your superiors and the person who sorts out the salaries. In China, however, it is regarded as not being private. Everyone on site knew what everyone else made and if they didn't know, they would ask. It was very strange when you considered that questions like: 'What does your father do?' or 'Are you married?' were reluctantly answered. Maintaining your outward façade and position was and is all-important to the Chinese and status is as important as money to them.

We were having difficulty in recruiting a shift supervisor until I had a brainwave and changed the title. 'Shift Manager' drew applicants from everywhere, even though the salary remained the same.

All in all, it's fair to say that I had a lot to learn when I went to China and I soon came to realise that this learning process would be painful, never ending and ongoing. Anyone who comes here must arrive with an open mind or they will be on an early flight back to home and sanity.

ALICE LI – A CHINESE
BRIEF ENCOUNTER

Alice Li, Alice Li! What brought her back into my mind? A brief meeting with another woman called Alice was all it took and everything came flooding back. Ships that pass in the night, or, in our case, ships that collide and scrape alongside each other before separating and leaving tangled pieces of wreckage on each other's decks.

I was summonsed from Shanghai to Anshan, to sort out a problem in the factory – I forget what it was now and, in any case, it doesn't matter. I arrived via Shenyang airport and a two-hour drive through the barren, brown, boring prairies of March maize fields which would change to an endless sea of waving green in the summer. It was cold; minus 10C and I had come from the near 30C degree heat of Shanghai. The welcome in the hotel was warm though, and dinner with my colleague, Gary, was good. We put the world to rights over a few vodkas and retired early.

Breakfast was the usual Chinese provincial fiasco, but I was used to it by now. Gary and I were dwelling over coffee and a cigarette when a petite, pretty Chinese woman came into the dining room. She had short black (what else?) hair and lovely doe eyes. Hmm... She spotted Gary, smiled, came over to us and Gary introduced us, "Oh, Russell, this is Alice, Alice Li. She's just joined the company as an accountant. Alice, Russell from Shanghai."

Alice had arrived the day before from Guangxi in Southern China and was staying in the hotel until she found a place of her own. She was bubbly, outgoing, very sharp and had a good appreciation of Western humour. She was thirty-two, but carried herself like a young girl. A nice lady.

Off to work in the company mini-bus through the drab, Russian built streets of Anshan. Arriving at the office Gary bounced out, as I did, but then I waited to help Alice get down onto the icy ground, gentleman that I am (true). I gave her my hand and as she took it I felt a jolt. I looked down at our hands in surprise and then up at Alice. She was rigid, her eyes staring into mine. Such eyes. She was in a state of shock and so was I. We couldn't speak and our breath hung between us, frozen in the chill air. After a few moments our eyes unlocked, Alice stepped down and we walked a few steps, still holding hands, letting go self-consciously. We kept our eyes to the ground and walked through the office doors side by side and then separated to go our different ways. We both turned and looked back at each other at the same time and a look of confusion and almost fear crossed Alice's face, then she turned sharply to go into her office, colliding with the doorjamb. My head was spinning and Gary jolted me back to reality. "In here you pillock. Fucking lost already?"

"Yes. What was I going to do doing today? A problem to sort out. Yes, sort it out. Yes."

The problem, whatever it was, was sorted out and the making sure it didn't happen again was cemented into the Chinese. I was on autopilot and floated through the day in a euphoric daze. I must have appeared even more laid back than usual, with my mind drifting back to the morning's encounter.

The day ended and we travelled back to the hotel, with Alice and me subdued, avoiding eye contact and not saying very much, except to give appropriate responses to Gary, who was babbling on in his usual way about nothing. Gary decided, for some reason, that we should go out for dinner and began to ring round to organise a crowd. He managed to get hold of three others - his translator, Maggie and two other Managers, Peter Li and Alex Wang. Then he informed us, "Seven o'clock, OK? Right? Sorted."

Dinner found Alice and me still confused and quiet, but we soon began to relax. We were sitting opposite each other, so it wasn't easy to avoid talking to or looking at each other even if, by then, we had wanted to. Our hands touched again, but this time we smiled at each other. An unspoken decision had been made. We were sitting at the end of the long table, making it easy to exclude the others, so we did.

The food, as ever in China, was in the middle of the

table and Alice began to transfer choice morsels to my bowl, hostess style, and then, very intimately, directly to my mouth, using her own chopsticks. Comments and laughter came from the other Chinese and I heard the words 'tai-tai,' Chinese for 'wife.' Alice smiled coyly, but carried on doing what she was doing. Gary gave me a searching look but I shrugged my shoulders, as if mystified.

The meal finished, the Chinese went to their homes and Geoff, Alice and I set off back to the hotel, with Alice and me secretly holding hands in the back of the car like school children. As we entered the hotel Gary headed for the bar, turning to me as he did and said, "You're going back in the morning, so we'd better have a talk before we go to bed. An hour should do it."

Shit. Alice mumbled a goodnight and headed for the lifts, giving me a blank gaze before she got in. Shit. Gary and I had our talk and then headed upstairs. My door hadn't clicked shut before I was on the phone to reception. "Miss Alice Li's room please."

"Have five Chinese lady name Li stay hotel, sir. What is Chinese name?"

Shit again. I stalked around the room, cursing Chinese hotels, hotel staff and China in general, before deciding to attack my mini-bar and was pouring tonic into a double, double vodka when there was a knock on the door. I knew who I wanted it to be and who it had to be. Please.

I opened the door and there she was; barefooted, arms by her side, with her eyes cast down. She tried to speak, but all that came out was, "I... I..." She looked up at me with a pleading, scared look in her eyes.

I took her hand and said, "I know" and led her inside.

We didn't speak and stood holding hands for a few seconds. We were both trembling. I kissed her upturned face and then her lips and she moaned as our tongues met. She smelt of jasmine and her hair was so soft I could hardly feel it. She was wearing a dark blue silk dress and, as I found out, nothing else. I slipped the dress off her shoulders and it slid down her body, catching briefly on her breasts and erect nipples. I lowered my head and took one of her nipples gently between my lips and she gasped and put her arms around my neck, letting me support all her weight. Her legs buckled as I slid my hand over her mound of silky, straight pubic hair and between her thighs. She was awash. I picked her up before she could fall, carried her to the bed and she was as light as a feather.

I don't remember getting undressed, but I must have. I held back from taking her right away and we explored each other's bodies. She reached down for me and her eyes widened and she gasped again before smiling. She was a small Chinese woman and had never been with a foreigner before. I couldn't hold on any longer, so I gently and slowly entered her. She stiffened as she felt the size of me inside her, then relaxed and wrapped herself around me like a baby monkey, clinging to its mother. It didn't last long – it couldn't – and we came together. It seemed to go on forever, deep inside her, as she thrust herself upwards to take as much as she could.

After, we lay in each other's arms not speaking – we hadn't said a word since she came in the room – until I felt tears on my chest. "What's wrong?"

"Nothing wrong, I'm just very happy."

We decided to take a shower and I watched her as she moved across the floor to the bathroom. She was perfect; not an ounce of fat on her, with skin that felt like velvet. Her breasts were just the right size – 'enough to fill an honest man's hand or a champagne glass' as they say – with dark brown, almost black nipples. Hips and backside? I've never seen better, and I've seen more than a few. The beautiful hands and feet it seems only Asian women have. Too much. Too much. I was in love already.

In the shower we soaped and then washed each other unselfconsciously, talking all the time, as if we'd been together all our lives, enjoying touching each other. Her nipples began to stiffen under my touch and she dropped to her knees to wash somewhere else – again. I reacted and she looked up at me smiling, "You're getting big again. You want?"

Before I could answer, she took me deep in her mouth and began to suck very slowly. After what seemed no time at all I had to say, "Stop! Stop! You'll make me come!"

She stopped, looked up at me with a smile, and said "So?" before kissing and licking me delicately and sliding her mouth back over me.

I exploded uncontrollably and she moaned and swallowed. She released me and looked up at me again. "I've never done that before."

She saw the look of surprise on my face and gave a laugh. "No, I mean I've never swallowed before. I've only ever sucked my husband, but I never swallowed for him. I didn't like doing it, but I do now."

She took me quickly in her mouth again and sucked hard for a few more seconds, draining me completely. She stood up, her eyes twinkling, and hugged me tightly before stepping out of the shower. "Take your time. See you in bed. You taste very good, by the way" and she skipped out of the bathroom, laughing.

I took my time, and when I went back into the bedroom Alice was already half asleep, spread-eagled like a starfish, face down on the bed. I sat down beside her and ran my hand down her back, thinking I'd never felt skin so soft – I really was in love already. She gave a sleepy grunt of pleasure, as I ran my hand down her back, over her buttocks and on down between her open thighs.

Suddenly she stiffened, raised her hips from the bed and thrust herself to meet my hand. She was wet again. I turned her over and found her wetness with my mouth and her small hands gripped my head, as if to make sure I didn't stop, her hips grinding up and forward to meet me. Her back arched and she let go of my head to clutch handfuls of bed sheet and she let out a long low wail and quivered before going limp. Eventually, she sat up slowly and reached for me. There were tears in her lovely eyes, but her face was smiling. She cupped my face in her hands and kissed me long and soft before pulling me on top of her, reaching down to guide me into her. We took longer this time – hey, I'm not a young man – and after, we lay exhausted and amazed.

We took another quick shower and went back to bed - to sleep this time. We lay touching each other and talking for a while and then drifted off, with Alice curled up like a baby, her head on my chest.

Alice had told me that she was divorced and had come to Anshan to start a new life. What a start. Her husband had divorced her because she couldn't have children and her family had been unhappy when she returned home to live with them, so she had decided to leave Guangxi. We'd talked about what happened in the morning when we touched for the first time. Neither of us had believed that something like it could happen and thought it was the stuff of romantic novels. She had been scared to death at first and had almost gone back to the hotel at lunchtime, to avoid seeing me. She hadn't been able to concentrate on work all day – tell me about it! – but had decided that she was going to come to my room as soon as we got back to the hotel. She hadn't been sure what she was going to say or do at that time, but she just knew she had to come and see me.

Gary spoilt her plan by arranging the dinner, but she had decided during dinner that she wanted me and had to be with me. She said she had almost cried when Gary kept me downstairs talking. She had come down to look from the second floor gallery every ten minutes, to see if we'd finished and, when we had, she phoned reception to see which room I was in. She also said she had stood outside my door for five minutes or more before she could get up the courage to knock and, after she had knocked, had almost run away before I opened the door.

We didn't talk much about what would or could happen next. It was dangerous because, if we were found out, Alice would be sacked and I would be repatriated. As it turned out we were right not to look too far ahead.

My alarm call woke us at 6.30 – we had only been asleep for three hours. It was the usual Anshan International recorded jingle, 'Ni hao. Thisa you wake up call. Wisha you have a nice day', spoken by a Chinese woman with a very, very sexy voice. I loved it and often listened to it twice and, as I've said before, for me, it was the best feature of the hotel.

We made love again, gently and slowly, with Alice astride me. She beamed down at me when it was over and said, "If I *could* have babies, I'd be sure to have one after this night."

We got ourselves organised and then walked out to the lifts together. Alice had to go back to her room and we had, sensibly, decided to be discreet and go down to breakfast separately, even though we felt like shouting it to the world. We arranged a time for me to call her when I got back to Shanghai and by then I would, hopefully, have some ideas about what we could do. We knew that we had to be together somehow and Alice said she was happy for me to decide what we should do. We kissed for the last time and said our private farewell and Alice got into the lift. I can still see her; radiant and happy, mouthing the words,

"Wo ai ni" (I love you) as the doors closed.

I joined Gary at breakfast and he grunted a good morning and then looked at me again and commented, "Christ, you look fucked. Bad sleep?"

"Yeah. Can't sleep in a strange bed. Not to worry, I'll sleep on the way back to Shanghai."

After a while Alice joined us and Gary said, "Alice you look wonderful. Pass your sleep secret on to Russell."

"Thank you. Maybe he should sleep in my bed" she said, with a smirk and a twinkle in her eye.

Gary looked at her sharply and then at me, but missed both her smirk and my sharp intake of breath as she ran her foot up the inside of my leg, under the table. Breakfast continued without further event, though Gary had one or two searching glances at both of us. He knew. There must have been a glow. We finished and went outside; they to the office and me to Shenyang airport.

The last time I saw her was as she turned to give me a happy smile and a wave, as the mini-bus pulled away. We had said all the right public things: "Nice to have met you", "Hope to meet you again" etc etc.

On the way back to Shanghai I worked it out. I'd already planted an idea with Gary at breakfast that I should come to Anshan more often and stay longer, to keep things on track, as was my working brief. He would suggest it to the CEO, Dennis, and take the credit for it, as he always did. To be honest, I should have been in Anshan more often, but it's too hot, too wet or too cold as well as being a shit hole, so I'd been avoiding it. Not any more.

I'd also worked out how to get Alice down to Shanghai; 'Cross-pollination of accounting procedures and systems between the joint ventures.' It would look good in a report. Brilliant! Full of this, I phoned the hotel at 9 pm as arranged. I'd even remembered to find out Alice's Chinese name. Thought of everything: "Room 613, please. Miss Li Wun Ming."

"Very sorry, sir. Miss Li leave hotel lunchtime." There was a pause, then "Are you Mr Russell? She leave message for you, sir. I read for you, sir. It say 'I have to go. I love you and I am sorry.' She cry very much, sir. Sorry, sir"

I put the phone down. What had happened? I couldn't call Gary, as that would have well and truly confirmed his suspicions.

I spent a long, sleepless night and in the morning I made the routine phone call to Gary, trying to sound casual, and I asked, "Hi. Anything going on?"

"Oh shit, yes. Great shame. Alice Li got the sack yesterday. Instant dismissal. Peter Li checked her qualifications and it turned out she'd lied about some of them. Pity. She was a nice woman. I think she fancied you a bit as well?"

"Oh, I don't know about that. Where did she go?"

"First flight back to Guangxi probably, but she was in a hurry to get away and could have gone anywhere. These northern bastards don't like southerners."

Gone? Gone! I was devastated. All her records had been ritually destroyed, Chinese style, so there was no way I could find her. She, I knew, wouldn't contact me because of the humiliation and loss of face she had suffered. That's the way they are. I'd known her only twenty-four hours and my heart was broken.

I carried a torch for her for months and even now, five years on, it hasn't completely gone out. I thought I'd seen her one day in Shanghai and followed a woman into a shop on Nanjing Lu, my heart racing, only to come back to earth with a blazing crash when it wasn't her. It was a lingerie shop as well. I got seriously shit-faced that night. Gone for good. It has taken a long time for me to bury her, even partially, and I know that writing about her will and has resurrected her, opened the wound and left me in turmoil, if only for a while.

Was it as good as we thought it was for those twenty-four hours, and would it or could it have carried on if we'd had the chance? It certainly couldn't have got better and that, in itself, should make me look at it with more realism and not through a rose-tinted haze. It was maybe too good. 'Too hot not to cool down' as the song says or – what was the other one from Bladerunner? – 'The light that burns twice as brightly burns half as long, and you have burned so very brightly.' All that may be true, but I wish I'd been able to find out. I hope that writing about her will help to 'lay the ghost', but do I really want to do that? What if I meet her again? Who knows?

I can smile now, though, albeit sadly, when I hear the Smokie song 'Living Next Door to Alice,' but I will forever sing the Chubby Brown chorus as 'Alice? Alice? Where the fuck is Alice?' Never 'who'.

CELEBRATIONS

Forget about Christmas, New Year, Fourth of July – everything – unless you roll them all into one and have one big bash. Nothing compares to Chinese New Year or, as they call it, Spring Festival. Because of Western influence and commercial awareness some Western festivals and special days are now observed in China, but they are half-hearted affairs. Christmas day is a non-event and everything dies after a Western style build-up – Christmas decorations on the streets etc – and everything goes flat. The millennium celebrations were the same. Midnight 1999 came and went, with the Chinese, while all going through the motions, not really knowing what to do next. You could see what they were thinking: "We're having a good time aren't we? What should we do now?"

Spring Festival is DIFFERENT. It begins with people going back to their hometowns from wherever they are in China. This takes time, and in the West it would be regarded as too much time. But in China it's accepted. Why? Back in the good old days of the Cultural

Revolution, Mao decided that people should return to the land and he made it happen – forcibly. The eldest child in the family was shipped out to God knows where in the Chinese countryside, usually hundreds and sometimes thousands of miles away from their hometowns. Furthermore, they were forbidden to return home except in times of National Holiday or for approved 'family visits.'

Special rules and conditions still apply to the people this happened to, and it is still difficult for them to return to their home cities and re-register to live out their remaining years as old people. This situation has added to the tradition and the need for people in China to 'go home' at holiday times.

Air travel is out of the reach of most Chinese people, though it is becoming more common, so most go by train. China is BIG, and if you want to go from, say, Shanghai to Harbin by train, you're looking at a two-day train journey. I know it takes two days because we had dealings with an engineering company there. Some of their equipment was faulty and they sent two engineers by train – two days. They finished their work in a day and went back – another two days. However, before they got back to Harbin the equipment broke down again, so they were met at the station and told return to Shanghai – another two days. Back in Shanghai again they spent another day making the necessary repairs, before returning, again, to Harbin – another two days. Eight days out of ten on a train. If you happened to come from Urumqi, Xin Jiang Province, then make it four days.

Trains are always packed with people of the same mind at this time of year, so travelling has to be started up to two weeks before the day or you can't get a ticket. The need and desire to go home is very strong and one of the worst things that can happen to a Chinese person is not being able to spend Spring Festival with their families. It's important and affects many things in China.

The Chinese New Year is a time for new beginnings and there is a reluctance to start anything new in the weeks leading up to it, with efforts being made to see that everything that can be finished is finished. This has a major effect on the Chinese economy as things can grind to a virtual halt for two or three weeks.

My first Spring Festival in China was spent in Harbin, Heilongjiang Province, at the invitation of a friend and colleague, Ma Shen You. I should have had more sense. Had I been in China for more than just a few months, I would have declined. My only recollections are of being fucking cold. Minus 25C fucking cold. Ice sculptures are very nice, but frostbite is not.

My next two SFs were spent in Shanghai, and they were special. Spring Festival 1999 saw me at Lao Xia's home, with his family and friends. It began with a banquet and booze, which was not unusual, but the quantity and the scale were the difference - The best of everything and lots of it. When midnight came the city exploded with fireworks, and it continued to explode until six in the morning. In many places it was impossible to see across the street because of the smoke. I had a thought. What a perfect time to invade China. No one would notice and many wouldn't care, even if they did notice.

I don't know how many deaths there are in China because of firework accidents at Spring Festival, but there must be a few hundred. Many of the fireworks are lethal, with only two-second fuses, and are little more than legalised hand grenades, capable of blowing your head off. The Chinese seem to have no regard for their safety or the safety of others and near misses, scorched fingers and vanished eyebrows are laughed at and treated as part of the fun.

In amongst all the celebrations there is genuine goodwill and everyone is 'nicer' to everyone else. Even beggars are treated better – not that they could be treated any worse.

I thought that after one night of craziness it would all be over, but no. It went on for the next week with sporadic bursts of fireworks at all hours all over the city. A week later I was staying in the Crowne Plaza for a couple of nights; the reason being that I'd lost all power in my apartment. I'd asked for it to be fixed, but it was Spring Festival, so all I got was a smile and an unkept promise. I shipped out.

I was awakened on Friday night, just before midnight, by another massive burst of explosive fireworks and looked out of my twenty-fourth floor window. The sky was ablaze with rockets and starbursts and continued that way until three in the morning. Even after that, there were sporadic bursts here and there.

That was it? Not quite. They have something like our Twelfth Night, called the Festival of The Lanterns, and in Shanghai, the place to see this was Yuyuan Gardens. Yuyuan Gardens is a tourist area of Shanghai that retains the flavour of Old China and it was festooned with hundreds of Chinese lanterns of every size imaginable. I still have a clear picture in my mind of Old China in the foreground with the ultra modern backdrop of the Jinmao Building and the Orient Pearl Tower, both lit up for the same celebration.

Chinese people love a party, whatever the reason, and they had a very good reason in October 99. China was fifty years old. It began with broadcast from Beijing, of the official ceremony to mark the occasion and it was done as only the Chinese can. There's a strange dichotomy about the Chinese. In most of the things they do there is chaos, lack of planning and confusion, but when they want to plan and organise something they do it better than anyone.

The parade in Tiananmen Square was impressive, and it was seen all over the world. I believe everyone who saw it would have been impressed and possibly a little disturbed by the extent and the precision of it all and, I have to add, for other reasons. I was watching it all in my apartment when my phone rang. "Yeah?"

It was a call from England. "Russ, are all the women in China the same as the ones on the front row in the army parade? If they are, I'm on my way."

It was Pete. We had been mates since we started school together as five-year olds and he was a dirty old man even then. Love him to death. I laughed and explained, "No, not all. The ones on the front two or three rows would have been handpicked."

"OK, but I understand now why you like it there. How much is a return ticket?" I laughed again. We talked for a while and then Pete realised how much the call was costing, or maybe it was his wife, Lorraine, screaming in his ear that made him stop running up a massive bill. I settled back down to watch some more, but the phone rang again. Same thing, only this time it was the Sales Manager, Ken Griffith, who I had worked with in South Wales. I talked to him for a lot longer – the company paid his phone bill.

The celebrations went on all over China in various ways and in Shanghai the main event was a firework display on the Bund, Waitan, down by the river. In common with a lot of people in Shanghai we, Amy and I, decided to 'go and have a look' – mistake. It was terrifying. Three million people were attempting to get into a space that could only hold half a million, at the most. Thankfully, we never got any closer than a mile from it. The police had realised, too late, that there were too many people and had blocked off all the streets leading to the river.

There must have been a few deaths and I myself saw four or five bodies being attended to by weeping friends and relatives. I couldn't tell if they were dead or not, but it seemed likely. We retreated and satisfied ourselves with the view of the display from the Club Lounge in the Crowne Plaza – a much better and eminently safer idea.

The evening, however, was not over. We had arranged to meet with some friends in Bats Bar in the basement of the Shangri-la hotel in Pudong, but we had to wait until the crowds thinned out and the police opened the roads before we could get across the river. Our friends were our next-door neighbours, Paul and Shelley. Paul was German and he was all right, for a German. He treated his girlfriend, Shelley, like a doormat and I could never understand why she stayed with the pig. She was fine too, apart from her habit of knocking on the door as soon as we had put food on the table. Maybe she had a very sensitive nose. She also used to visit us in some very 'casual' clothes – a loose, sleeveless top and no bra. "Honest, I never noticed she has big black nipples and that one breast hangs lower than the other." Hmmm.

Shelley was a frequent visitor and was very, very friendly. She called one day when I was alone, again wearing the aforementioned casual clothes. We sat and talked, with me trying not to look – too much. She noticed me not looking and laughed, "I make you not comfortable? It's OK. You can look. I like you look. Not shy."

I looked, with my mind working overtime and my jeans beginning to swell. She noticed and moved closer. She peeled off her vest and said, "Now you can feel." After I had 'felt', she moved onto the floor between my legs and began unzipping me. "I can look?" She 'looked', then said "Is wrong time for me, but can make comfortable."

She began with her mouth, but changed to her hand, explaining, "If in my mouth always sick. Paul makes me do and always sick. Sick this morning before he go to work. You can on my face and on my here." She indicated her breasts.

It ended, as it always does, with the inevitable explosion, which sprayed onto her neck and ran down on to her breasts. She was very happy with the result and said, "Very much. Good. Hope Amy don't want, when she finish work. Haha." Bad girl.

She went to the bathroom to clean herself up and when she returned she decided she would go. "Better I go now. Paul will come back." I showed her out and she gave my groin a parting squeeze and a peck on the cheek and said, "I like you, Russell. I want do something for long time."

We were never to be alone together again. Amy was suspicious – woman's intuition? – and seemed to sense that something had gone on, but she never went any further than the observation, "I think she like you very much. You be careful. OK?" Hmmm.

Where was I? Yes, on the way to Pudong. We got there late and the place was packed. Fortunately, though, Paul had been watching the display from the top floor of the Shangri-la with some colleagues and had got there early, so we had good seats. As we made our way to them, I glanced at the band – Philippino again, but I didn't know any of them, which was strange. I got a drink and settled in to listen to the music and do some people watching.

I like people watching. Very soon I was lost in my watching and connected thoughts and observations, along the lines of, "He must be a newcomer. You don't buy drinks for that many girls – unless, of course, you're investing for the future." and "I wouldn't have picked that one" etc.

I was jerked away from my favourite pastime by the sound of my name over the speakers. "We have a guest singer in the bar tonight. Will Russell please come to the stage?"

What the fuck? Who the fuck? I sat tight, but they called for me again. "We know where you are. Come on! Come to the stage."

I was dragged and pushed out of my seat by a laughing Paul and Shelley, with Amy sitting frosty faced. She didn't like me to sing. "Too many women see you when you sing. Don't like."

I made my way to the stage and found out how they knew my name. I had blamed Paul, but when I looked closer I saw that the drummer was someone I knew from the Crowne Plaza. It was 'Bing-Bong', the bastard. He gave a laugh and then asked: "Hey, man, I saw you come in. What you gonna sing?"

I was caught flat-footed and, without thinking, I said, "Anything by the Eagles." Mistake. Too late.

They began. 'Hotel (fucking) California.' I got through it and received an ovation, but refused to sing another – 'always leave them wanting more?' It was the largest audience I had ever sung to; there must have been close to a thousand in the place. I made my way back to the table, receiving slaps on the back and offers of drinks all the way. Amy spent the rest of the evening in cold silence, as women floated over to the table to tell me how much they'd enjoyed my singing.

After a couple of hours we decided to move closer to home and headed for the Manhattan bar on Ju lu Lu, a notorious place on a notorious street. It got no better and we went home early after Amy returned from a visit to the toilet, to find an enthusiastic fan from the Shangri-la wrapped around me. Of course she trusted me. No she didn't really, and had made it her business to ask most of the staff in most of the places I frequented to keep an eye on me. It became normal for a woman showing an 'interest' in me to suddenly go cold, after a whispered conversation with a barmaid or waitress. No problem. In most places there were girls who liked a challenge – 'If I can't have it, I want it.'

I've mentioned Christmas as being a non-event in China, but how was it for me? As my first Christmas approached, I was apprehensive. Would I be sad? How much would I miss it all?

When it came to it I had no real problems. Had I been in Britain and alone I would probably have been suicidal, but in China life was going on and it was just another day. There was no 'Christmas spirit' and nothing except the street decorations to remind me that it actually was Christmas. Some others were not as fortunate; there are two or three Christmas suicides among ex-pats in China every year. Can it ever get that bad? Yes it can, believe me.

CHOCOLATE FIREGUARDS
AND AUSSIES

As an ex-pat resident of Shanghai I was, supposedly, part of the British community living there. I soon found, however, that it was made up mostly of people whom, had it been a normal environment, I wouldn't have entertained more that ten minutes. It all smacked too much of the British Raj, with coffee mornings, social evenings and cocktail parties. Maybe they were right and how they lived was normal and I, and those of like mind, were out of step. I tried to join in and become part of it, but it grated on me to the extent that I only went to a couple of functions before throwing in the towel. Thereafter, I confined myself to accepting Consulate freebies and invitations from people I liked.

The rest of the ex-pats seemed to live their lives much as they would have anywhere, by creating Little Britain, complete with house servants – a Little Britain that just happened to have a huge Chinatown close by. The place was unreal enough, without creating your own illusion. My choice of lifestyle and my general attitude were probably major contributors to my company's view that I had 'gone bush' and their subsequent decision that they wanted me out of there. At least my life was as normal as it could be and, as a result, I probably got to know and understand China a lot better than most.

Apart from my contact with the British end of the company my other regular contact with things British was the Commercial Section of the British Consulate in Shanghai – namely Joseph (Joe) Woodall, the Commercial Consul. Joe was very Home Counties and 'hurrah', but all right. All right and absolutely useless, hence the term 'chocolate fireguard'.

It seems that British embassies and consulates are the same everywhere. Primarily, they are there to represent Her Britannic Majesty's Government and control the issuing of British visas, with everything else being, or seeming to be, subordinate. They are supposed to be there to help and advise too, but getting them to do either can be difficult and costly. Crowbars would have been very useful in trying to get anything from them.

Conversely, they were very, very good at getting people to do things to help them. A phone call from Joe. "Russell, old chap, any chance of you giving me a bit of a hand?"

"Well, I…"

"Yes? Great. I've got a group of British Industrialists with some chaps from MAFF (Ministry of Agriculture, Food and Fisheries) coming over next week. Any chance of looking after them for a couple of days – letting them visit your factory and two or three Chinese companies? That sort of thing?"

"Well. I..."

"Jolly good. Give me a call when you've got it sorted out." Screwed again.

In the event, it wasn't too bad – the first time. The second time, however, only six months later, when I did it again, I found that it was exactly the same people again. I asked Joe about this and was informed, "Yes, they felt that they needed to do a re-appraisal."

Re-appraisal? More like another free 'jolly' and seven days in a five star hotel. I was very glad I had become a non-taxpayer.

Joe stitched me up a number of times and I ended up not trusting him, or anybody from the Consulate, any more. The first time he did it, it was a massive breach of trust and I never forgave him for it. He called me early one morning with a request. "Russell, we've heard that there's been an outbreak of foot and mouth disease in Shanghai. Do you think you could find out how true it is and, if so, how bad it is?"

I told him I would see what I could do and get back to him. I called Frank into the office, put him in the picture and asked him to see if Lao Song, our 'dairy' man, knew anything and I was surprised at Frank's reply: "Lao Song will not tell you anything about number five disease and neither will any other Chinese member of staff."

"What?"

"Yes, it is a criminal offence to talk about this disease to a foreigner and when we talk about it we refer to it as 'number five disease'."

It was true. In typical Chinese fashion there was a refusal to officially admit the presence of foot and mouth in China to the rest of the world. China was riddled with it and it reared its head frequently. They wouldn't even call it by name. It began to make sense, as I recalled the times when the Bright Dairy Company had cancelled farm visits, with the excuse 'We are concerned about the current risk of disease being introduced to our farms from outside.' Exactly the opposite was true. They were so twitchy about it that they wouldn't even speak about it in Chinese if I were in the same room. China!

Anyway, I found all this out later. Back to Frank, who continued, "No, Lao Song will not tell you anything, but I will, as long as I can be sure that your friend in the Consulate does not tell ANYONE where the information came from. I could get into a lot of trouble."

I gave Frank my reassurances – 'British Diplomatic Service confidentiality' etc. – and he told me. It seemed that there had been a major outbreak in the Shanghai dairy-cow population and 20,000 cows had been slaughtered and incinerated in a pit in Nanhui County, south of Shanghai. The rest of the cows had been vaccinated, but the vaccine was known to be not very effective, so the outbreak was not, in reality, under control. It was never 'under control', and re-occurred every six months or so. It was laughable when China refused to import British dairy or beef products after Britain had its last outbreak in 2002. China!

I thanked Frank and told him not to worry about anything. Then I phoned Joe and gave him the information and told him of the risk Frank had taken in telling me. Joe was very pleased. "Thank you, Russell. Don't worry. Mum's the word."

I didn't give it any more thought until my phone rang about two hours later. It was an Aussie friend, Mike Boddington, who worked for a company called PIC, the Pig Improvement company, which specialised in pig breeding and genetics. I was stunned when he opened the conversation with, "G'day, Russ. I've just had a call from Joe Woodall. He said to call you if I wanted to know anything more about this foot and mouth outbreak?"

Joe, the bastard, had spilled his guts. There was nothing I could do except hope that fear of further publicity would stop Frank from getting into deep shit. Thankfully, though, the news broke worldwide after an article was published in the *New York Times* a couple of days later. Panic over and me better informed and wiser.

Joe, however, screwed me again shortly after. He called me early one morning – again. Another phone call and an invitation. "Russell, we're having a little soiree tonight for some visitors from Blighty and I thought you might like to join us." I accepted – it was free. "Jolly good. Michael Boddington and a few others you know will be there too. See you at six. Third floor in The Hilton. Bye."

I called Mike to see if we could meet up and go

together, as his office was close to my apartment, and he agreed, "Great mate. See you around 5.30."

I met up with Mike as arranged and off we went in a taxi. Then Mike said something that surprised me. "Hope they've got power-point on their computer. I need it for my presentation."

"You're giving a presentation?"

"Yeah. Joe asked me to. What are you doing for yours?"

"Mine?"

"Yeah. Joe said that you would be saying a few words as well. You're first on."

"The bastard" I thought.

I glared at Joe when we arrived and he was very apologetic – too fucking late. I managed to spout some bullshit for five or ten minutes and just about got away with it. Joe was very grateful, but I made him very aware that I wasn't happy. Boddington thought it was all highly amusing, until it was his turn and the computer crashed. Served him right, the smug Aussie bastard.

We then both proceeded to disgrace ourselves and behaved as badly as we possibly could, without being thrown out. It was close, though, and I think Joe breathed a sigh of relief when we left – even though it was with two cute Chinese Consulate staff members.

They were bad girls – well, mine was and had my dick out in the taxi and half completed a blowjob in the lift before we even got into my apartment. She would not be denied and completed the job as soon as the apartment door was closed. She was a strange girl and had a food fetish thing. She got off on eating while we were in the act – messy. Different, but messy. Cucumber, banana, ice cream and crisps. Use your imagination. Unfortunately, we hadn't behave badly enough and Joe continued to invite us to Consulate functions.

My lack of trust and faith in Consulate service continued, and it reached a climax during the time of the US bombing of the Chinese Embassy in Belgrade. If you remember, this was when the USA 'accidentally' dropped one on the Chinese Embassy because they were passing on military information. We received no advice from the Consulate on what to do. It was an American problem, but being their closest allies put us alongside them in the eyes of the Chinese. US citizens were advised to leave the country or stay out of sight to avoid reprisals. British citizens the same? You are joking!

The risk was real, but it was exaggerated. The Chinese were angry, but the 'spontaneous' demonstrations and stonings of US Embassies and Consulates in China was orchestrated and controlled by the Government. This was very well demonstrated in Guangzhou, where the police stopped some people on the way to the US Consulate and asked, "Where are your rocks? How can you demonstrate when you have no rocks to throw?"

It went on for a couple of weeks and then stopped very, very suddenly. It was getting close to the anniversary of the Tiananmen Square massacre, so the government closed things off before the mob could turn. They would have, for sure. If you get Chinese people pointed and moving in a direction, they will follow it and follow it blindly. My conversations with Chinese friends about the 'Belgrade incident' were scary. "We are not afraid of America. If the Chinese Government tells us to fight America we will, and we will die for China."

Their view of the Tiananmen Square massacre was also interesting. They, of course, didn't know very much about it, but there general opinion was, "Yes, maybe the Government over-reacted, but the students showed great disrespect for authority. They brought it upon themselves and deserved what happened to them." Once again – scary.

There were no major problems in Shanghai during this time, apart from one American tourist, who went along to the US Consulate on Urumqi Lu to see 'What wuz goin' on.' I was told that he arrived there wearing a stetson, jeans and with a camera hanging round his neck. Apparently he got a fair amount of shit before the police rescued him. Pillock.

In Shanghai things wrapped up pretty quickly, after a misdirected rock laid out a policeman. Great. Anyway, a couple of weeks later, after it was all over, I got a phone call from Joe. He enquired, "Russell, old chap, any problems during the recent situation?"

"No, Joe. What about you?"

"Oh, as soon as it happened, we shipped out to Hong Kong. Just come back now. Glad all was well with you. Jolly good. Bye."

Women, children and diplomats first. I repeat – 'chocolate fireguards.'

Joe continued his uselessness until he left, but his 'leaving' was done under unfortunate circumstances. Joe played squash and he and I had had a few games, which I always won. Joe was keen, though, and would always be an exhausted ball of sweat by the time we finished. I called him one day to ask him for some information and he gave me the "I'll get back to you on that. Call you tomorrow" response. This meant that he didn't know, again, and would have to find out. To be fair to him, he always did call back, except that this time he didn't. After a couple of days, having not heard from him, I gave him a call, only to be told by his secretary, "Sorry Russell, he snapped an Achilles tendon playing squash the other night and had to go to Hong Kong for surgery."

"Sorry to hear that. Was he winning or losing when it snapped?"

"Losing."

"Seems a bit of an extreme way of avoiding defeat."

"We thought so too."

A week later I called again to see how he was and they told me there had been complications. He had had a blood clot, almost died and had been shipped back to the UK. He never returned and I regret not having been able to say farewell to him and give him some shit.

I'll stay on this 'demonstration' period for some more goings on. I had to make six-monthly trips to Hong Kong to get my visa renewed by the British Sugar office there. British Sugar and my company were part of the same group and they had several operations in South China.

They seemed to have no cash restraints, so they had a plush, virtually unused office in the central business area of Hong Kong. My stays were only ever for a couple of days and I was happy about this. I do not like Hong Kong. It is, dare I say it, too British. There are big red buses and everyone drives like maniacs on the 'wrong' (opposite to China) side of the road. The cars in China will try to miss you when you cross the street, but in Hong Kong they would kill you. The people are also a shower of thieving, lying, cheating bastards. I used my Visa card to pay a bar bill one time and became suspicious when it disappeared from my sight. As a result, I telephoned the credit card company as soon as I got back to the hotel and told them I thought my card had been used fraudulently. They called me back in a couple of days to tell me that the bar had tried to extract £3000, as well as £25. Bastards. The only good thing was that they didn't even get the £25 I should have paid.

Hong Kong just doesn't feel like China, but maybe it does, if it's the only part of China you've ever been to. For me, though, it's a poor copy. My view may be jaundiced and might improve if I could see more of it. Maybe I will some day. I did, however, like Macau and will go there again when I can. It feels older, has more character than Hong Kong and is more laid back and peaceful. I like it there. Back on track now. I was sitting in my room in the Furama Hotel - very expensive – when my phone went. "Yeah?"

"Russell, glad I've caught up with you. Do you feel

safe?" It was Rick Kimble, the Personnel Director, phoning from the UK, and he was concerned. He was one of the more sensible Head Office types and was a 'friend' of sorts. Was he trying to warn me about some impending doom or something? I thought for a few seconds before answering, wondering what was wrong. Maybe I had I fucked up? I made a quick memory check on recent things I'd done. No, they wouldn't know about that. Could it be...? No. They'll never find out about that. No, nothing came to mind, so, still wondering if I'd fucked up, I said, with some hesitation, "Yeah, I feel safe enough, Rick. I think so anyway."

"Oh, good. We were worried about you because we hadn't heard from you. The demonstrations and things?"

"Oh, that. No problems, Rick."

"Good. British Sugar have called all their people back to Hong Kong and we've made Clive [Finance Director for China] in Anshan the Evacuation Co-ordinator if you all need to get out of China for a while." I suppressed my urge to laugh and he carried on, "Seeing as how you are already in Hong Kong, why don't you stay there for a few more days until it quietens down?"

I told him I would give it serious consideration and would let Clive know where I was to see what he advised, while still trying not to laugh out loud. I thought it better not to tell him that the biggest anti US demonstration of the day had been In Hong Kong. I'd witnessed the 'spontaneous outpouring of the anger of the people of Hong Kong' as I'd been on my way back to the hotel. All the demonstrators were wearing the same spontaneous baseball caps and T-shirts.

After I finished talking to Rick I thought I would have a bit of a wind-up with my colleagues in Anshan, so phoned and said, "Hi, it's Russell. Could I speak to the Evacuation Co-ordinator, please?" I waited for Clive to come to the phone and then, in a panicky voice, "I want to fly home. It's not safe here any more. Get me out."

I'd made a mistake. I'd forgotten that Clive had undergone a humourectomy in early life, as part of his accountancy training, and, apart from a vestigial mixture of infantile rude schoolboy toilet jokes and Benny Hill, he had nothing left. He took me seriously and said, "OK, don't worry. Stay where you are and I'll come down there tomorrow. I think we should all get out."

I was stunned, stuck for words. It took me more than ten minutes to convince him that I was joking. He wasn't happy and the next thing he said was, "I think we should go and go quick. It really isn't safe."

After I'd managed to convince him I was all right and put the phone down, I decided to phone Gary and find out why he was so keen to be away. Gary scoffed, "You know what he's like. Any excuse to do fuck all. HE asked them to make him Evacuation Co-ordinator and he's been pestering me for the last three days. If I'd agreed with him, we'd have been gone two days ago. He's got everyone in the UK on high alert waiting for us. Stupid cunt."

Gary was right, he was a stupid cunt, but sometimes he was only a cunt – a dog in the manger, holier than thou, backstabbing, two-faced, hypocritical cunt. Oops! I forgot to write sanctimonious. You will gather that I didn't like him. He didn't like me much either, or my life style, and, as I found out later, was instrumental in my departure from China. The fact that he was fucking Ava, the translator, every time he visited Shanghai, was an unspoken and often not unspoken secret, even though he fed tales to the UK about everybody else. Gary even bailed out of the Anshan hotel they lived in to get away from him. As he put it, 'I'm had enough of him clocking me in and out and reporting on my every move.'

Clive finally showed his true colours and was disgraced and sacked when he left his wife for his Anshan translator, the aptly named Bunny. Unfortunately this this was after I had left China, so I missed Gary's celebration party and the pleasure of gloating. I believe he may still be in Anshan running an English School, but I don't really care. I hope he burns in hell. Slowly.

Anyway, I took advantage of the situation for a couple of days, got bored and headed back to the Shanghai 'danger zone.'

A couple of weeks later, after all was calm, Gary came down to see me. We were having a fairly relaxed meeting in the lobby of the Crowne Plaza and had just about finished when my phone rang. It was Boddington. "Russell, you baaastard, git yoreself darn to the Long Bar. It's Melbourne Cup Day and we need some poms to kick."

I told him I was just finishing a meeting with Gary, but would be there as quick as I could. "Bring the big fat fucking pommie baaastard with you. We can give him shit as well."

We quickly got through what we needed to and headed off for the 'kicking.' Unexpected drinking sessions are always the best, and this was to be a good one. The Long Bar was heaving with Australians, all the worse for alcohol, and we received a jeering cheer of welcome as we entered. It went as expected and we suffered the usual round of insults and gave back our fair share.

You have to be careful with Australians, though, and not use big words or anything too intellectual or technical. Three syllables are about the limit for words, with nursery rhymes and ring pull cans for the other two. Stick with those and they don't feel too intimidated.

Ask a British man on the street to name a poet and they would probably respond with Wordsworth, Coleridge or even Kipling. An American would probably give you Longfellow or Dickinson. Australians, however, would probably say, "Only pouffes write poetry."

Also, avoid talking about romance and love, if you can, as they struggle with these concepts; eg, Aussie romantic conversation:

"Hey, Sheila, d'you fuck?"

"Well, not till I met you, you smooth talking baaaastard."

They are improving I suppose, but you have to be wary of any country that regards pavlova as the high point of its culinary achievement and has a National Anthem called 'Advaaance Awstraylia Faaaair.' I'm not sure if they have a patron saint or not, but if they had to choose one, they would have difficulty. How on earth could you make a choice between Les Patterson, Ned Kelly and Kylie Minogue? Very, very difficult.

When challenged they always fall back on their sporting prowess, which in turn gives the opportunity for comments about their lack of alternative cultural stimuli. You then have to explain the meaning of 'culture' and 'stimuli,' so that they have half an idea of what you're talking about. Sad.

I must say here, though, that I do have some very good Australian friends, but as a race they are way too far up their own arses. As individuals they are fine, but get a bunch of them together…

Anyhow, back to the Long Bar. The evening progressed and Gary and I caught up with them very quickly and even managed to bring our conversation down to their level without too much effort. It was a good night and passed without incident, apart from a brief episode involving Boddington. There was an ageing, predatory 'sheila' there who decided that she was going to have him. She moved in and got close before making a grab for his tackle. Mike was terrified and literally climbed over the girl sitting next to him to escape. He was very pissed off with me, because I kept trying to push him back. He was like a drowning man, desperately trying to reach the surface of the water fifty feet above him. I let him make his escape eventually, but by that time he was white and sweating. He was very upset with me. "You baaastard. She must be fucking sawdust from the navel on down. Fuck! Don't tell any fucker."

I promised not to, but held the threat over him for months to come. I did make quite a few new acquaintances there and even found some intelligent Australian women, oxymoronic, though it sounds.

CHAPTER TWENTY

TRAVELS

For two years I was fairly well tied to Shanghai, Minhang and my work there, with occasional stints up to Anshan, to oversee and advise on operational issues at our other joint venture. My brief in Shanghai was to gradually hand over responsibilities to the Chinese staff and let them run everything, the aim being total withdrawal of all foreign staff. Payback on the operation was not happening as quickly as some poorly-informed and 'China ignorant' individuals had hoped and predicted, so ongoing costs had become an issue. I was a cost and my time in China was coming to an end, unless something else was found for me to do. It didn't look good.

There is always something round the corner. The corner arrived one day when I was talking to Gary, the General Director for China, who was in Shanghai on one of his escapes from the Anshan shithole.

It was very strange about Anshan. My contract allowed me to go back to England every eight weeks, spend two weeks there and return to China. It was felt that this would help to maintain sanity and perspective. For those in Anshan, however, it was different. They could go back to England every SIX weeks because it was a harsher working environment than Shanghai. Crazy. I suppose you could compare it to the difference between falling a hundred and fifty feet, as opposed to only one hundred, ie you're still dead when you hit the ground, but have less time to think about it. I found it to be a pain in the arse to do and very disruptive work wise, so I gave up after six months.

Apart from the jetlag factor, it took two weeks on returning to China to get things back on track, as in our absence, the Chinese had changed everything. Gary and the accountant tosser Clive in Anshan thought I was stupid, and religiously exercised their right. They even argued about their holiday entitlement. They thought that the thirteen weeks 'off' their contracts gave them should not impinge upon their annual holiday entitlement of six weeks. Nineteen weeks off in a year plus Chinese Holidays? Please! I was saving the company a lot of money by remaining in China – £15,000 a year – but was viewed with suspicion, which gave rise to the comment, "He's leaning too much towards the Chinese."

"Fuck them all" I thought.

Anyway, Gary was rabbiting on in his usual way about nothing when he dropped something into the conversation. "Oh, by the way. There's a guy coming over from the UK next month. He's David Sutton from Volac and he wants us to set up some meetings with people in the Chinese dairy sector. If everything works out, Volac want us to represent them in China and market and distribute their products."

I knew Volac and their people from the UK and had used their products – animal feed supplements and such – and they were a good company with good products. I'd also heard of David Sutton before, but had never met him. Geoff continued, "Yeah, but there's a problem. I'm going back to the UK next week and I haven't got time to sort anything out. I won't be here when he arrives, either."

"Well, who's going to organise it and look after him then?"

"You are. See what you can put together over the next couple of weeks."

That was it. I was off on yet another tangential trip, and this one was to lead me to most of China's Provinces over the next year. Maybe it's just the way things always are, but I wish something would happen to me on purpose just for once.

Coincidence then stepped in and lent a hand. The next day I was pondering and planning what to do about my visitor when translator Frank came into my office with Lao Song, the Sales Manager. They had come to tell me that Bright Dairy Company of Shanghai wanted to meet us, with a view to possible co-operation. Lao Song, it turned out, was a cattle specialist, had contacts all over China in the dairy industry and had been courting Bright for a month or two already. I listened and then put Lao Song in the picture about Volac. He was excited about one of their products in particular, Megalac, and before the morning was over we had worked out an itinerary for David Sutton that covered Shanghai and Beijing. By mid afternoon, visits and meetings had been arranged with six different companies and organisations in Shanghai and Beijing. Sorted.

Just before I was about to leave for home, Gary called me and asked, "Hi. Any thoughts yet on what you're going to do with the man from Volac?"

I played it cool. "Oh, yeah. You'll get a fax of the itinerary for your approval tomorrow."

He was silent for a few moments, then, "Fuck off. Seriously, what do you think you can sort out for him?"

"It's done, Gary. Have a look tomorrow."

"Ok, but this had better not be a wind-up."

Before lunch the next day he phoned again and there was suspicion in his voice when he said, "You knew about this before I told you, didn't you?" I indicated to the contrary and he continued, "OK, then. I'm impressed. It's all yours now. Go for it."

Over the next week I got my head down and had a good look at Volac's products, to see where they would fit into China. I had used one of their products, Megalac, regularly back in the UK, so I knew it worked. Without getting technical, it's a product that is added to feed to give extra energy to dairy cows. This helps them to maintain milk yield and improve fertility – always a problem with the mutated animal that is the modern dairy cow. Anyway, this was the product that had got Lao Song all excited and it definitely looked like the one that would feature.

In the UK I had just 'used' it and not bothered to try and understand what it did or how it worked, but now I had to know or look stupid. I also found out about the Chinese dairy industry and was staggered. It was HUGE. Knowing the size of China, I shouldn't have been surprised, but I was.

The Commercial Section at Consulate in Shanghai gave me a contact in Beijing, who was Co-Ordinator for the EU Dairy Project, a guy called Cliff Black – 'Criffa Brack' to the Chinese – and he was a gold mine of information. Facts, figures, history, herd distribution, plus contacts in every province. It was the one and only time that the Consulate ever 'gave' me anything useful. Chocolate fireguards.

By the time David Sutton stepped off the plane at Shanghai I was well on the way to being the company's China dairy expert. I knew a fair amount about cows anyway, having been responsible for feeding them, successfully, for twenty odd years. I prefer them to the other domesticated farm animals – pigs, sheep, chickens, turkeys and the like - which all have a great proclivity for falling over dead at the drop of a hat. Turkeys, in fact, are veritably suicidal. Cows, on the other hand, are bigger and stronger animals that can take a bit of stick.

I went to meet 'the man from Volac' at the airport and get him to the hotel. I'd been told to look out for a Samsonite suitcase being towed by somebody who looked like a farmer. I missed him at first and was wondering where the fuck he was, when I heard a Cheshire voice talking to another 'waiter' and asking, "Are you Russell Nash?"

I made myself known and had a look at him. Short, slightly portly, bespectacled, bushy moustache and a broad smile. I liked him immediately. I got him to the hotel, sorted his room out and was about to leave him to 'crash' when he enquired, "What time is it here?"

"12.30."

"Good. The bar'll be open. Let's have a couple of beers. They'll help me to sleep."

"OK. Follow me." a small alarm bell had rung, but you have to be a good host, don't you?

Seven pints of Kilkenny later I decided I had better go home and by then we were mates and he had become 'Sutty'. He too was impressed by what he thought I had sorted out for him. "Didn't know what to expect. Thought you might be another of those fuckin' tossers from your head office. Most of 'em couldn't organise a piss-up in a fuckin' brewery."

I left him in the bar finishing his beer at two and told him I would be back around seven, if that was all right, to eat with him. He thought it was a good idea and agreed, "OK. See you then. Going to bed after this one."

Around seven I went back, as promised, but couldn't find him. Couldn't find him, that is, where I expected him to be, ie jetlagged in his room. Mystery, until the small alarm bell jingled again. I made my way down to Charlie's and he was still in there and, by then, fending off ladies of the night. He greeted me effusively, as you would expect, with, "Russell, decided to push on through and have a really good sleep tonight. Done it before and it usually sorts out the jetlag. Do you want a pint?"

I don't know how many he had had, but it must have been a LOT. Sutty could drink and I was to be the one with whom he did most of his Chinese drinking. It was a dirty job, but... We had a few more and decided to give food a miss, before he finally called it a night around 10.30. Thank God it was Saturday night.

Sunday lunchtime came and I headed for the Crowne Plaza to meet up with Sutty, as promised. We were to have lunch, talk about the 'plan' and have a quick look at Shanghai. That's what we were supposed to do, but... 'the best laid plans of mice and men gang aft aglay', and so it turned out. We did have lunch and we did go through the 'plan' quickly before we decided that it was too hot to venture out. What to do? Stupid question. We decided to go and meet up with our mutual friend Kilkenny and continue our 'bonding'.

We found that we had a lot in common and couldn't understand how we had never bumped into each other in the UK, in, what was a relatively small industry. Anyway, we made up for lost time. I also found out that Sutty's normal practice in dealing with jetlag was to have a two-day bender. He said that this sorted him out best and, apart from the hangover, was more enjoyable than other methods. To assist in this he always tried to time his long-haul flights so that he arrived wherever it was on either Friday or Saturday – very well organised.

Drink, however, was his only vice and unlike me, he steered clear of other sins of the flesh. He enjoyed women's company in bars and things, but that's as far as it ever went.

Being able to drink is a more than useful attribute when doing business in China, and it speeded up the 'getting to know you' process for him and endeared him to the Chinese during his ten-day stay. We stayed in Charlie's for most of the afternoon before deciding to have a look in some of the other drinking haunts - Hard Rock, O'Malley's, Long Bar - rounding off the evening with a visit to the Step Bar, across the road from the hotel. The girls loved him and Sutty, being on expenses, wasn't too averse to throwing his hospitality around. He became a regular during this and subsequent stays in Shanghai. He liked the place and the place liked him. As we were leaving at the end of the night, he stopped me and said, "Listen. They're playing my song."

I listened and heard a Chinese version of 'Yellow River' coming over the speakers. There was a mispronunciation that made it more than appropriate: 'Yellow Liver.'

Monday morning saw us visiting Bright Dairy Company and getting our first customer – a flying start. Bright had about forty thousand dairy cows in and around Shanghai, so they were very important. We had to go through the usual rings and hoops of course, to get them to do business, but I was surprised that we did it so quickly. Giving them a couple of tonnes of free product and extended credit terms was what did it, but it was worth it.

Over the next three days we made visits to other

companies and to the Shanghai Dairy Federation, with equal success. Sutty was happy and it didn't do my credibility any harm either. Again, there was a lot of 'hospitality' that had to be coped with, but it made a pleasant change to see someone else on the receiving end. He was lucky though, because I was there to guide, assist and advise on his trip through the Chinese business minefield. Still, he spent a fair amount of time in slack-jawed amazement - and this was a man who had done business on all continents. However, he was adaptable and got into the swing of it quicker than most. We had a good time and more than once we were the 'last men standing,' when the Chinese had surrendered to our superior drinking capacity and so it continued.

Next we were off to Beijing to continue the quest. It was much the same as Shanghai, apart from Sutty's run in with Chinese 'unofficial' officialdom. He needed to get his product, Megalac, registered, and had organised an appointment with the necessary department. Off he went to see 'the man', leaving me in the hotel. He was away for about three hours, during which time I busied myself sampling Beijing beer. He returned and sought me out. He was not happy. "Get me a fucking beer. Quick." Beer was supplied – quick.

"What's wrong? You couldn't get it registered?"

"Yeah, registered OK, but it cost me a thousand dollars 'under the table' before they would do it. Thieving bastards and, of course, no fucking receipt. They're worse than the fucking South Americans and Russians. Bastards."

We put the world to rights thereafter, and all was well by the end of the night. By the time Sutty departed we had a 'plan' – fairly ambitious, but we figured that if we managed to crowbar 30% of it from our respective companies, we would be doing OK.

I spent the next couple of weeks gathering more information (thank you, Cliff Black) and assembling a business plan, which I tentatively submitted. Much to my amazement, it was accepted. The attractive 'bottom lines' were probably what did it. I set about assembling a team, which consisted of Lao Song, Zheng Xi and Peter Li, an escapee from Liaohe. Peter (Li Guozhi) had been Human Resources Manager in our Northern JV until he had fallen foul of the Chinese partner, Mr Huang. There seemed to be no reason for Huang's dislike and persecution of Peter, other than the fact that Peter was not 'his man' and leaned too much towards the Western way of doing things. Peter was too good a man to lose, so he had been sent down to Shanghai, in the hope that I could find him something to do. The timing was just right. My by then assistant Zheng Xi was too young and had no business experience, so he was a good man for the home base. It suited him and gave him time to fuck about on his computer, which he loved.

Peter was full of enthusiasm and we became and still are good friends. Our friendship was cemented by the time we spent together over the next year or so, flitting about here and there in China. We went virtually everywhere and it all became a blur of flights, hotels, meetings and banquets. Looking back on it, I could have been visiting the same place repeatedly, for all the difference there was from one to the next. Sad really. There were, however, some places that were worthy of note and for a variety of reasons. Qingdao and its Province, Shandong, were my favourite place and Beijing and Chendu were both memorable.

Qingdao. Ah, Qingdao! I think I liked it because it and its weather reminded me of my home town by the sea. That and the people. The people there are more straightforward than those in the rest of China because of a historic German influence. The Germans, God bless them, also showed them how to make beer and Qingdao beer is the best in China, as well as being famous worldwide. We made several trips up there to visit dairies, dairy organisations, government departments and the Nestle company. Nestle were trying, patiently, to educate peasant dairy farmers into the ways of Western dairy culture. Good luck! Not worth talking to for another five years – at least. We courted the others with a fair modicum of success and had some good times into the bargain – most of them, I have to admit, with the help of alcohol and 'company'. We were lucky in that Qingdao was one of Lao Song's old stamping grounds and he already knew most of the people we visited and revisited.

The hospitality was immense and at times, overwhelming. This resulted in quite a few lost or very blurry hours, with Lao Song suffering most, as his capacity was very low. It was on our third or fourth visit that he suffered the worst. Cliff Black just happened to be visiting

Qingdao at the same time as us, so we arranged to meet and have a chat. Our meeting was to be in the Qingdao Holiday Inn at 4 pm. After yet another lunchtime banquet at which there was a lot of 'hospitality,' we made it to the hotel in time and I introduced Peter and Lao Song to Cliff. Lao Song then performed a double pirouette before collapsing, full length and comatose, on a lobby sofa. We left him there for the course of our meeting and at the end Cliff's only comment was, "That's got to be the most impressive entrance to a hotel I've ever seen."

Apart from Lao Song's knowledge of the place, we also benefited from the services of a regular taxi driver. We'd used him on our first trip and thereafter Peter used to call him when we were going there again. He would meet us at the airport, stay with us for the day and, very often, the night. He took us to some 'interesting' places and I think he enjoyed himself as much as we did. I'm putting an insert here of something I wrote at the time that was the result of one visit to an 'interesting' place. Before anyone reads this let me state for the record that it is pure fiction, based upon observations made by both Chinese and Westerners – honest. Who am I trying to kid?

Her first "White Ghost"

Shy and unsure. Apprehensive and scared but filled with curiosity. Young and beautiful, with hair like silk and skin as soft as a baby. A Chinese child woman. Lying together in the half dark, she was tentative and coy, still torn between fear and curiosity. Small hands reached down exploring. "Wah." She gave a small wail and her body quivered. "Slow, gentle, no hurt me. Me small, me small. You big, you big." Slow and gentle it was – to start.

The clenched hands and rigid body relaxed and melted and the look of fear in her eyes and on her face changed to surprise, wonder and pleasure as places within her were touched and awakened for the first time. Sighs and moans of pleasure grew in number and volume and legs encircled waist as she rose to take and to give. Deeper, stronger, faster. It finished and she clung, not wanting it to end.

"Again! Again!" Again, again after she used hands and mouth to bring me back.

"No condom. Want all!"

Again, again, impaled with her body arched and perspiring above me, caught in the moonlight streaming through the window. Her dark nipples erect and her face a mask of mixed ecstasy, lust and pain. Taking all, giving herself sweet pain until she collapsed, limp and panting on my chest after a screaming orgasm, then sliding off into exhausted, contented sleep, with an arm and leg draped over me.

The morning. "Again? Again?" Again, again. After – "You go?"

"Yes, I go."

"I want you come back quick. See you again. You come back? OK?"

"OK I come back."

Another 'Westernised' Chinese Maiden?'

– Anon.'

The 'child woman' in question was Wu Xiao Jing, who was a secretary at the Qingdao Dairy Federation. We had had a meeting in the afternoon which ran on into a banquet and then to karaoke – our taxi driver knew a good place. Xiao Jing had been in our meeting as translator (she wasn't very good) for their side and had come with us to the banquet. When it was time to go on, much to everyone's surprise, she came with us. Surprise, because karaoke is normally a male thing, particularly after business banquets. Her boss wasn't too happy about her going, but she was determined and would not be dissuaded. I didn't give it much thought, apart from being amused at her boss. She was obviously going to cramp his style.

Once we were in the place, her reason for going became very clear to all. She was after me. I am a gentleman and always try to make women happy, so what else could I do but go along with her and help her in her quest?

As the evening progressed it became apparent to all what was going on, as she sat tight up beside me with her hand on my knee, feeding me snacks and choosing songs for me. It was no surprise to anyone when, at the end of the night, she squeezed into our taxi and went back to the hotel with us. She was lovely, if a little small, and was as tight as a tube of smarties. Mmm. We had a busy night and morning and by the end of it she could hardly walk. She was happy, though. Sadly, it was to be our one and only.

We went back to Qingdao three months later and I met her again. She was very happy to see me and friendly enough, but said "Russell, I have boyfriend now. Serious boyfriend."

That was it. She was twenty-six, so she had reached the age, for a Chinese woman, where she 'needed' to get married or be regarded as being 'strange'. Old China is still very much alive, though things are changing – slowly.

Beijing. Beijing is a place I am not too keen on. It's smaller than Shanghai, as most places are, but still BIG. It seemed that every time I went there I had a bad or not too good experience. Also, it always seemed to be either too hot or too cold, with no happy medium – my own fault for going there at the wrong times. It's grander than Shanghai, though attempts are being made to make Pudong a place of wide boulevards and open spaces. I think my view of Beijing has always been jaundiced since my first contact with its airport – nightmare. First impressions etc. Maybe not, though, as something bad inevitably seemed to happen – delayed flights, ripped off by taxi drivers (always), lost hotel reservations and cancelled appointments.

Taxi drivers, in particular, pissed me off – often. Airport taxi drivers everywhere assume that because you are a foreigner who has just arrived you are fair game. In Beijing, though, they still assume that you are a halfwit, even after you have told them where to go in Chinese and had a brief conversation with them about where you are from and how long you have been in China. They then make their attempts to rip you off, one way or another, whether it be with a detour, a 'broken' meter or by slipping you some dud money in your change. It's best never to give them a 100rmb note, as you will almost certainly get a forged 50 in your change.

I did all the touristy bits of course – Great Wall, Forbidden City, Tiananmen Square and the rest. I almost got sunstroke walking across T Square in mid July and then frostbite in February. The people aren't too good either. In Shanghai you know you will get ripped off and cheated sometimes and Shanghai people are fairly open about the fact. In Beijing, however, they try to give the impression that they are as pure as the driven snow. Hypocritical, and dishonest about their dishonesty.

In amongst it all, I did manage to get some business done and make some useful Ministry contacts, so it wasn't a total loss. There were other 'things' as well – of course. The ongoing Yellow Fever sampling and testing procedure continued unabated. Again, though, while Shanghai admits to its problems and shortcomings and turns a blind eye – 'live and let live' - Beijing takes a very much 'holier than thou' attitude, accompanied by an outstretched palm. Hotel and security staff are very strict on 'entertaining' until you slip them an aid to blindness and forgetfulness.

It was a cold, cold February evening and I was at a loose end. Meetings finished, business done and on my own in the bar of the Jianguo Hotel. The rest of the 'team' had gone back to Shanghai, but I had to stay for a meeting with a Junior Agricultural Minister the next day. I wasn't going to see him alone and had elicited the services of our company Nutritionist, Alex Wang, from Anshan. He had gone to university with the man I was to meet and was to arrive the following morning. Alex was a good guy and had done his doctorate in Australia, so his English was good.

Good, that is, for someone with an ocker accent. 'G'day, mate' from a Chinese mouth was slightly incongruous. A bit like Glaswegian Italians – 'Nae chipsa left, ye ken.' Or 'I woulda lika to go back to the land ova my faithers.'

I was pleasantly surprised by the bar and its name – Charlie's. The same as my local in Shanghai. It also had a live band, who were belting out the usual mix of Philippine band music – 'An' now, by special request, (liar), we'd like to sing a classic song by the Eagles, Hotel (fucking) California'. I like that song when the Eagles sing it, but have heard it done badly too many times in China and now I shudder every time a band begins to perform it. The bar had its usual collection of 'ladies' trying to score and brighten up someone's evening, but nobody was biting – too early.

I had a brief, one-sided conversation with a loud, drunk, Texan American in which he extolled the qualities of Chinese women and Asian women in general. He was preaching to the converted, but wouldn't shut up and I finally got rid of him by making an extended visit to the toilet. When I came back he was curled up in a corner, snoring. He was probably one of the most objectionable people I've ever met on my travels. A real pig. I dumped his business card and had been sharp enough to make sure I hadn't given him one of mine. As Groucho Marx put it: "I've had a wonderful evening, but this wasn't it". or "I never forget a face, but in your case I'll make an exception".

Anyway, I'd just about decided to call it a night when an up to then silent, solitary woman introduced herself.

"Hi. You look as if you're on your own. Want some company?"

She was tall and slim with the usual other Chinese bits – brown eyes and long black hair. Nice and very, very good English. She didn't wait for my answer and slid into the stool next to me. She began our conversation with a deck clearing statement. "I'm not a prostitute" she said. Then, "My name's Linda Xu and I come from Dalian. What about you?"

I supplied the necessary response as well as telling her that I knew Dalian, in Liaoning Province, fairly well. She seemed pleased and said, "I haven't been back there for three years, so maybe I won't know the place when I do go back."

We talked thereafter and I found that she worked for an advertising company in Baoding, just outside Beijing, and was staying in the hotel for a couple of nights while she attended a training course. She was twenty-seven, unmarried and had broken up with her boyfriend about three months before – a German. Lucky escape, I thought, but didn't say. She was still rebounding and maybe looking for a soft, hard landing - or something. It was strange in that there was no conversation about spending the night together. It just seemed to be assumed, almost as if it had been prearranged.

We left the bar around ten o'clock and made our way upstairs. My room was the choice, because it was on the Executive Floor, but as we left the elevator she stopped and said, "Wait a moment". I watched as she made her way to the security guard, who was sitting at the end of the corridor. There was a brief exchange and she returned, smiling, "OK. Fifty yuan. Now no problems."

I was puzzled for a moment until I realised that she had just 'squared' things with the guard. Apparently she had stayed in the hotel with her German boyfriend and knew what was required to 'smooth the way'. I offered her the fifty, but she declined with, "No problem. You bought all the drinks".

Inside my room it was as if we had known each other for ages. There was no shyness or hesitation and we showered together as if we did it every day. Her body was good and firm with upturned dark nipples on small breasts. She was muscular for a woman, with a flat, hard stomach and strong legs – very strong, as my ribs would attest to later. Her pubic hair was silky and straight – love it. She gave me a quick appraisal and her approval: "I'm looking forward to this. It's been a while. I tried a Chinese man last week, but no good. Couldn't feel anything. I think I'll feel you."

In bed she asked me a question. "What do you like?"

"Everything."

"Good. We can do everything." So we did.

She was good. Not amazing, but good. We didn't sleep until one o'clock and in the morning I was awakened to her taking advantage of my 'morning glory.' Mmm. What a way to start the day. We went down to breakfast together and then I walked her out to her ride to work and we said 'Goodbye.' Over. There was no deep feeling, but we kept in touch for a month or two by phone and email, until it faded away of its own accord. 'Ships that pass in the night'. Ah well…

Next on the 'places to remember' list was Chendu in Sichuan Province. Many people think the population in China is centred on the eastern and southern areas, but the largest concentration of Chinese is in Sichuan and Chongqing. At one time Chongqing was part of Sichuan, but because of its population density it was given municipality status – the same as Tianjin in the north. The city of Chongqing is heading towards a population of twenty million with another twenty or so in the surrounding area. When you add this to Chendu's ten million plus, you come up with a number not too far away from the total population of Britain. That's a lot of people and an important place to go if you want to hit a big market. That's why we were there.

Peter and I made the trip from Shanghai to meet up with the Chendu Dairy Federation – thanks, yet again, Cliff Black. We arrived and checked into the Chendu Holiday Inn around 7 pm. Peter was more excited and enthusiastic than usual for some reason and was bursting to get out and about in the city; something to do with 'Sichuan Sisters', or so he said. As usual my checking in took longer – photocopying of visa and passport – and Peter was impatient. "I'll go up to my room now. Call you later. OK?" Off he went and I followed about five minutes later.

As I got into the room my phone was ringing – Peter already. As I picked up the phone, I thought I would try something, so I said, "Wei, ni hao. Ni shen yao shenma?" ('Hello. What do you want?' in standard Chinese receptionist speak.)

Much to my surprise Peter responded with an apology. "Dui bu qi, dui bu qi." (Sorry, sorry) and hung up, only to call back a few seconds later. "That was you before, wasn't it? Fuck. Your Chinese is getting good."

We hit the town, but it was a big letdown, as it was new to both of us and we didn't know the places to go. We also had an early morning meeting about half an hour away from the hotel, so we gave up at about eleven and returned to the hotel. There would be another time and there was.

The next morning we set off at 7.30 and headed to the outskirts of the city. Boring. All Chinese cities look the same to me now and this was just another one on the list, as far as I was concerned. We were to meet a Madam Wang, who was President of the Chendu Dairy Federation and one of the few women, then, in a position of leadership and control in China.

She was impressive, but not for the reasons you would think, ie she wasn't a power or control freak. She was practical, direct, intelligent, matter of fact and very perceptive, and her English was good enough for her not to need a translator. (Very often English-speaking Chinese will use a translator in meetings, so that they can hide behind them and give themselves more time to think.) The way she looked wasn't bad either. She was about five foot four and well put together for her age, which was about forty.

The meeting and the day that followed, visiting dairy farms and dairy companies, went well. We met up with Madam Wang again around 4.30 and discussed what the next moves should be in our co-operation and it went well again. Job done. She finished off with an invitation to dinner, as expected, to seal our co-operation agreement. I was tired, having had a bad night's sleep, and could have done without it, but it had to be done. Maybe it wouldn't be too bad. She was only a woman after all. How wrong can you be?

We met up with her and some of the other people we had met during the course of the day at around six o'clock. Hopefully, if things went the usual Chinese way, everything would be wrapped up around eight. The meal followed the usual pattern, but there was a surprise. Madam Wang could drink. She could drink a LOT. It was one of the very few times I was under pressure in China, and she almost saw me off. I was relieved and very, very tired when it came to an end, as expected, around 8 pm. There was the standard invitation to go to karaoke, which I declined, unusually. Peter, however, was very keen to make up for his unsuccessful night before, so he accepted their invitation.

Madam Wang said that she had had enough to drink as well and didn't like singing anyway, so said she would go home. She turned to me and said, "Russell, my home is on the way to your hotel, so we can share a taxi, if you want."

"Sure. Good idea." So off we went in a taxi.

As we neared her home she said, "It's very early. Would you like to come in for a drink?" Then she laughed and said, "Not alcohol. I think we have both had enough." I agreed.

As we were walking from the taxi to her apartment I said, "What does your husband do?"

"He works for the Chongqing Municipal Government. I don't see him very much because we are both so busy." Small alarm bell.

"Do you have any children?"

"Yes, a daughter. She's in boarding school in Beijing." Bigger alarm bell.

In the apartment she busied herself squeezing some fresh orange juice, while keeping up a conversation with me from the kitchen. She joined me with the drinks and the conversation continued along normal lines until she said something out of the blue, "How many Chinese women have you slept with?"

"A few. How many foreigners have you slept with?"

Her answer was good. "Not enough, and I like sleeping with foreigners."

"Once more into the breach for God, for Harry…" I thought it best to find out what her full name was before we went any further and she said, "It's Wang Ling." and then, "You want to stay on the sofa or go to bed?"

I indicated that I didn't mind either way, so she stripped off in front of me and helped me with my undressing. Then she sat me back down and dropped to her knees, where she observed, "I don't think you will come very quick. Too much to drink. Good." She kept her head down for a couple of minutes and then straddled me, laughing, "Big. Good. I'll have to measure you and tell my girlfriends. Ha ha. I want you to come now. Fill me."

Her body was on the soft side, but still good for a forty year old and still very good to touch. She coped OK with me saying, between gasps, "Biggest one so far. I like. Stay all night?"

I didn't and couldn't answer, as my mouth was full of raspberry nipple, but I thought, 'so far?' I did stay all night and we got to know each other, in a manner of speaking. I thought she'd been joking when she said she would have to measure me, but she produced a tape and, after making sure I was as big as I could be, she did the deed: "Wah. Twenty-one centimetres. I'll have to tell my friends. You could get a job in yellow movies. Wah!"

She decided she liked doggy style the best. "You feel biggest like this" was her explanation. She also liked to suck and suck and suck. I didn't complain. She also liked me using my mouth on her and commented, "Why can't Chinese men do it right?"

We must have gone to sleep around one o'clock and the last thing I remember was her saying, "Don't worry. I'll get you back to the hotel for breakfast."

The morning came and we showered together before she took me back to the Holiday Inn. She was sore. "Too much. I want you again, but I don't think it would be comfortable. Will you kiss me there again and I will suck you?" After, she complained, "Not very much to eat."

I told her that this wasn't surprising, given what she had already 'eaten' with both of her mouths the night before. She giggled and said, "Mmm. You're right. You need rest and food now." Then, laughing, "Milk is good."

She took me back to the Holiday Inn and decided she would stay for breakfast. Luckily, Peter didn't arrive in the restaurant until we were almost finished. If he'd seen us arrive together two and two would definitely have made five. He didn't seem surprised to see her there and it is fairly normal for business people to meet for breakfast in China.

She left shortly after Peter arrived, saying she had a busy day ahead, but was looking forward to our future relationship. This last was said with a smirk. After she left Peter was quiet for a while and then asked, "How was she?" I gave him a raised eyebrow look and he continued, "Everybody knew what she was going to do. They said she does it all the time with foreigners. Come on. How was she?"

Laughingly, I gave up any pretence of innocence and indicated that she had been 'Very OK.' Chendu would be and was visited again – and again.

Most of the travelling I did was by air, but I did make quite a few trips by road to places within easy distance of Shanghai. I spent a lot of time in Hangzhou, in Zhejiang Province, south of Shanghai, but most of this was recreational and I've written about it separately. However, I did make many trips into Jiangsu Province that were mostly work related. Trips to Wuxi, Suzhou and Nanjing were regular and 'there and back' was always completed in one day, so nothing to report. Nothing except boring highway trips, meetings and banquets. Most of the trips back were spent in sleep after too much beer and or baijiu, but one day I was awake for most of the time, letting my mind wander where it would, and the result was the following. Incidentally, this was the piece that the CEO picked off the fax machine in the UK, giving rise to him expressing his concern about me:

'A dip into insanity. Went to Jiangsu yesterday to look at a new sieving machine. The journey was three hours plus, there and back. On the way back, everyone started to nod off, except me and the driver, I hasten to add. Nothing to do except look at the countryside and reflect. I began to hum bits and pieces of songs to myself and among the selection was an Elvis Presley song — Occupation G.I. Blues. Not prompted by anything, it just popped in there, as songs do. They do with me anyway. I began to mess around with the words in my head and what follows is the result. Apologies to Elvis fans and the original writers, Tepper & Bennett.'

Expat Shanghai Blues

I've got the one, two, three, four Expat Shanghai Blues
(Chorus) From the top of my head to the heels of my Western shoes
And if I don't go to the UK soon I'm gonna blow my fuse.

We try to make money but all that we do here is wait.
We try to make money but all that we do here is wait.
But if it don't happen soon Mr Weston will say "Too late."
(Gary Weston – owner)
I've got the one, two, three, four Expat Shanghai Blues

From the top of my head to the heels of my Western shoes
And if I don't go to the UK soon I'm gonna blow my fuse.

The women are lovely as flower but be careful of those,
The women are lovely as flowers but be careful of those.
After two weeks they start looking at wedding clothes.

I've got the one, two, three, four Expat Shanghai Blues
From the top of my head to the heels of my Western shoes
And if I don't go to the UK soon I'm gonna blow my fuse.

The food here is fine but there are times when it gives me grief.
The food here is fine but there are times when it gives me grief.
Sometimes I'd give my right arm for a slice of British beef.

I've got the one, two, three, four Expat Shanghai Blues
From the top of my head to the heels of my Western shoes
And if I don't go to the UK soon I'm gonna blow my fuse.

Sometimes it gets lonely as if I don't even exist.
Sometimes it gets lonely as if I don't even exist
Well that's a real good time to go out and get pissed.
(Clean version) And I often wonder if I'm ever missed.

I've got the one, two, three, four Expat Shanghai Blues
From the top of my head to the heels of my Western shoes
And if I don't go to the UK soon I'm gonna blow my fuse.

Don't get the impression that I want to be on my way.
Don't get the impression that I want to be on my way

Because there's nowhere else on Earth I'd rather stay.

But I still get those one, two, three, four Expat Shanghai Blues
From the top of my head to the heels of my Western shoes
And if I don't go to the UK soon I'm gonna blow my fuse.

Expat Shanghai Blues. Expat Shanghai Blues.
Expat Shanghai Bluuueees…
Zai jian..

I did, however, have one extended trip deep into Jiangsu that is worth mentioning. We were contacted by a company from Xinhua County who asked us to go and see them. They had a feed mill they wanted me to look at and pass an opinion on. What they really wanted was our money and technology – as usual. Still, it was worth a trip. It was a six-hour drive and by the time we were there it was dark. The dark was good because it gave me a sight I will never forget. As is normal in China, they were burning off the stubble in the rice fields – totally against the law. It was as if we were driving through a corridor of fire with the colour of the flames distorted to deep orange by the tinted windows of the car. The effect was amazing. It was like driving through a Dali painting or Dante's Inferno. Beautiful.

As soon as we got there it began. The hospitality was overwhelming – they really wanted our money. Our time there was a blur of meetings, visits, baijiou and more baijiu. They even offered me a house, if I would go and help them. Maybe I should have and maybe I would have, if it hadn't been so 'sticksville'. There was one thing, however, that really got to me. Fish. Xinhua is famous for its fish farms – there are acres of them - and supplies about a thousand tonnes to Shanghai every week. They are proud of it and try to get you to sample every variety of aquatic food that they produce. I like fish, but… too much.

Thankfully, we had the second night off and were left to our own devices. What to do? We hit the high spots of Xinghua City and covered them all in about a minute, before deciding to go bowling. I'd only ever bowled once before, so Frank took it upon himself to show me how. Do you believe in beginner's luck? I do now. After an initial, abortive, attempt, I proceeded to hit four strikes in a row – a 'turkey'. Frank probably still doesn't believe it was only my second time.

We were on the way back to the hotel when a strange thing happened. I was propositioned by a woman. Not strange in itself, but in strange circumstances. It was a one-horse town and, as we waited to cross the street at the only set of traffic lights, a brand new black Audi pulled up beside us. A very nice car, but it looked totally out of place. Then the window slid down to reveal the driver. It was a woman and a very attractive woman. She smiled invitingly at me and said something in Chinese which I couldn't understand. Frank then had a conversation with her for a couple of minutes, after which she gave me another beautiful smile before driving off. I was intrigued and asked Frank, "What did she say?"

"She wanted to know if you would spend the night with her. I told her no."

"No? You bastard!" I could have killed him. I often wonder what she was doing there and whether she was a professional or an opportunist. Thank you, Frank.

The hotel we were staying in was the best one in the city, but it was still shit. It's the only hotel I've ever been in where I was let into my room and not given a key, ie if you left your room after they had let you in, you couldn't get back in again unless the receptionist opened the door for you. All to do with ensuring there were no immoral goings on, so Frank said. He probably chose it for that reason, good Christian boy that he was. Never mind.

Next morning we were up early and ready for the six-hour drive back to Shanghai. Let's go. No - our hosts met us at the hotel door and insisted that they take us for breakfast. I resigned myself to it, but insisted that there would be no alcohol – still hung over. They had laid on a banquet breakfast for us, which was nice, but way over the top. There was also a karaoke machine in the room – No! Yes. A waitress began to sing screechy Chinese karaoke and I made the mistake of applauding. She was very happy and did it again. Too early. Frank began to laugh, so I asked, "What's so funny?"

"They want you to sing an English song."

"Tell them to fuck off." I resisted and then gave in. "OK, but only one. Give me the song book."

I looked through the book and there was only one song. Shit. It was 'My Heart Will Go On'. At the time, the movie 'Titanic' and its 'song' were very, very popular in China and Celine Dion could have stood a fair chance of being elected as Party Chairman. I hated it and avoided listening to it whenever I could. If a band began to sing it, the audience would applaud wildly and then give them another ovation when they finished. I, on the other hand, used the beginning of the song as a cue to make an extended visit to the toilet, returning only after I'd heard the second ovation.

I also hated, or came to hate, two other songs; the Philippine or Chinese rendition of 'Hotel California' – love it by the Eagles – and another dire song called 'Sha-la-la-la-la'. This second one really raised my hackles and even managed to followed me back to Britain; I arrived back in the UK on a two-week visit, jumped into the car provided for me, switched on the radio and… 'Sha-la-la-la-la. Sha-la-la in the morning….' Arrrg. No escape.

Anyway, I performed my song and got away with it. Frank laughed again, "They want you to sing it again."

"Really tell them to fuck off this time."

Breakfast over, we went on our way, but not before they gave me a 'gift'. I was apprehensive because, on an exploratory visit to them, they had given a gift of twenty soft shell turtles to some Chinese representatives of the company – live soft shell turtles. I breathed a sigh of relief when they gave me four small traditional Chinese pictures. We went on our way and sadly, for them, we decided not to pour any money into another Chinese black hole.

All in all I visited every Province bar two, Guizhou and Xi Zang (Tibet), and unfortunately, I can remember very little of any of them. It was flight, hotel, meeting, banquet, hotel and flight for most places. It reminded me of the Simon and Garfunkel song 'Homeward Bound' in many ways. Xin Jiang, Gansu, Ningxia, Qinghai and Inner Mongolia were memorable because I never want to go back there. Shitholes all. Others, like Heilongjiang and Jilin, are remembered because they were fucking cold and Guangdong and Guangxi because they were fucking hot.

Of all the Provinces I visited because of work, I think I liked Shandong and Yunnan the best. Shandong because it reminded me of home and Yunnan because it was beautiful. The rest of them were much of a muchness and a blur of high-rises, airports, people and traffic and I doubt whether any of them would improve if I were to revisit as a tourist.

As a tourist I only went to Zhejiang and Hainan Island. I liked Zhejiang and escaped to it whenever I could from Shanghai, spending many weekends in Hangzhou and Ningbo. Hainan was good and seemed to be a different world to the rest of China. It's a tropical paradise and a great place to laze about and do absolutely nothing. I'm good at that.

SHANGHAI LIMBO

All good things come to an end, and the day dawned that heralded my 'good thing' ending in China. I was being sent home, the reason being that, while I had successfully launched Megalac in China, it was considered that I didn't know enough about cows to carry it further. The real reasons, I found out later, were that I was rumoured to have a drinking problem and that I was 'too Chinese' in my lifestyle. All this came to light much later, after I had left the company, when, as I've said elsewhere, Arsehole Clive in Anshan showed his true colours by shacking up with his translator, Bunny. He it was, that had put the poison into the CEO's ear. I won't forget him.

I freely admit to going native and I have to say, I found it an advantage when dealing with Chinese people. Others thought this too, but, unfortunately, they weren't the ones who were whispering in the CEO's ear. Drinking? Yes, I used to drink, but it never interfered with work, except when it was a necessary part of it. I was to return to the UK, to run a new project that was more in line with my 'core skills.' My company specialised in 'buzz words' and phrases and they cropped up frequently – words like 'synergy' and, the aforementioned, 'core skills' were the ones on the go at the time.

There was nothing I could do about it, so I prepared myself. Part of my preparation was a quick round of farewell emails to contacts and friends in China and, out of the blue, a response came from a friend, Chris Helm, in Hong Kong. He asked, "Would you be interested in gong to work in Hanoi?"

"Yes" was my brief answer and then things began to happen - very quickly. I got an early Saturday morning phone call (what a hangover) followed by a trip to Hong Kong for an interview with the company owner, Jack Brown, and the job was done. I was to be Deputy General Director and Chief Financial Officer for the American Feed company, Vietnam. All this took place in April and it was agreed that I should start in August, after I had separated myself from my old company.

I returned to England to wrap things up at work and I was looking forward to telling them to stick it up their arse. It worked out better than I could have hoped, as the 'job' I was earmarked for didn't materialise. This meant that instead of resigning, I became entitled to a redundancy payment. A tidy sum. Plus, I was also given three months' salary in lieu of notice. I decided to escape from the UK early, both to avoid tax liability and to get away from a country that had begun to depress me more than I can say. So it was back to Shanghai for a month or so of R&R.

It was a strange month and a forerunner to my life to be in Hanoi. I relaxed and decided to enjoy myself. Big Ron lent a hand, but he was working, so could only join me at the weekends. I kept myself busy.

One of the more memorable escapades started as a quiet Tuesday night in Charlie's. I was at my usual place in the bar and was talking to an Australian guy, I forget his name, when two women entered the bar. By their uniforms they were United Airlines Stewardesses and they were roaring drunk. United Airlines used the hotel for layovers – remember the term 'layover'.

They spotted us and made a beeline to our corner of the bar. They were both in their mid thirties – one black and one white and blonde. The black one, who I found out was called Jodie, was immediately all over me. She was beautiful, so I didn't mind at all. The blonde one, Kaye, tried to give the same treatment to the Australian, but he wasn't having any and left the bar after about five minutes. Fucking coward. Jodie carried on and Kaye made an attempt to join in, but couldn't get near me, so she decided to go back to her room. I was grasping the edge of the barstool and Jodie manoeuvred herself until my knuckles were right on the button and she went for it saying, "Yeah, that's the spot. That's the spot. Don't move your hand." Then, "I'll go first. I don't want this to look like a pick up thing." Too late. "My room's 1202. I've got some condoms if you want to use them. I don't care. Don't be long."

She left, but before I followed, five minutes later, one of the bar staff, Angel, approached me and asked, "Russell, is that woman hooker? If she is Chinese, we ask her go. Bad, bad woman." I agreed. Bad, bad woman.

Five minutes later I knocked on her door and she opened it, pulling me inside quickly. She was half undressed and grabbed my crotch as her tongue flashed down my throat. "C'mon. Shower quick." We showered and she continued her attention, "Hey, not bad for a white boy an' you ain't even all the way hard yet."

It was my first black experience and I was fascinated. I can still see her black hands and her bright red nails touching me, the crispy wiriness of her pubic hair and feel of her skin. Her skin. Ohhh!

When I was hard enough, which was quickly, she hoisted herself on to me and went for it. I hesitated and asked, "What about a condom?"

"Fuck it, I can always give you a blow job if I change my mind. I will anyway, before we're done."

We decided that things would be easier on the bed, so we disengaged. On the bed she told me, "You can do anything you want to me, but I don't like it up the ass. Fuck it, you can do that to me too, if you want."

We had only just started again when there was a knock on the door. Jodie was angry and shouted, "Fuck! Who is it?" It was Kaye, so Jodie said, "Hey, I think my buzzer is in your room. Go get it and bring your own. Bring a bluey as well. I've got a live one here."

Buzzer? Bluey? All was revealed when she let Kaye in shortly after. The buzzer was a vibrator and the bluey was Viagra. Kaye said, "Better take it now. You're gonna need it. I've got some catching up to do."

She stripped off quickly and grabbed Jodie, pushed her onto the bed and sank the full length of her vibrator into her. They moved into a 69 position as I watched and worked on each other with mouths and machines. I wish I'd had a camera. Both had fantastic bodies, though Kay had had a boob job – a good boob job. Jodie's breasts were real, with the left slightly bigger than the right. The plantation boss had been involved in her ancestry and she was very dark, but her facial features were not negroid and she reminded me of a very dark Halle Berry.

Black and white. Hope I do it again sometime. Bad girls. I joined them. It was my first and only time to try Viagra and I was glad I did. We had a good time and they finished off with a double blowjob, sharing the proceeds. Bad girls. By that time I had had enough and, I think, so had they. We slept and I woke around three in the morning and took my leave. They were leaving at eight in the morning and I never saw them again. Ah well. At least I found out why they are called 'layovers.'

With regard to 'adventures', this one was the high point. There were others and they all seemed to just happen, rather than be sought after or organised. I had an interesting afternoon with an old friend called Annie (not the boss of the Step Bar) which is touched on in another part of my writings, so I won't repeat it. She was very good, though.

Another dalliance was with a young lady called Joy. She was from Guangdong and had come to Shanghai to make her fortune – so she said. Her efforts, however, seemed to be more directed in trying to get her hands on somebody else's fortune. She was looking for a husband – any nationality, as long as they were rich. She wasn't a hooker, but was well on the way down that path. Our 'relationship' was one of convenience and we were, almost always, together when we each had nothing better to do.

Our first time together was just such an occasion. It was a quiet Monday night in Charlie's and the band's night off, so there were only three or four people tucked away in corners. I had my back to the door and, in the bar mirror, I caught the sight of a pretty face peering through the door. The face scoped the place and frowned before spotting me. She paused for a moment before bringing the rest of herself through the door. Very nice. She took a seat at the bar and ordered a Long Island iced tea – expensive. I watched in the mirror, as she pulled a packet of cigarettes and a lighter from her bag and then saw her drop the lighter back in. Aha! A few seconds later she was beside me, saying, "Excuse please. Could you give me light?"

"Sure."

She had a soft silky voice, which immediately grabbed my attention. "Can I sit an' talk? Practik my English? I am Joy."

I thought, "Mmm. Joy? I bet you could be." I was about to answer, "sure" to her request to join me, but she was already on her way to retrieve her Long Island iced tea. She came back and climbed onto the stool next to mine and began to 'praktik' her English. She had only been in Shanghai a week and was still finding her way around, so she didn't know that Charlie's was quiet on Mondays. She looked at her watch and asked, "When more people will coming?" I put her in the picture and she shrugged, then said, "Is OK. Maybe is too much noisy. Can talk with you more easy."

We talked and found out about each other and she seemed disappointed when I told her I was only staying for a few weeks. She, on the other hand, said she wanted to live in Shanghai and make a lot of money. However, she seemed to have no plan as to how she was going to do it and seemed to have no qualifications or skills to get her foot on the ladder. I was wrong about the skills.

She had been alone since she was seventeen and had worked in various bar jobs and karaokes for five years, before venturing to the Shanghai land of opportunity. On digging deeper, I discovered that her plan revolved around finding a rich foreign sucker, who would 'take her away from all this' to a better life. I was safely out of the frame – not rich. The night passed quickly, but her Long Island iced teas went slowly and I commented, "You drink very slowly."

"I don' like drink, but these 'spensif and make people think I rick."

She was cute rather than beautiful, with the usual Chinese attributes – long black hair, neat figure, tiny hands and big black eyes. Not bad. Not bad at all and, as I was to find out, well named. I asked her where she was staying and she frowned and said, "Not sure. Don' wan' go back my hotel. Bad man there wan' fuck with me las' night.

Fraid. Go morrow an' get things an' fine 'nuther place."

"You can stay with me tonight, if you want" I said to her unspoken request. "The bed is big enough."

"OK, I like big bed." She grinned.

We made our way up to my room and her eyes widened as we entered. "Wah. Very good! Bes' place I ever stay." then she poked around, checking everything out, before throwing herself at me and saying, "Sank you. I make you happy now. We shower quick." Then she slipped out of her clothes quickly and gave me a twirl, "I am OK?"

She was OK. Dark skin all over, perky breasts with upturned nipples, tiny rounded bottom and well-muscled, shapely legs. She was an LBFM (little brown fucking machine, for those who don't know). We showered and she began to make me happy. To be fair, though, I did my fair share of happiness-making too. She liked reverse cowboy the best, but issued me with a warning, as we were negotiating the position for the first time, "No in my bum. Hurt much. Make me cry."

I reassured her and kept my word. I'm not a believer in, nor a lover of, anal sex anyway, except if options are limited or if it's requested – I never like to disappoint a lady. We safely negotiated a fair selection of the Kama Sutra before, eventually, calling it a night. She had had enough by then and was happy. She said, "Full now. Very full. You big enough." We slept.

Morning came, I ordered breakfast and she asked, "How long food will coming?"

"Fifteen, twenty minutes. Why?"

Then she dragged me out of bed and pulled me to the shower saying, "Enough time."

In the shower she washed the appropriate part and gave me a standing up blowjob, which buckled my knees and had me gasping. She had done it before and often.

Breakfast arrived – full American – and she ate her own and half of mine and I don't think she'd eaten properly for two or three days. She sprawled on the bed, laughing. "Full again. I lucky girl."

We spent the rest of the morning in bed, watching TV and - you know. We wandered down stairs at lunchtime to eat and she trawled the buffet, twice, in the Orient Express, before declaring that she was full again. After lunch she decided that she needed to go back to her hotel and move to another, but she thought she would make a play to see what I could or would do help her. She put on a sad, sad face and said, "Russell, I no money now. Help me?"

I helped and gave her a thousand, which lit up her eyes, and then I asked where she would go. "Need look, look. Many cheap hotel." And with a raised eyebrow query, "I like this hotel."

I had expected it and was ready with the answer, "A night or a couple of nights here and there is OK, but the hotel doesn't like it if somebody stays with you all the time."

She gave me a soulful look and said "I want come tonight again."

I gave in and said that one more night would be all right, but only one, and followed up with my back-up excuse, "I'm going away tomorrow for a couple of days, to see some friends in Hangzhou, before I leave for Vietnam." Half true. We exchanged phone numbers and she left.

She arrived back in Charlie's at 8.30 and we did it all again. We did it again often, a couple of times a week maybe, until I left Shanghai three weeks later. It always followed the same pattern - A phone call from one to the other. "You doing anything tonight? No? OK, see you in Charlie's later."

As I said, it was all about convenience. I gave her money now and again, if she asked, but there was never a regular, mechanical transaction. Now and again she would come into Charlie's with new hopefuls and she always came over to chat, before going back to her prospecting. When the time came for me to leave she shed a few tears and even offered to go with me to the airport, but I told her no. I hope she found what she was looking for.

During my last week in Shanghai I had another opportunity-cum-offer of an 'encounter' of sorts, but not the kind I was, ever have been, or will ever be interested in..

I was in Charlie's, again, and the place was fairly full. A good night. The band had asked if I would sing later, but, for some reason, I wasn't feeling up for it. Not enough to drink maybe? Anyway, somebody else got up to sing. He was a young coloured guy and he was one of a group of United Airlines air crew, on yet another layover, who were getting roaring drunk in one of the booths. He was good. Later, as I was on my way out to the toilet, I paused at his booth and told him that he was the best singer I'd ever heard in the bar. He was. He thanked me for the compliment, returned to his beer and I thought that was it, but... I came back from the toilet to my stool and he came over, "Hey, buy you a drink my friend?"

I said, "Sure." and invited him to sit down.

His name was Verne and we sat and talked about this and that – music mainly – and then another crew member came over, whom he introduced as Scott. They were flight attendants and both from Los Angeles. The rest of the crew drifted off to bed, so we sat and talked some more. I can't remember what we talked about, but it was probably bullshit. As was normal for the time of night and alcohol, Charlie's began to thin out and Scott asked if there was anywhere else to go. I suggested the Step Bar, and off we went.

The Step was fairly quiet, but welcoming, as usual. Scott went in pursuit (fruitless) of one of the staff and Verne and I talked some more. After a while Verne said, "Russell, I sense that you're searching for something in your life. Am I right?"

I thought for a moment or so, laughed, and replied, "You could be right. Any suggestions?"

His suggestion was, "My room number's 1213."

I was stunned. Then I thought, "Flight attendant." I should have known. If he'd worked for Quantas now, I would have expected it. How to handle this, other than smack him in the mouth? I shook my head and said, "Sorry, but your judgement is very, very off."

He grinned, shrugged his shoulders and was about to

say something else when, to my relief, Scott rejoined us, having decided to give up on his quest for the bar staff. Change the subject and quick. Scott, God bless him, supplied the required new topic by asking me about the ins and outs of Chinese females. Ins and outs? A very well chosen phrase and something I was, and still am, eminently qualified to talk about. After about half an hour, they decided that they should head back to the hotel. It was 2.30 and they had to be sober and on their way by nine, so... They said their goodbyes, with Verne, of course, giving me a lingering handshake and a raised eyebrow query, which I ignored. I was tired myself, but hung around for another hour before deciding it was safe to go back to my room. I was still rather wary, so I took an added precaution and persuaded Annie, the boss woman, to come and have a farewell drink in my room. She'd been trying to get there for the last month, so it was her last chance. She took it with both hands, in a manner of speaking. Average.

My time drifted by in Shanghai, until my leaving took me almost by surprise. I'd done the rounds of goodbyes to friends, Big Ron in particular. "Hanoi? Cain't help you, Sundance. I've only ever seen it from the air."

Favourite places were revisited to fix the pictures of them in my mind – the view of West Lake from the Shangri-La in Hangzhou for one. It was with mixed feelings that I walked out of the Crowne Plaza and on my way out of China, for what could have been the last time, for all I knew. Would I ever be back? Time would tell, as it always does. Vietnam here I come.

PRONUNCIATION GUIDE

I thought it might be a good idea to give the readers of this book, if there are any, some clue as to how to get their tongues round Chinese and words. It was very confusing for me at first because Pin Yin pronunciation, the Romanised representation of Chinese, doesn't follow Standard English phonics and phonemes. However, I got used to it, but had to throw what I'd learned out of the window when I went to Vietnam.

I've made certain assumptions about some of the better-known names, so you won't see Shanghai, Beijing etc. in the list. See how you get on.

Ai – Love. I.

Aiya - My God. Eye-yah.

Anshan – City in Liaoning Province in NE China. As it looks – one of the few.

Ayi - Aunt or housemaid. Eye-ee or 'I E'.

Ba – Eight. Bahh – as in 'Bahh, bahh black sheep.'

Baijiu – Chinese liquor. Evil stuff. Buy-joe – as in Joseph. Or Buy-jew – as in Shylock.

Bi - Family name. Bi – as in 'bid.'

Bi – Cunt. Bee – as in honey.

Baoding – City close to Beijing. Bow-ding – as in 'bow-wow-wow.'

Bu – No. Boo as in boom.

Bu yao - Don't want. Boo-yow – as in 'cow.'

Bu zhi dao – Don't know. Boo-jer-dow – as in 'how.'

Cao – Fuck exclamation. Tsow – as in 'now.'

Chang Ko – Small village in Zhejiang Province. Chang – as it is. Co as in Co. Ltd.

Chen Fei – Name Chun-fay.

Chendu – Capital of Sichuan Province Chun-doo.

Chongqing – Municipality in Central China. Chung-ching.

Chongming – Island close to Shanghai. Chung-ming.

Da – Big - Dah – as in lah-de-dah.

Datsuwai – Shanghainese for 'turn left.' dat-sue-way. Almost 'that's the way.'

Dai – Family name of a local mafia boss friend. Die – very appropriate.

Dalian – Port in Liaoning Province. Nice place. Dah-lee-en.

Du – Family name Doo.

Dui bu qi – Sorry Dway-boo-chee.

Er – Two. Ar.

Fapiao – Receipt. Far-p-ow.

Fu – Family name. Foo – as in fool.

Fujian – Province in SE China. Foo-jee-en.

Fu Yi Gang – Name. Foo-yee-gang.

Gansu – Province in NW China. Shithole. Gan-sue.

Guangdong – Province in SE China. Gwang-dung.

Guangxi – Province in SW China. Gwang-shee.

Guanxi – Relationships (how things get done in China). Gwanshee.

Guangzhou – Capital city of Guangdong. Gwang-joe.

Gubei – District of Shanghai where I lived. Goo-bay.

Guiling – Name. Gway-ling.

Guizhou – Province in SW China. Gway-joe – is Joe gay?

Guo – Family or first name. Gwo.

Hainan – Island Province off the coast of S China. Nice place High-nan.

Hangzhou – Capital of Zhejiang Province in East China. Hang-joe – poor Joe.

Hao – Good. How.

Harbin – Capital of Heilongjiang Province. Fucking cold. As it looks.

Hen – Very. Hun – as in Attila The…

Heilongjiang – Province in NE China. Fucking cold. Hey-lung-jyang.

Hua Hai Lu – Major street in Shanghai. Wha-high-loo.

Huang – Family name. Whong.

Huinong – My company in Shanghai, Whay-nung.

Haode – OK. how-de – with 'e' the same as in 'the.'

Ji – Chicken or prostitute, Jee.

Jiba – Cock or dick, Jee-bahh – as in 'black sheep' again.

Jiangsu – East China Province, Jyang-sue.

Jilin – Province in NE China. Another fucking cold one. Jee-lin – as in 'Linda.'

Ju Lu Lu – Notorious street in Shanghai, Jew-loo-loo.

Lao – Old or well respected. Me, in both instances Lou – as in 'loud.'

Laowai – Foreigner. Me As above, plus wye as in letter 'Y' sound.

Lanzhou – Capital City of Gansu Province. Shithole Lan-joe.

Li – Name, Lee.

Liaohe – Joint venture partner in Anshan. Lee-ow-her.

Liaoning – Province in NE China. Yet another fucking cold one. Lee-ow-ning.

Lingyi – Buddhist shrine near Hangzhou. Ling-yee.

Lu – Family name, or 'road.' Loo – as in toilet.

Luhui – The village close to the factory in Shanghai. Loo-whay.

Mai – Buy or sell, depending on the tone. Confusing. My.

Mao Zedong – Chairman Mao. Mow – as in 'how.' Dzur- tung.

Moutai – Expensive baijiu. Mow – as in now. Tie – as in round your neck.

Meiyou – No or negative. May-yeo – as in yeoman or yokel.

Meiyou wenti – No problem. as above, plus wun-tee.

Nanhui – County to the south of Shanghai. Nan-whay.

Nanpu – One of the major bridges over the river in Shanghai. Nan-poo.

Ni – You. Nee.

Ni hao – Hello Nee-how.

Ni hao ma? – How are you? as above plus Ma – as in mother.

Ningbo – Home in Zhejiang. Ning-bwo.

Ningxia – Small Province in North Central China. Shithole. Ning-sha.

Pudong – Eastern side of the river in Shanghai. Poo-dung.

Puxi – Western side of the river in Shanghai. Poo-shee.

Qi – Seven. Chee.

Qing – Please. You don't hear this much in China. Ching.

Qingdao – Port in Shandong Province in NE China. Ching-dow – as in how.

Qinghai – Province in Western Central China. Very big shithole. Ching-high.

Shandong – Province to the S E of Beijing. Nice place. Shan-dung.

Sei Ling – Name of one of the translators in Shanghai. Sailing.

Shenjingbing – Crazy. Shun-jing-bing.

Shen – What – as in what I want is… Shun.

Shenma? – What? Shun-ma.

Shenyang – Capital of Liaoning Province. Terrible place. Shun-yang.

Sichuan – Province in Western Central China. Search-wan.

Song – Family name. Sung.

Suzhou – City in Jiangsu Province. Sue-joe – Joe's having a bad time of it.

Ta – He, she or it. Tar.

Tai, tai – Wife. Tie, tie – as in knot. Very apt.

Tian – Family name. TN.

Tianjin – Municipality on the coast to the East of Beijing. Tee-en-jin.

Ting – Stop, taxis. as it looks.

Tsai qi – Martial arts discipline. Tsigh-chee.

Urumqi – Capital of Xin Jiang Province. Awful place. Wool-oo-moo-chee.

Wang – Family name. Wong.

Wei – 'Hello' when answering the phone in China. Way. Way-ee. Why-ee.

Wei Gao Chao – Free Trade Zone in Shanghai. Way-gow-chow.

Wo – I or me. Woe. as in woe is me.

Wodemaiye – Oh my God. Woe-da-mire.

Wo xi huan – I like. Woe-shee-wan.

Wu – Family name. Woo.

Wu shu – Martial arts discipline. Woo-shoo.

Xia – Family name. Summer or prawn, depending on tone. Shee-ya.

Xia bi – Stupid cunt. Shee-ya-bee.

Xi'an – Capital of Shaanxi Province. Shee-an.

Xie, xie – Thank you. Shay, shay.

Xiao – Young or small. Shou – as in shout.

Xiao tsu wai – Shanghainese for 'turn right.' Shout-sue-way.

Xinhua Lu – Street in Shanghai. Shin-hwa-loo.

Xinghua – Small city in Jiangsu Province. Shing-wha.

Xin Jiang – Most westerly Province of China. Shin-jyang.

Xi Zang – Tibet. Shee-dzang.

Xu – Family name. Shoo or shoe.

Xupu – One of the major bridges across the river in Shanghai. Shoo-poo.

Yao – Want. Yow – as in wow.

Yao Lin Dong – Cave complex in Zhejiang Province. Yow-lin-dong.

Ye Feng – Name of my main translator in Shanghai. Year-fung.

Yi – One. Eeeee.

Yi yuan – Hospital. Eeee-yoo-an.

Youguai – Turn right. Yeo-gu-eye.

Yuan – Chinese money. Yoo-an.

Yunnan – Province in SW China. Yoo-nan.

Yunnan Baiyao. – Magic medicine. Yoo-nan By-yow.

Yuyuan Gardens – Tourist attraction in Shanghai. Yoo-yoo-an.

Zai jian – Goodbye. Zy-tee-en – Zy as in my.

Zhejiang – Province in East China to the South of Shanghai. Dzur-jyang.

Zhang Minhe – University Dean in Xi'an. Jang Min-her.

Zheng Xi – My assistant, Xiao Zheng, in Shanghai. Jun Shee.

Zher shi – This is…. Jer-sher – as in jerk and shirt.

Zhi – Family name. Jer – as in 'jerk.'

Zhongguo – China. Jung-gwoe.

Zhongwen – Chinese. Jung-wun.

Zhou – Family name. Joe.

Zouguai – Turn left. Zoh-goo-eye